DISASTER MANAGEMENT IN ARCHIVES, LIBRARIES AND MUSEUMS

DISCLAIMER

No undertakings, express or implied, are given concerning the use of the contents of this book and neither the individual authors or publishers will accept liability for losses which might arise directly or indirectly from use of information herein.

Disaster Management in Archives, Libraries and Museums

GRAHAM MATTHEWS

YVONNE SMITH

GEMMA KNOWLES

ASHGATE

Published by
Ashgate Publishing Limited
Wey Court East
Union Road
Farnham
Surrey, GU9 7PT
England

Ashgate Publishing Company
Suite 420
101 Cherry Street
Burlington
VT 05401-4405
USA

www.ashgate.com

British Library Cataloguing in Publication Data
Disaster management in archives, libraries and museums
   1. Libraries – Risk management 2. Museums – Management
   3. Emergency management
   I. Matthews, Graham, 1953– II. Smith, Yvonne III. Knowles, Gemma
027'.00684

Library of Congress Cataloging-in-Publication Data
Matthews, Graham, 1953–
   Disaster management in archives, libraries and museums / by Graham Matthews, Yvonne Smith, and Gemma Knowles.
       p. cm.
   Includes bibliographical references.
   ISBN 978-0-7546-7273-9
   1. Libraries--Safety measures. 2. Libraries--Great Britain--Safety measures. 3. Archives--Safety measures. 4. Archives--Great Britain--Safety measures. 5. Museums--Safety measures. 6. Museums--Great Britain--Safety measures. 7. Library materials--Conservation and restoration. 8. Archival materials--Conservation and restoration. 9. Cultural property--Protection. 10. Emergency management. I. Smith, Yvonne. II. Knowles, Gemma. III. Title.

Z679.7.M38 2009
025.8'2--dc22
                                                                2008045373
ISBN 978-0-7546-7273-9

Mixed Sources
Product group from well-managed forests and other controlled sources
www.fsc.org Cert no. SA-COC-1565
© 1996 Forest Stewardship Council
FSC

Printed and bound in Great Britain by
MPG Books Ltd, Bodmin, Cornwall.

Contents

List of Tables

About the Authors

Graham Matthews is Professor of Information Management in the Department of Information Science, Loughborough University. Prior to this he was Professor of Information and Library Management, Head of Research, School of Business Information, Faculty of Business and Law, Liverpool John Moores University. In 1995–1996, he led a British Library Research and Development Department funded project that reviewed disaster management practice in British libraries (Matthews, G. and Eden, P. (1996) *Disaster Management in British Libraries. Project Report with Guidelines for Library Managers*, Library and Information Research Report 109, London: The British Library Board). He is co-editor, with John Feather of *Disaster Management for Libraries and Archives* (Ashgate, 2003). In 2005–2006, he led an AHRC funded project, 'Safeguarding heritage at risk: disaster management in UK archives, libraries and museums'. He has written and presented widely on this topic and preservation management in general. He is Chair of the Chartered Institute of Library and Information Professionals Preservation and Conservation Joint Committee.

Yvonne Smith has considerable experience in project management and business analysis, a degree in Information Systems and a MA in Information and Library Management. She is currently working as an Information Advisor at Edge Hill University.

Gemma Knowles has a degree in Archaeology, a MA in Museum Studies, and a MA in Conservation of Historic Objects. She has worked in the museum domain since 1999 and has experience of disaster management from a 'care of collections' perspective. She is currently working within the National Conservation Centre for National Museums Liverpool as an Organics Conservator.

Yvonne Smith was senior researcher on the project, Gemma Knowles, researcher. They worked with and under the supervision of Graham Matthews in the School of Business Information, Faculty of Business and Law, Liverpool John Moores University.

Acknowledgements

We are grateful to the Arts and Humanities Research Council (AHRC)[1] for an award that funded the research on which the book is based.

The book has depended greatly on the contributions of many individuals, including archivists, consultants, conservators, curators, disaster recovery company experts, librarians, managers, and others from outside the sector, including those working in fire services, insurance companies, etc. Our particular thanks go to all those individuals and their institutions in the UK and around the world who have contributed so generously to the research in many ways, especially those who responded to our questionnaire and e-mail surveys, those who agreed to be interviewed by the research team, and those who provided information or contacts. We are also grateful to those who invited us to take part in or attend conferences and similar events during the research and after. We have not included lists of individuals and institutions to help us preserve the anonymity we assured when seeking their participation. This should not diminish how greatly we have valued the information they have provided to us.

We are also grateful to the members of the Project Advisory Panel for their advice and support throughout the project (institutional affiliations are as at that time): Sue Cole, English Heritage; Fiona Macalister (and Nick Jordan), The National Trust; Linda Ramsay, National Archives of Scotland; Najla Semple (and Maggie Jones), Digital Preservation Coalition; Alison Walker, National Preservation Office; Carol Whittaker, CyMAL: Museums Archives and Libraries Wales; Peter Winsor, Museums, Libraries and Archives Council; Christine Wise, M25 Consortium of Academic Libraries.

We are grateful to Dianne van der Reyden, Director for Preservation, Library of Congress, for her invitation to Graham Matthews to attend a meeting in Washington in 2006 which facilitated access to individuals with experience of different aspects of disaster management in the US. We are also indebted to senior managers at Heritage Preservation in Washington for their contributions. And, to Randy and Gary, for their company and sharing advice over a beer … We are also indebted to senior staff at ICOM and the Netherlands Institute for Cultural Heritage, for sharing their expertise on emergency planning in the wider cultural heritage.

---

1   The AHRC funds postgraduate training and research in the arts and humanities, from archaeology and English literature to dance. The quality and range of research supported not only provides social and cultural benefits but also contributes to the economic success of the UK. For further information on the AHRC, see: http://www.ahrc.ac.uk/Pages/default.aspx.

We are grateful to Bob McClelland, Reader, Liverpool Business School, Liverpool John Moores University, for his advice on statistical analysis, and to all our former colleagues there for their encouragement and support.

After the research had been completed and the book was being finalised, areas of England suffered severe flooding. We are grateful to those who provided us with information about the impact of this on the cultural heritage. Thanks go to Fiona Spiers, Head of Heritage Lottery Fund, Yorkshire and Humber, for an invitation to attend an event disseminating information about the impact of the flooding and for providing information about what had been learned. Similarly thanks go to Ann Chumbley, Registrar Museums Sheffield, for information on her experience at Kelham Island Museum, and lessons learned.

We also wish to thank Susan Lansdale, Executive Officer, East Midlands Museums Service, coordinator of its Regional Emergencies and Disaster Support (REDS) Service, Gerry Boulton, Business Continuity Manager, Department of Culture Media and Sport, and members of its London Emergency Planning Group who provided us with updates, contacts and information in the period after the completion of the research.

Our thanks are due to Dymphna Evans and Claire Jarvis, Commissioning Editors, and Gemma Lowle, Senior Editor, Ashgate, for their patience and support.

Any omissions or errors are those of the authors.

List of Acronyms and Abbreviations

AAM	American Association of Museums
AFRICOM	International Council of African Museums
AHRC	Arts and Humanities Research Council
AIC	The American Institute of Conservation of Historic and Artistic Works
AIC-CERT	American Institute for Conservation – Collections Emergency Response Team
AIM	Association of Independent Museums
ALA	American Library Association
ALM London	Archives, Libraries and Museums London
AMOL	Australian Museums OnLine
CARBICA	Caribbean Regional Branch of the International Council on Archives
CARDIN	Caribbean Disaster Information Network
CARTAS	Caribbean Archives Taskforce for Disaster Protection
CAVAL	CAVAL Collaborative Solutions
CCI	Canadian Conservation Institute
CDERA	Caribbean Disaster Emergency Response Agency
CMA	Canadian Museums Association
CoOL	Conservation OnLine
CoSA	Council of State Archivists
COSADOCA	Consortium de sauvetage du patrimoine documentaire en cas de catastrophe
CyMAL	Museums Archives and Libraries Wales
DCMS	Department for Culture, Media and Sport
DISACT	Disasters ACT [Australian Capital Territory]
EEMLAC	East of England Museums, Libraries and Archives Council
EMMLAC	East Midlands Museums, Libraries and Archives Council
EmmS	East Midlands Museums Service
EPSRC	Engineering and Physical Sciences Research Council
ESARBICA	East and Southern Africa Regional Branch of the ICA
ESRC	Economic and Science Research Council
FEMA	Federal Emergency Management Agency
GCI	Getty Conservation Institute
HDRS	Harwell Document Restoration Services
HEFCE	Higher Education Funding Council for England
HLF	Heritage Lottery Fund

ICA	International Council on Archives
ICA / PDP	International Council on Archives Committee on Disaster Prevention
ICBS	International Committee of the Blue Shield
ICCROM	International Council for the Study of the Preservation and Restoration of Cultural Property
ICOM	International Council of Museums
ICOM MEP	ICOM Museums Emergency Programme
ICOMOS	International Council of Monuments and Sites
ICON	Institute of Conservation
ICRC	International Committee of the Red Cross
IFLA	International Federation of Library Associations and Institutions
IFLA PAC	IFLA Core Activity on Preservation and Conservation
LIC	Library and Information Commission
LISC	Library and Information Services Council
LISC (NI)	Library and Information Services Council Northern Ireland
MDA	Museums Documentation Association
MGC	Museums and Galleries Commission
MLA	The Museums, Libraries and Archives Council
MLA North West	Museums, Libraries and Archives North West
MLA West Midlands	Museums, Libraries and Archives West Midlands
NEDCC	Northeast Document Conservation Center
NEH	National Endowment for the Humanities
NEMLAC	North East Museums, Libraries and Archives Council
NERC	Natural Environment Research Council
NICH	The Netherlands Institute for Cultural Heritage
NIMC	Northern Ireland Museum Council
NPO	National Preservation Office
RCAHMS	Royal Commission on Ancient and Historical Monuments
REDS	Regional Emergency and Disaster Support
SEMLAC	South East Museums, Libraries and Archives Council
SLIC	Scottish Libraries and Information Council
SWMLAC	South West Museums, Libraries and Archives Council
TNA	The National Archives
UCL	University College London
UKIRB	United Kingdom and Ireland Blue Shield Organisation
UNESCO	United Nations Educational, Scientific and Cultural Organisation
WET	Worcestershire Museums Emergency Task Force
YMLAC	Yorkshire Museums, Libraries and Archives Council

Preface

The book is based largely on the findings of an AHRC funded project, 'Safeguarding heritage at risk: disaster management in UK archives, libraries and museums', undertaken March 2005 – October 2006. Select material from that date up to Summer 2008 has also been incorporated. Dissemination at conferences and similar events has both provided up to date information and feedback on findings and recommendations of the research. The idea for this research came out of Matthews's wish to build on previous work he had undertaken in this field and to broaden its scope.

It is hoped that readers will benefit from the range of advice and views offered to the research team by practitioners and experts in the field. We hope we have done justice to their generosity in sharing their experience and views with us. Whilst the book is research based we have tried to write it in a style that incorporates the practical aspects that were emphasised by those who contributed. This, however, is not a 'how to do it' manual; but references to such sources are provided. Our purpose is to disseminate the results of the research in a way that reflects the insights into various aspects of disaster management that we have gathered and analysed, and make them of use to those working in the field. We hope that practitioners and managers will be able to take information provided and use it to support advocacy for initiating or developing disaster management in their particular context. We also hope that the contents will offer ideas and practical tips for those seeking to sustain or move forward existing policy and practice. Whilst there are differences between archives, libraries and museums, there are many common issues they face with regard to disaster management. Likewise, size and type of institution can play a part in how it is addressed but similar approaches may be taken. From an international perspective, circumstances in particular regions and countries will differ but there are lessons that can be shared. We thus hope that the book will stimulate both planning and action in disaster management in archives, libraries and museums through the sharing of contemporary experiences and views.

Graham Matthews, Loughborough
Yvonne Smith, Liverpool
Gemma Knowles, Liverpool

Chapter 1
The Research Project and Disaster Management: Introduction

Aim of the Book

The book aims to provide a contemporary overview of disaster management in archives, libraries and museums in the United Kingdom, and an insight into activities elsewhere in the world. It does so on the basis of primary research into real-world experience and activity that has provided a greater understanding and knowledge of current disaster management/emergency planning activities within and across the UK archive, library and museum domains.

It reports primarily on the findings of a research project, 'Safeguarding heritage at risk: disaster management in UK archives, libraries and museums', undertaken at Liverpool John Moores University from March 2005–October 2006, by researchers Yvonne Smith and Gemma Knowles, under the supervision of Graham Matthews. The research was funded by an award from the United Kingdom Arts and Humanities Research Council (AHRC). In writing the book, the authors have also incorporated information relevant to the topic beyond the end of the project, up to Summer 2008. The research is the first study of a cross-domain nature that provides an overview of the sector, the individual domains, as well as an international perspective.

Digital resources and services were not within the direct remit of the research on which the book is based. This was decided at the proposal stage of the project as its scope was determined. Reviewers of the proposal influenced this decision which was confirmed later by the Project Advisory Panel. Not only would this have added to the already wide scope of the project but others were already addressing this (for example in the UK, the Digital Preservation Coalition).

Audience

The research reviewed current disaster management practice in the UK and abroad and sought lessons from other fields like business and computing and events such as 11 September 2001. It aimed to provide an up to date overview of good practice that would inform cultural heritage strategists and offer practical advice for managers. Information to assist managers and policy-makers has been identified. It was hoped consideration of results could lead to sharing of innovative approaches in practice.

It was also intended that project findings would inform practitioners' and trainers' prioritisation of training topics and contribute to educators development of courses. The audience of the book is thus wide, including archivists, librarians, curators, managers, trainers, consultants – very much reflecting the range of individuals who contributed to the research. Students should also find the contents helpful and complementary to the kind of information on the topic they will find in 'how to do it' publications on their reading lists.

In academic terms, the project was timely as it took place when there was a wider move to interdisciplinary and academic/practitioner research in this field (e.g. the *Preserving Our Past* event (March 2006), funded by the AHRC, Economic and Science Research Council (ESRC), Engineering and Physical Sciences Research Council (EPSRC), Natural Environment Research Council (NERC), English Heritage, to encourage cross-disciplinary collaboration amongst the historic environment research community (AHRC *Preserving Our Past Workshop*). As such, the research should provide researchers in other disciplines with an insight into disaster management in this sector and thus facilitate potentially creative initiatives involving several disciplines (addressing, for example, buildings, environment and climate change).

The project has already had an impact on policy, through, for example, informing and facilitating the development of collaborative support networks (e.g. participation in the DCMS's London Emergency Planning Group meetings and its development of AGORA, an extranet to promote collaboration and sharing of experience; and liaison with East Midlands Museum Service Regional Emergency Disaster Support). The newly established Renaissance South East Emergency Response Units has included project findings in its procedural manual.

The project continues to increase awareness and understanding of disaster management in archives, libraries and museums among practitioners and those in other fields with whom they work (e.g. civil emergency planners, fire service) through a range of dissemination activities including publications and presentation of conference papers.

The Research Project

Background

The national cultural heritage in museums, archives and libraries is at risk from natural and man-made 'disasters'. These may cause damage to collections and buildings, with unique material lost forever. Effective disaster management can prevent or reduce this.

Since the mid 1980s, Professor Matthews has had a considerable research interest in preservation management. Through this he became particularly interested in one of preservation management's key aspects, disaster management. The findings relating to disaster management in a broader investigation of preservation policy and practice in libraries he was involved in in the early 1990s (Feather, Matthews and Eden 1996), led to him directing the last major UK review of the topic, *Disaster Management in British Libraries*, funded by the British Library Research and Development Department, 1995–1996 (Matthews and Eden 1996).

Since then, however, there have been considerable developments across the cultural heritage sector. In the area of disaster management, these include: ongoing professional and institutional activities, their promotion on websites, research projects, applications from other disciplines, and, unfortunately, yet more experience of disasters, from fire, flood and terrorism, for example. Over the period, government in the UK has encouraged increasing collaboration between domains – archives, libraries and museums (and the private sector). It is acknowledged now that the sector incorporates a broad range of institutions, small and large, local and national, each with varying disaster management requirements, levels of provision and resources. Matthews has continued to monitor developments (Matthews and Feather (eds.) 2003; Matthews 2005a) and undertake research (Matthews, et al. 2004; Matthews 2005b) in this field.

Since the turn of the millennium, there has also been a growing international dimension as, firstly, the Internet has offered opportunities for greater sharing of advice and experience from around the world, and, secondly, the impact of terrorism and war has been seen to be widespread and far ranging. In spite of developments to assist disaster control planning, and reminders of the impact of incidents large and small, Wellheiser and Scott noted that the '"current" ... reality is that many organisations, despite their good intentions, have yet to realise these intentions in the form of a disaster plan or integrated planning' (2002, 4).

Indeed, disaster prevention and preparedness are activities which some may put off to a later date, the likelihood of experiencing a disaster thought to be remote, the 'it won't happen here' attitude. Unfortunately, there are many incidents of varying cause and scale from around the world to suggest this may not be the case. Well publicised examples include the flooding in Florence in 1966 and its effect on the National Library (*The Florence Flood* 2008), the destruction by fire of Norwich Central Library in England in 1994 (Creber 2003), the devastating fire at the eighteenth century Duchess Anna Amalia Library in Germany in 2004 (*Help for Anna Amalia* 2006). Archives, libraries and museums are not immune from critical, region-wide incidents, for example, the floods in the Czech Republic in 2003 (Vnouček 2005), the 2004 Indian Ocean earthquake and the ensuing tsunami's impact on South and Southeast Asia (IFLA PAC Regional Centre for Asia and National Diet Library, 2005), and Hurricane Katrina's devastation on the Gulf Coast of the United States in 2005 (American Library Association 2008). War and terrorism, likewise – for example, the terrorist attacks in the United States on 11 September 2001 (Heritage Preservation 2002), war in the former Yugoslavia (Teijgeler 2006), and Iraq (Johnson 2005). It was thus felt timely to consider disaster management practice in this context, including reaction to such disasters, and what might be done to foster good disaster management practice across this sector which has responsibility for what are increasingly recognised as key economic as well as cultural assets. Existing practice within the UK sector needed to be identified and reviewed to inform the development of effective disaster management to meet the needs of museums, libraries and archives in the 21st century. To achieve this, it was also relevant to consider activity in archives, libraries and museums elsewhere in the world, and to look beyond the sector at other disciplines and sectors for different approaches and lessons.

Aim and Objectives

So, what did the project set out to do, and how did it achieve this? It aimed to:

- achieve a contemporary overview of disaster management practice and issues in the UK cultural heritage sector
- identify relevant practice in other countries and sectors
- inform strategists and managers in museums, libraries and archives
- make recommendations for the effective development of disaster management.

Specific objectives included, to:

- identify and review the literature of disaster management in the UK and international cultural heritage sector
- identify and review practice (good and bad), gaps and issues within the UK sector domains: archives, libraries and museums
- identify and review examples of good practice and theory outside the UK and in other disciplines
- compile and make available an up-to-date bibliographic resource of worldwide documentation (including websites) and practical information on disaster management
- recommend how sector-wide development in the UK might be planned and implemented to achieve effective disaster management in individual institutions and sector-wide.

Method

To achieve these aims and objectives, the project employed a variety of methods, including literature and website searches and review, document analysis, questionnaire surveys and analysis, visits to select organisations, and interviews with key individuals/groups.

The literature review emphasised that there is a vast amount of information available, including that from international and outside the cultural heritage sector organisations and, increasingly, this is available on websites (e.g. International Council of Museums (ICOM), *Risk Management*; International Committee of the Red Cross (ICRC); The World Bank, *Disaster Risk Management*). Indeed, most initial approaches to 'non-cultural heritage' institutions seeking information about disaster management were met with a response to 'see website'. A review of such websites in the UK with a focus on civil emergency planning, risk management and business continuity (including IT) was undertaken. The review highlighted sources of information and advice, tools, services, examples of good practice and models that could be used in the cultural heritage sector, such as those available on the Collections Link website. (Collections Link is a recently established national advisory service for collection management managed by MDA (Museum Documentation Association) in partnership with the Institute of Conservation (ICON) and the National Preservation Office (NPO) and funded by The Museums, Libraries and Archives Council (MLA).) Analysis of a sample selection of disaster control plans also contributed to the overview.

Literature and website searching also provided insight into practice and initiatives in other countries and sectors. The project coincided with major events (e.g. 7 July 2005 terrorist attacks in London, Hurricane Katrina August 2005) that led to a further increase in information and advice on emergency planning, business continuity, risk management (including IT) on government and other websites, in addition to that initiated by response to previous man-made and natural disasters worldwide.

A contemporary overview of disaster management practice and issues in the UK was achieved through a questionnaire survey sent to a representative sample of UK archives, libraries and museums. The survey results were enriched by data from interviews, and an e-mail survey of regional MLAs and national equivalents. Analysis of a sample selection of disaster control plans has also contributed to the overview, which was also informed by a thorough literature and website search. In addition to investigating the UK situation, the award allowed the project team to contact key institutions around the world. An e-mail survey of institutions/ individuals outside the UK was carried out. Select visits outside the UK afforded opportunities to meet individuals with whom the researchers had already been in e-mail contact as well as new contacts. Interviews with international experts took place.

Individuals who contributed to the project as interviewees or respondents to the questionnaire and e-mail survey were assured of personal and institutional anonymity, including attribution of quotes in publications resulting from the research. To maintain this anonymity, no lists of individuals or institutions are provided. The authors in no way wish to underplay the contribution of the many participants who have contributed greatly to the project but wish to respect the confidentiality assured.

Team members' attendance at, or participation in, a range of events, both during the course of the research and after it as part of the dissemination of findings have enabled them to gather, share and discuss information and views and to keep abreast of developments, and as such have contributed not only to the research but to the broader content of the book. They are grateful to individuals and organisations who have invited them to participate and for the information and discussion that has contributed to the research and the writing of the book. Such events (in chronological order) include:

Disaster Preparedness Planning – Stage 2. Museums, Libraries and Archives Council, London, 19 April 2005.

Savings Plan: Emergency Planning for Museums. Museums Association, London, 25 April 2005.

Rising from the Rubble: Tsunami Devastates Sri Lankan Libraries. Presentation by Premila Gamage, Member, Sri Lanka Library Association (SLLA) Tsunami Library Development Project; Secretary, Twinning and Adoption Task Force of the Sri Lanka Disaster Management Committee for Libraries, Information Services and Archives, Career Development Group, London and South East Divisions, with International Library and Information Group, CILIP, London, 24 August 2005.

From Parchment to Pictures to Pixels. Society of Archivists Conference 2005, University of East Anglia, Norwich, 6–9 September 2005.

Has Preservation Come of Age? 21 Years After the Ratcliffe Report. National Preservation Office Annual Conference, The British Library, London, 31 October 2005.

The 3-Ds of Preservation: Disasters, Displays, Digitization, Symposium co-sponsored by the Bibliothèque nationale de France and the International Federation of Library Associations, Preservation and Conservation (IFLA PAC) Core Activity & IFLA Section on Preservation and Conservation, Bibliothèque nationale de France, Paris, 8–10 March 2006.

Capturing Katrina: Collections – Recovery Experiences and *Future Directions in Safeguarding Document Collections*, Library of Congress, Washington DC, 20–21 April 2006.

Disaster Management for Libraries and Archives, CILIP University College and Research Group East Midlands Section, University of Leicester, 27 April 2006.

Department for Culture, Media and Sport London Emergency Planning Group (meetings October 2006-).

Practitioners' Panel, East Midlands Museums Service, Castle Museum and Art Gallery, Nottingham, 8 December 2006.

Responding to Climate Change, Institute of Conservation. Care of Collections Group. Responding to Climate Change. Annual meeting, Tate Britain, London, 25 April 2007.

Safe and Sound: New Approaches to Emergency Planning, Museums Association, London, 21 May 2007.

Information Providers Coping with Disaster in Asia-Oceania, IFLA Asia and Oceania Regional Section Open Session, 73rd IFLA World Library and Information Congress, Durban, South Africa, 19–23 August 2007.

Differing Directions: Challenging Communities, Society of Archivists Conference, The Queen's University, Belfast, 28–31 August 2007.

10th World Forum for Motor Museums, Haynes International Motor Museum, Sparkford, nr Yeovil, 16–21 September 2007.

Beyond the Deluge: Moving Forward, Heritage Lottery Fund Yorkshire and the Humber, Government Office Yorkshire and the Humber, Leeds, 26th November 2007.

Don't Panic! Planning an Effective Disaster Response, The Midlands Federation of Museums and Galleries, RAF Museum Cosford, 2nd July 2008.

Further information about methods used is provided in appropriate chapters in the book.

What is Disaster Management?

Disaster

'Disaster' can be an emotive term. The definition used in the project was that determined in a previous investigation of disasters and their management in libraries:

> any incident which threatens human safety and/or damages, or threatens to damage [or destroy], a library's buildings, collections, contents, facilities or services. (Matthews and Eden 1996, 4)

Disasters can result from a range of causes, man-made and natural, including: arson, burst pipe, electrical fault, leaking roof, poor maintenance, earthquake, hurricane, flooding, terrorism, war. They vary in scale and impact. Some may cause minor inconvenience, others can have enormous consequences for the library and its parent organisation, with catastrophic damage to stock, equipment, buildings and disruption to services, with considerable financial implications. If the incident is major and/or region wide and life threatening, emergency services will give priority to human safety and re-establishing the local infrastructure.

Disaster Management (Emergency Planning)

Archives, libraries and museums should take measures to prevent disasters. Not all, however, can be prevented, so they should also prepare for them, and how to react to them to minimise their effect. This should be done in a flexible, not a prescriptive manner. Activities aimed at achieving these ends constitute disaster management. It should be noted that whilst 'disaster management' is a term commonly used in libraries and understood by archivists, in the museum domain it is normally referred to as 'emergency planning'.

Disaster Control Plan

At the centre of effective disaster management is the disaster control plan:

> a clear, concise document which outlines preventive and preparatory measures intended to reduce potential risks, and which also provides details of reaction and recovery procedures to be undertaken in the event of a disaster to minimise its effect. (Matthews and Eden 1996, 4)

Over the last thirty years or so, the disaster control plan has been the basis on which disaster management has been founded and developed.

> Any disaster, even a minor one, will cost time and money, cause other work to be delayed and possibly inconvenience users. Good disaster management, whilst it can never totally prevent disasters occurring, will reduce their likelihood and enable the library to deal more efficiently and effectively with them. (Matthews and Eden 1996, 72)

The disaster control plan normally addresses four stages:

1. Prevention
2. Preparedness
3. Reaction
4. Recovery.

However,

> disaster management includes much more than the formulation of a written disaster control plan. It encompasses broader management issues such as finance, risk assessment and training. (Matthews and Eden 1996, 4)

It is, therefore, vital that the plan is not just words on paper, it should be a blue print for action, and so preparedness should involve familiarisation with all of its aspects. Training for all staff is vital so that they are aware of its contents and know their roles, individually and in teams. Appropriate stores of equipment and material for dealing with incidents should be maintained. With regard to reaction, staff should know how to raise the alarm, who to call in, how to identify material for appropriate treatment, and to protect undamaged material. Recovery will include activities such as arranging insurance assessment, drying or treating materials, offering counselling to staff, providing a temporary service, and returning storage areas and services to normal. The plan, which should be a concise document for ease of use, should be regularly reviewed and updated. Specialist advice, such as that from conservators, external consultants or disaster recovery companies may be sought as appropriate. Digital materials and computing facilities will require separate attention and within larger institutions may be the responsibility of another department with whom the archive, library or museum should consult. Outside the heritage sector, it is important to liaise with the local fire service and civil emergency planners to familiarise them, for example, with the archive, library or museum and its collections, for advice on security and business continuity.

Risk Assessment and Management

Disaster control plans should be based on risk assessment and management of those risks. Potential hazards, risks and threats inside and outside the library, archive or museum need to be identified, actions relating to them prioritised, and strategies put in place for their removal or response to them to minimise their impact. This must be an ongoing, regular process as external and internal circumstances will change.

Busines/Service Continuity

Disaster control plans should include or be developed alongside business or service continuity plans. Whilst the disaster control plan will facilitate response and reaction to an incident, if the incident threatens to stop or disrupt delivery of services (or business), then this must also be addressed as well as dealing with the aftermath of, for example, the flood or fire. Disruption to, or cessation of services to readers or visitors will not only cause them inconvenience, but may also contribute to financial loss for the institution. Contingency arrangements, therefore should be in place to provide temporary services to minimise negative impact on institution's business plans and income generation.

Archives, Libraries and Museums

A list of the types of archives, libraries and museums included in the survey is given in Chapter 3.

Arrangement of Chapters

Chapter 2 considers the context of disaster management in archives, libraries and museums. To help readers put the following chapters in perspective, it offers a broad overview of the cultural heritage and disaster management. It then moves on to focus on archives, libraries and museums and introduces the international context and key international agencies working in that. Next, the UK context is outlined, followed by a brief review of developments in disaster management there.

Chapter 3 provides a summary of the findings of a questionnaire survey of archives, libraries and museums in the UK, and a survey of regional MLAs.

Chapter 4 provides a select overview of activity worldwide and nationally, based on the findings of an e-mail survey of institutions and individuals, the literature, and select websites. It highlights key developments and issues.

Chapter 5 focuses on the disaster control plan and, based on analysis of disaster control plans and responses to the UK questionnaire, considers its significance and what it should cover, with examples. It also looks at why some institutions do not have plans.

Chapter 6 pulls together key themes that have emerged from the research and illustrates them with comments from interviews and survey responses.

Chapter 7 reflects briefly on achievements and whether lessons are learned before moving on to consider aspects of disaster management that need to be addressed in planning for future activity, including working with others beyond the cultural heritage sector.

Chapter 8 lists sources of information on disaster management, under broad headings, for archives, libraries and museums.

References

AHRC, *Preserving Our Past Workshop* [website], (updated 2008) <http://www.ahrc.ac.uk/FundingOpportunities/Pages/PreservingOurPastWorkshop.aspx>, accessed 18 Sep. 2008.

Collections Link, Collections Link [website], (updated c.2006) <http://www.collectionslink.org.uk/>, accessed 30 Aug. 2008.

Creber, J. (2003), 'Aftermath – service continuity and recovery', in Matthews, G. and Feather J. (eds.) (2003), 191–211.

DCMS, *Business Continuity Planning Guide. Business as usual. A step by step guide to introducing and maintaining a business continuity plan*, (London: DCMS), (published online 2005) <http://www.culture.gov.uk/images/working_with_us/10231stegbystepguide.pdf>, accessed 20 Sep. 2008.

Digital Preservation Coalition, *Welcome to the Digital Preservation Coalition* [website], (updated July 2008) <http://www.dpconline.org/graphics/index.html>, accessed 2 Sep. 2008.

Feather, J., Matthews, G. and Eden, P. (1996), *Preservation management. Policies and practices in British libraries* (Aldershot: Gower).

'The Florence Flood. News, Archives and Photos of the Florence Flood of 1966' [see *November 4th 2006 40th anniversary of the Florence flood*] [website], (updated 14 Jan. 2008) <http://www.florence-flood.com/>, accessed 14 Aug. 2008.

Gorman, G. E. and Shep, S. J. (eds.) (2006), *Preservation Management for Libraries, Archives and Museums* (London: Facet Publishing).

'Help for Anna Amalia' [website], (updated June 2006) <http://www.anna-amalia-bibliothek.de/en/index.html>, accessed 29 Aug. 2008.

Heritage Preservation (2002), *Cataclysm and challenge. Impact of September 11, 2001, on Our Nation's Cultural Heritage. A report from Heritage Preservation on behalf of the Heritage Emergency National Task Force*, [Project Director Ruth Hargraves] (Washington, DC: Heritage Preservation), (published online 2002) <http://www.heritagepreservation.org/PDFS/Cataclysm.pdf>, accessed 29 Aug. 2008.

ICOM. *Risk Management* [website], (updated 25 Oct. 2006) <http://icom. museum/risk_management.html>, accessed 30 Aug. 2008.

ICRC, *International Committee of the Red Cross* [website], (updated 29 Aug. 2008) <http://www.icrc.org/>, accessed 30 Aug. 2008.

IFLA PAC Regional Centre for Asia and National Diet Library, Tokyo, Japan (2005), *Open seminar on the documentary heritage damaged by the Indian Ocean Tsunami and the meeting of Directors of the IFLA/PAC Regional Centres in Asia and others, National Diet Library, Tokyo, December 6, 2005.* [website], (updated 2006) <http://www.ndl.go.jp/en/iflapac/news.html>, accessed 29 Aug. 2008.

Johnson, I. M. (2005), 'The impact on libraries and archives in Iraq of war and looting in 2003: a preliminary assessment of the damage and subsequent reconstruction efforts', *International Information and Library Review* 37:3, 209–71.

Matthews, G. (2005a) 'Disaster management and libraries; planning into action: an institutional perspective', in Wellheiser, J. G. and Gwinn, N. E. (eds.) (2005), 61–77.

Matthews, G. (2005b) 'Disaster management: sharing experience, working together across the sector', *Journal of Librarianship and Information Science*, 37:2, 63–74.

Matthews, G. and Eden, P. (1996), *Disaster Management in British Libraries: Report and Guidelines*, (British Library Research and Innovation Report 109) (London: British Library Research and Development Department).

Matthews, G. and Feather J. (eds.) (2003), *Disaster Management for Libraries and Archives* (Aldershot: Ashgate Publishing Ltd).

Matthews, G. et al. (2004), *An Investigation into the Work of REDS (Regional Emergencies & Disaster Squad). A Report to East Midlands Museums, Libraries and Archives Council (EMMLAC) (Leicester: EMMLAC)*, (published online 2004) <http://www.mlaeastmidlands.org.uk/templates/temp_cor_rep_index.rm?category=keywords_root.taxonomy.corporate.documenttype.Report&category=keywords_root.taxonomy.corporate.subject.Collections&id=589&sort_type=date&num=5&term=&submit.x=11&submit.y=13&from=6>, accessed 27 Aug. 2008.

Teijgeler, R. (2006), 'Preserving cultural heritage in times of conflict', in Gorman, G. E. and Shep, S. J. (eds.) (2006), 133–65.

Vnouček, J. (2005) 'The Prague flood diary', in Wellheiser, J. G. and Gwinn, N. E. (eds.) (2005), 103–8.

Wellheiser, J. G. and Gwinn, N. E. (eds.), *Preparing for the worst, planning for the best: protecting our cultural heritage from disaster. Proceedings of a conference sponsored by the IFLA Preservation and Conservation Section, the IFLA Core Activity for Preservation and Conservation and the Council on Library and Information Resources, Inc., with the Akademie der Wissenschaften and the Staatsbibliothek zu Berlin. Berlin, Germany, Jul 30–August 1, 2003*, (Munich: K G Saur).

Wellheiser, J. and Scott, J. (2002), *An Ounce of Prevention. Integrated Disaster Planning for Archives, Libraries and Record Centres*, 2nd edition (Lanham, Maryland, and London: The Scarecrow Press, and Toronto, Ontario: Canadian Archives Foundation).

The World Bank, *Disaster Risk Management* [website], (updated 6 Aug. 2008) http://web.worldbank.org/wbsite/external/topics/exturbandevelopment/extdismgmt/0,menuPK:341021~pagePK:149018~piPK:149093~theSitePK:341015,00.html>, accessed 30 Aug. 2008.

Chapter 2
Disaster Management and Archives, Libraries and Museums: Context

Introduction

The chapter begins with a brief outline of the broader cultural heritage in which libraries, archives and museums form one sector. It then considers disaster management and emergency planning from a general perspective. It is thus intended that the wider context in which disaster management in libraries, archives and museums functions is introduced before looking at the sector itself and developments there since 2001. The major international non-governmental agencies and their work is outlined, followed by an introduction to the context of archives, libraries, museums and disaster management in the United Kingdom.

Cultural Heritage and Archives, Libraries and Museums

> Cultural heritage is understood to mean everything that has been transmitted from the past which informs us about how people lived, worked and thought, and may still influence the way in which we do these things ... (Feather 2004, 2)

> In its traditional sense, heritage, whether tangible or intangible, can be defined as monuments, cultural and natural sites, museum collections, archives, manuscripts, etc., or practices that a society inherits from its past, and which it intends to preserve and transmit to future generations. (Abid 2007, 2)

Feather (2006, 4) posits a typology for 'the heritage sector' which helps 'to define and locate those parts of the heritage which are in the domain of the heritage institutions: libraries, archives, museums and galleries'. He breaks down the sector into three aspects: 'Built Environment (buildings, townscapes and archaeological remains), Natural Environment (rural landscapes, coasts and shorelines, agricultural heritage), and Artefacts (books and documents, objects, pictures)'.

This research has focused on the latter of these, Artefacts – books, documents, objects and pictures, but can not ignore the other two as many artefacts are housed in Buildings and these are subject to the Natural Environment.

Whilst there are similarities between the three domains, there are also differences, but there is much they can learn from each other in terms of disaster management.

Disaster Management – General

What is the context of wider disaster management and emergency planning, i.e. beyond the cultural heritage sector? Minor incidents or faults (for example leaking pipes, faulty electrics) within an institution can cause damage and disruption to service and may be dealt with in-house or with minimum external assistance. Major disasters, however, natural and man-made, can strike with massive region-wide effect and impact on the whole of society. In such cases, human life and safety take priority, with emergency and relief services occupied with this and reinstating the infrastructure. In such cases, heritage institutions, whose staff are likely to have been caught up in the disaster and have been affected by it, may have to 'go it alone' for some time. In terms of natural disasters, UNESCO (2006) reports that, 'Today the world is facing disaster on a record scale. Since the 1990s, disasters kill 58,000 people on average each year and affect another 225 million people. In 2005 alone, there were more; 92,000 people died in 150 disasters'; and,

> The past year has reminded people everywhere that no place in the world is immune from natural disaster. From the massive Indian Ocean earthquake and tsunami to the drought- and locust-ravaged countries of Africa, from the devastation caused by hurricanes and cyclones in the United States, the Caribbean and the Pacific to heavy flooding across Europe and Asia, hundreds of thousands of people have lost their lives, and millions their livelihoods, to natural disasters. (UNESCO 2005a)

To these natural disasters must be added man-made disasters caused, for example, by war and terrorism, and their impact (recent examples include war in Iraq and 11 September 2001).

Those working to restore archives, libraries and museums in the aftermath of a major region-wide disaster, man-made or natural, must work with international and national emergency organisations and services, representatives of government, the armed forces, civil emergency planners and the emergency services dealing with the emergency and its aftermath. Organisations such as the International Committee of the Red Cross (ICRC) (see, for example, ICRC *National Implementation of International Humanitarian Law: Protection of Cultural Property*; and *International Review of the Red Cross, 2004 – No. 854*); the World Bank (see Taboroff 2001; The World Bank *Cultural Heritage and Development*), and the Getty Conservation Institute (GCI), (see, for example, *Field Projects. Iraq Cultural Heritage Conservation Initiative*) are increasingly involved in disaster management and the cultural heritage. For examples of the wide range of organisations involved (countries, non-governmental organisations, the private sector, etc.), see *Humanitarian Response to the Indian Ocean Earthquake 2004* (2008*); International Response to Hurricane Katrina* (2008).

Archives, Libraries And Museums – International Context

Since the mid 1990s, there have been considerable, ongoing professional and institutional activities within disaster management across archives, libraries and museums. These activities have included awareness raising, training, conferences, publications, development of disaster control plans, websites, research projects and applications from other disciplines. The Internet has offered greater access to and sharing of advice and experience internationally. The impact of terrorism, war and natural disasters around the world is now broadcast worldwide in real time via various media.

2006 saw the 40th anniversary of the flood that occurred in Florence on the 4 November 1966 (see, *The Florence Flood. News, Archives and Photos for the Florence Flood of 1966*). The flood resulted in a tremendous international response as noted by Feather:

> Among the flooded buildings was the Biblioteca Nazionale, where nearly half a million books and manuscripts suffered from the inflow of water and mud. A huge international rescue effort was mounted by Unesco, with binders and conservators recruited from all over the world to help in restoring the library's treasures. (Feather 1996, 3)

The flood, certainly, had far-reaching impact. Wellheiser and Scott (2002, 3) call it

> … a pivotal point in disaster planning and recovery for archives, libraries and record centres, and indeed, the entire field of preservation. Response to the flood and recovery of the damaged collections of the Biblioteca Nazionale generated new thinking, collaborative approaches and a wealth of innovative advances that continue to be used and adapted worldwide.

Since then, the devastating natural disasters, war and terrorist attacks of recent years have without a doubt had an impact on how disaster management is viewed and acted upon – lessons are there to be learned and strategy reviewed. Considerable disaster management activity had grown up gradually in the cultural heritage sector since the 1970s. Talking with archivists, conservators, curators, and librarians during the course of the project underlined the view that major disasters, reawaken interest and activity, at least for a time. As one interviewee in the U.S. put it:

> … there has been a great deal of attention on disaster management and emergency planning. Certainly after September 11th there was a little flurry of activity, but after Katrina it's been huge.

The impact of the 11 September 2001 terrorist attacks in the US on heritage institutions has been well documented (Heritage Preservation 2002). Other major disasters worldwide have followed on a regular basis. In 2002, floods in Europe (see H-Museum) caused considerable damage, for example in Prague, Czech Republic (see, Balik 2002; Balik and Polisensky 2004; Vnouček 2005). The 2003 war in Iraq and subsequent civil disorder caused major damage and destruction of heritage sites and institutions (see, for example, British Library 2007, Johnson 2005; Spurr 2007). In 2004, the Indian Ocean earthquake and tsunami of December 2004 (see, Goonewwardena and Aho 2007, IFLA PAC Regional Centre for Asia and National Diet Library, Tokyo, Japan 2005), struck with devastating effect and loss of life. The impact of Hurricane Katrina, which struck in August 2005 on cultural heritage has been well documented (see, for example, American Library Association (ALA) *Libraries and Hurricane Katrina* 2008; Delehanty 2006; Frost and Silverman 2005; Society of American Archivists *Hurricane Katrina Recovery Information*; and Weinstein 2006). Later that year (October), an earthquake devastated Pakistan, October 2005 (Shaheen 2007).

Key International Agencies

UNESCO
The United Nations Educational, Scientific and Cultural Organization (UNESCO) supports the cultural heritage and its preservation in various ways. For example, through its *Memory of the World* Programme (UNESCO *Memory of the World*) which includes *Lost Memory: Libraries and Archives Destroyed in the Twentieth Century* (Hoeven and Albada 1996) and *General Guidelines for Safeguarding of the Documentary Heritage* (Edmondson 2002). With regard to armed conflict, it offers an information kit (UNESCO Culture 2004). It has also published a strategic guide to risk management in heritage collections (Blanco et al. 2007).

A conference co-organised with the International Federation of Red Cross and Red Crescent Societies and the United Nations Children's Fund, *World Conference on Disaster Reduction. Cultural Heritage Risk Management. 18– 22 January 2005, Kobe, Hyogo, Japan* (UNESCO 2005b) had broad disaster management coverage, but included the cultural heritage within its thematic sessions: Governance: institutional and policy frameworks for risk reduction; Risk identification, assessment, monitoring and early warning; Knowledge management and education: building a culture of resilient cultures; Reducing the underlying risk factors; Preparedness for effective response.

International Council on Archives, International Council of Museums, International Federation of Library Associations
The key international non-governmental organisations for archives, museums and libraries are the International Council on Archives (ICA), International Council of Museums (ICOM) and International Federation of Library Associations and

Institutions (IFLA). They all have preservation, conservation and disaster and emergency planning within their scope.

International Committee of the Blue Shield
ICA, ICOM and IFLA, along with the International Council of Monuments and Sites (ICOMOS) in 1996 formed the International Committee of the Blue Shield (ICBS), with the intention that it should become the cultural heritage equivalent of the ICRC. ICBS works closely with UNESCO, the International Centre for the Study of the Preservation and Restoration of Cultural Property (ICCROM) and the ICRC. There are National Committees of the Blue Shield in countries throughout the world. For further information on the development of ICBS, see Shimmon 2005, and the ICBS website. Recent articles in the journal *Alexandria* also considered its development internationally (Shimmon 2004) and nationally (Cole 2004), the importance of planning (Varlamoff 2004), financial initiatives (van der Plas 2004) and legal aspects (Carducci 2004). More information can be found in proceedings of an IFLA PAC and Section on National Libraries open session (Koch (ed.) 2003).

International Centre for the Preservation and Restoration of Cultural Property
The International Centre for the Preservation and Restoration of Cultural Property (ICCROM) 'is an intergovernmental organisation (IGO) dedicated to the conservation of cultural heritage. It exists to serve the international community as represented by its Member States, which currently number more than 125'. (ICCROM). It was established in 1956; its creation '... was very much a reflection of conditions in the aftermath of World War II, when destruction of cultural properties was fresh in memory' (Jokilehto 2000). A concise account of its development since then is provided by Jokilehto (2000).

For further information about the international organisations mentioned above, and their activities, see Chapter 4, 'Worldwide Situation'.

United Kingdom Agencies

Overall Organisation
Responsibility for, and funding of archives, libraries and museums in the UK is complex and dynamic. In this respect, the authors are sympathetic to Babbidge's view in a recent report (2007) (available on the Association of Independent Museums website (AIM 2008)) on local authorities and independent museums

> As even a brief and simplified explanation of these arrangements takes many
> pages, it has been necessary, at the risk of the reader losing the will to live,
> to give over a larger part of the report than otherwise would be desirable to
> describing local government as it is now, and how it is likely to change. (p. 6)

and as such would suggest that those wanting more detail look at his report as it provides a concise introduction to local government in England, Wales and Scotland, including taxation and funding, partnerships, non-governmental organisations, museums and independent museums. National institutions receive funding from central government departments. Funding from national governments and local authorities supports archives and libraries and museums (to different levels) throughout the UK. (Lawley (2003) provides an interesting insight into museums and local authorities.) There are different statutory requirements; the devolved administrations (Scotland, Wales, Northern Ireland) have their own roles and legislation, too. (UK Resilience. *Recovery Guidance – Infrastructure Issues. Historic Environment*, provides guidance on this particular topic in a way that illustrates national, including devolved administrations, regional and local roles and responsibilities.) Over the years, there have also been various initiatives, which have encouraged institutions to apply for one-off non-core project funding, too. (Harrop et al. (2002) illustrate the growth and challenges of competitive funding in the archives domain.) Some institutions are run as independent charities. There are also those run as part of commercial organisations, and some which operate as private, independent concerns. (For further information on funding, see: Greenwood and Maynard (comps.) 2006, which outlines the type of institution in each domain, how funded, and levels of income and expenditure (2–9) ; the National Council of Archives (2005) which includes a section, *Context – the last five years* (20–2); University Museums UK Group (2004 24–30)).

For the development of the cultural heritage, Selwood (2001) provides an overview. The websites of the government departments agencies considered below should also be consulted (see, for example, MLA *Renaissance* and regional museums). Collections Link, the 'national collections management advisory service' offers information on legal requirements (Collections Link. *Comply with the law*) including charity law, independent status and governance, and fundraising (Collections Link *Raise Funds*) including Arts Council England, and the Heritage Lottery Fund (HLF) and other national lottery sources.

The Museums, Libraries and Archives Council (MLA) 'is [the] government's agency for museums, galleries, libraries and archives', they 'deliver strategic leadership in England and in each of its regions' (MLA, *About Us*). There are regional councils throughout England and national equivalents exist in Northern Ireland, Scotland and Wales.

English Regional MLAs
At the time of writing, the MLA in England is undergoing a restructuring. In England,

> The MLA Partnership is government's agency for museums, galleries, libraries and archives. [It] delivers strategic leadership in England and in each of its regions and ... collaborates with partners [for example, The Collections Trust] across the UK ... [It is] a Non-Departmental Public Body (NDPB), sponsored

by the Department for Culture, Media and Sport (DCMS). Launched in April 2000 as the strategic body working with and for the museums, archives and libraries sector, tapping into the potential for collaboration between them, MLA replaced the Museums and Galleries Commission (MGC) and the Library and Information Commission (LIC), and includes archives within its portfolio (MLA About us).

There are nine regional MLA's in England.

CyMAL: Museums Archives and Libraries Wales
CyMAL: Museums Archives and Libraries Wales (CyMAL) supports the development of local museums, archives and libraries services and: provides the Minister for Heritage with authoritative policy advice; gives advice and financial support to local museums, archives and libraries; develops and implements policies appropriate to Wales.

> ...[it] was established as a new division of the Welsh Assembly Government on 1 April 2004 ...[it] represents a significant investment by the Assembly Government in the development of local museums, archives and libraries services which meet 21st century needs. It builds on the strategic agenda outlined in the Assembly Government's strategic agenda, 'Wales: A Better Country'. (CyMal: Museums Archives and Libraries Wales)

Museums Galleries Scotland
> is the lead body for the funding, development and advocacy of over 340 museums and galleries in Scotland ... [It is] the recognised representative of and advisor to a membership which includes all 32 local authorities, 162 independent trusts, 7 regimentals and 9 universities. (Museums Galleries Scotland)

It replaced the Scottish Museums Council on 31 March 2008.

Scottish Libraries and Information Council
> The Scottish Library and Information Council [SLIC] is the independent advisory body to the Scottish Government and Scottish Ministers on library and Information matters. SLIC members include all local authority, higher education, further education organisations, NHS Trust library services, as well as other specialist library and information organisations. SLIC was established in 1991 and is funded by organisational membership subscriptions. The Scottish Government partially funds the Council in its work and The National Library of Scotland also contributes financial assistance. (SLIC *Introduction*)

Scottish Council on Archives

The Scottish Council on Archives was established in May 2002 to co-ordinate national policy on archival issues in Scotland. The formation of the Scottish Council on Archives was one of the principal objectives of the Scottish National Archives Policy (1998) in recognition of the need for an independent body which would represent and promote the interests of Scotland's broad archival community.

The council is a non-executive body and embraces all the major Scottish professional groupings. It also includes our main user groups, such as family and local historians, teachers of history, as well as representatives of private owners. For the first time, the full range of archival stakeholders will be able to work in partnership with major client groups in one single, all-inclusive national body. In recognition of the need to forge cross-sectoral partnerships, the Scottish Museums Council (SMC) and the Scottish Libraries and Information Council (SLIC) will be included as observer members.

The Scottish Council on Archives is committed to developing a national strategy to take the archival community in Scotland forward. (Scottish Council on Archives *About the Scottish Council on Archives*)

Northern Ireland Museums Council

The Northern Ireland Museums Council [NIMC] is a company with charitable status that was established under Ministerial order in 1993. It is managed by a Board, composed of representatives from the regional museums in Northern Ireland, the National Museums & Galleries of N. Ireland, District Councils in N. Ireland, nominees of the Minister of Culture, Arts & Leisure, a nominee of the universities in Northern Ireland, and representatives of the independent museums. The Council is principally funded by the Department of Culture, Arts and Leisure for Northern Ireland, although it also receives support for its work from its membership, a wide range of trusts, foundations and other grant bodies. (NIMC *The Council*)

Library and Information Services Council Northern Ireland

LISC Northern Ireland is the umbrella body for libraries and information providers from the public, academic, government, voluntary and commercial sectors. LISC promotes high standards in library and information services throughout Northern Ireland by: providing advice and consultation to the Department of Culture, Arts and Leisure and to other Government Departments advocating on behalf of the whole library and information sector in Northern Ireland, promoting innovation, partnerships and the sharing of good practice among library and information providers. (LISC (NI) *Library and Information Services Council Northern Ireland*)

Disaster Management – Development

In the UK, since the publication in the mid-1980s of the Ratcliffe report – a seminal report on the state of preservation and conservation in UK libraries – (Ratcliffe with Patterson 1984) there have been many professional and institutional developments in preservation. These have included disaster management. Ratcliffe noted that there were ' … very few libraries which have any kind of contingency plans formulated to meet emergencies, large or small' (Ratcliffe with Patterson 1984, 53). Since then things have developed gradually. Early on, Anderson and McIntyre's *Planning Manual for Disaster Control in Scottish Libraries and Record Offices*, published by the National Library of Scotland in 1985, was very influential in promoting disaster planning and providing guidance (internationally, too, according to Harvey (1993, 122)) as was the NPO video, *If Disaster Strikes!* produced in 1988. Another major influence was the fire that destroyed Norwich Central Library in 1994 (Creber 2003; Kennedy 1995). This timescale in libraries and archives is underlined by a comment from one of the contributors to the project:

> I've been here in [town] since 1982. When I first came we were physically separate from the library next door, but in 1990s, the building was reconstructed, and we are now physically attached to the library, although we still maintain our administrative distinctness. I suppose if you go back to the 1980s, disasters weren't much talked about, it was later, in the 1990s that we began to take them more seriously, and become more aware of what was happening elsewhere. (Local Authority archive)

For further information about the development of disaster control planning and disaster management, see Matthews, Smith and Knowles 2007.

A key milestone for museums was the establishment in 1991 of REDS (Regional Emergencies and Disaster Squad), an EmmS (East Midlands Museums Service) initiative under the direction of EmmS' then Assistant Director, Fergus Read, to co-ordinate pre-planned response and specialist support to museums, libraries and archives in the East Midlands region in the event of disaster or emergency (Read 1991). Since then it has continued to provide subscribers with an emergency manual outlining procedures and actions to enable institutions to produce their own plan and the facility to call out trained emergency squad members to disasters for immediate response, with access to emergency stockpiles throughout the region. These services have been consolidated and developed to varying degrees since 1991 (Matthews et al 2004, 8) and have served as an exemplar to others. For further information on REDS and more recent developments see its website (EmmS).

Others have investigated the state of emergency planning in museums. A survey of museum training needs (McKinley and Reynolds 1999) revealed that disaster planning was not a high or medium priority, but was mentioned as a training need in some museums. In a review of needs in museums and galleries for the Heritage Lottery Fund and Resource, Paine (2000, 27) noted that:

> There appears to be no information available on the incidence of fire damage to museum collections. There were 53 incidents of water damage to collections between 1988 and 1998, of which building defects were responsible for 26 and inadequate storm drains for 13.

HEFCE, in collaboration with the Association of University Chief Security Officers has recently published *Planning for and Managing Emergencies: a good practice guide for higher education institutions* (Easthope and Eyre 2008).

The other main example of a UK network to address disaster management has been the M25 Consortium of Academic Libraries, Disaster Management Group. This consortium focuses on developing disaster preparedness support including promoting awareness and best practice in disaster management, assisting in dissemination of disaster control management information and, more recently, arrangements for service continuity. Participants sign up to a 'Multilateral agreement for mutual subject support in the event of a disaster' – this support may include provision of services (e.g. access to special collections, borrowing rights) in addition to those offered in the 'general' M25 mutual support agreement (study space, basic enquiry service). It does not offer support for disaster response (but it does offer advice and information on disaster control management via its website, email discussion list and training events). Perhaps the best known product of the M25 Consortium's work in disaster planning is the disaster control plan template. Initially created in 1997, it has been revised and enhanced to reflect changes and initiatives in good disaster planning practice and to incorporate new areas (M25 Consortium of Academic Libraries. Disaster Management Group).

Wise (2006) provides more information and echoes the 'drivers' (fires, floods, terrorist attacks) mentioned above that have influenced activity in disaster management. She adds an additional one that reflects developments in the area she works, higher education:

> In addition to greater awareness in the library sector generally of the need for disaster planning on sound principles, significant institutional drivers for academic libraries, have been risk management, risk registers and organisational resilience in general. The Higher Education Funding Council's *Guide to Risk Management in Higher Education* being notable in this regard [HEFCE, 2005]. Colleagues will be familiar with risk assessment exercises and risk registers as part of the increasing institutional priority accorded to business and service continuity planning. (p.1)

Accreditation Scheme

A driver for museums to develop effective emergency planning, is the Accreditation scheme, which towards the end of 2004 replaced the previous Registration scheme, that sets out agreed national standards for museums in the UK. It is administered by the MLA in collaboration with the regional MLAs and their counterparts in Northern Ireland, Scotland and Wales. Emergency planning is included as part of the standard:

> 1.7.1 Museums must have an emergency plan (or disaster plan as these are sometimes called), and must show a copy to their assessing organisation on request. The plan must include:
> (a)   the arrangements for staff and visitors
> (b)   the arrangements for collections and buildings
> (c)   a risk assessment of threats such as fire, water, theft and vandalism or other disasters
> (d)   procedures to be followed by staff on discovery of an emergency.
>
> 1.7.2 Museums must review emergency plans every five years as a minimum. The date of the last review must be provided. (MLA 2004, 18)

Appendix 4 of the document, provides guidance on drafting an emergency plan and outlines an 'effective approach'. This includes, for example, appointing 'a crisis management team to assess the risks and produce the Plan', analysing the current situation and removing or reducing risks, researching the experience of others, recording contact details of other relevant organisations, devising a call-out system, publicising the plan, and practising and improving it. It goes on to indicate what a full emergency plan 'may usefully include' in addition to the required elements in 1.7. These elements include: membership and responsibilities of the Crisis Management Team, the Incident Management Team, assessment of risk, alert, evacuation and safety procedures, contact details of on-call staff, departments and services, floor plans, suppliers of specialist equipment, checklists of routine maintenance, and staff awareness procedures. Additionally, it suggests museums might also find it useful to produce an Overview Emergency Plan to facilitate getting the right people to the right location to make the decisions necessary in the first 24 hours of the crisis and to initiate the recovery process (MLA 2004, 45).

Such requirements were likely to result in a need for more advice and support for further development of disaster management / emergency planning in museums and galleries, particularly smaller ones, throughout the UK, to help them meet the demands of the new Scheme. This was the case and regional agencies and consultants have undertaken much of this.

Designation Scheme

At the end of November 2004, the designation scheme for museums was extended to libraries and archives. The scheme is administered by MLA on behalf of the Department for Culture, Media and Sport (DCMS); it identifies and celebrates the pre-eminent collections of national and international importance held in England's non-National museums, archives and libraries. (MLA *Programmes Designation*). It aims to raise standards. Institutions must apply for Designation status and these are considered by an expert panel.

The application guidance notes require that evidence that institutions have carried out a self-assessment using *Benchmarks in Collection Care for Museums, Archives and Libraries* (Re:source 2002) and that they are working towards the standards there. (MLA 2008) The Benchmarks document includes 'Emergency Preparedness' (65–9) and indicates criteria under 'basic', 'good', and 'best' headings. Institutions should have achieved 'good' or 'best'. Applicants must also demonstrate that they are working to relevant standards: for example, museums must meet the Accreditation standard, archives be working towards The National Archives (TNA) standard for archive repositories (2004) – see MLA 2008, p.11, for further information relating to appropriate standards. The TNA standard (2004) advises institutions should have a disaster control plan and addresses specific aspects such as fire prevention.

Other Organisations

The regional branches of professional associations such as the Museums Association, the Society of Archivists, and the Chartered Institute of Library and Information Professionals occasionally offer training events and occasional publications on disaster management. Other key heritage organisations such as English Heritage, The National Trust, Historic Scotland, and Cadw have their own disaster management arrangements for their properties and sites, including response teams. They play a much wider role with their expertise and experience. They offer a ranger of information and guidance, for example, technical advice notes on various aspects of conservation and related issues such as fire (Kidd 2005) and flooding (see, for example, English Heritage 2004). They also address policy and legislation (see, for example, English Heritage. Research and Conservation. Heritage Protection 2008), and research into topics such as climate change (see for example, The National Trust 2008). As well as in-house training, they also engage in training with others (for example, a short course, *Surviving a Disaster*, English Heritage in partnership with the Centre for Sustainability, University College London), (UCL *Short Courses from CSH*).

Since 11 September 2001 there has been a considerable increase in government activity at national, regional and local level relating to civil emergency planning, with wide dissemination of advice and support. Ongoing terrorist attacks worldwide, and recent severe flooding in Europe and the UK have kept such planning high on political agendas. Activity in this area includes co-operation between government agencies and other bodies at national and local level and much of the work in this area is pertinent to those charged with responsibility for disaster management/ emergency planning in the cultural heritage sector.

In the UK, websites such as UK Resilience, MI5, and Communities and Local Government offer advice on threats, fire prevention, how to deal with flooding, and provide links to other useful sites. Since the Civil Contingencies Act 2004 (Great Britain) local authorities have also developed their planning and offer advice on their websites. For example, The London Resilience Partnership's *London Prepared* offers advice and links on various aspects of preparation and prevention; Leicestershire County Council's *Emergency management* website pages provide details of contacts and responsibilities, training, leaflets on emergency management, including business continuity and a news update. The UK and Ireland Blue Shield Organisation (UKIRB) website has also been developed in recent years. This website is being hosted by the NPO and was developed by a secondee from English Heritage.

Disasters

Unfortunately, in the UK, as elsewhere in the world, since 2001, there have been significant incidents in individual archives, libraries and museums; and flooding has been region-wide in some areas with impact on the cultural heritage. In 2002, fire destroyed the world famous Artificial Intelligence Library, University of Edinburgh (Richardson 2002), and the National Motorcycle Museum, Solihull, West Midlands, was struck by fire (Norman 2004) in September, 2003 (now reopened); Ramsgate Library, Kent, too, was destroyed by fire in August 2004 (BBC *Call for library protection boost*); floods at Boscastle, Cornwall caused major damage to the Museum of Witchcraft there in August, 2004 (Museum of Witchcraft 2008); in January 2005 floods badly affected Tullie House Museum and Art Gallery in Carlisle, Cumbria (Museums Association *Tullie House Museum reopens after gallery flood*); the Cutty Sark, a clipper ship, was damaged by fire at Greenwich, London, in May 2007 (24 Hour Museum *Cutty Sark fire. Trust launches online appeal for restoration*) and in July floods – across large areas of England – caused considerable damage (for example, to Kelham Island Museum, Sheffield (Sheffield Industrial Museums Trust 2008)).

There is not the space within the book to provide detailed information about other countries. Some aspects of this are, however, covered in Chapter 4, *Worldwide Situation*.

Conclusion

Disasters, small or large, can happen anywhere; some areas are more prone to large-scale natural disasters; new threats, natural and man-made can impact anywhere.

Approaches to disaster management in different countries will be affected by this, but they are also influenced by, for example, the cultural, financial, political, social, technical context of individual countries. Within the cultural heritage sector, there are several international agencies that look to work with others to promote and coordinate effective disaster management internationally and regionally and to influence national initiatives. With regard to archives, libraries and museums, 1966 and the flooding in Florence was a key point in modern times in focusing attention on disaster management and motivating activity. Since then, there has been considerable development, much of it, unfortunately, based on the experience of yet more disasters. Achievements, developments, and work still to be done will be addressed in the following chapters.

References

24 Hour Museum, *Cutty Sark fire Trust launches online appeal for restoration* [website], (updated 22 May 2007) <http://www.24hourmuseum.org.uk/nwh_ gfx_en/ART47486.html>, accessed 5 Aug. 2008.

Abid, A. (2007), *Preserving our Digital Heritage: the UNESCO Charter*, (published online 29 May 2007) <http://portal.unesco.org/ci/en/ev.php-URL_ ID =24673&URL_DO=DO_TOPIC&URL_SECTION=201.html>, accessed 24 Jul. 2008.

AIM, *Welcome* [website], (updated 2008) <http://www.aim-museums.co.uk/>, accessed 23 Aug. 2008.

ALA, *Libraries and Hurricane Katrina* [website], (updated 2008) <http://www. ala.org/ala/cro/katrina/katrina.cfm>, accessed 5 Aug. 2008.

Anderson, H. and McIntyre, J. E. (1985) *Planning manual for disaster control in Scottish libraries and record offices*, (Edinburgh: National Library of Scotland).

Babbidge, A. (2007), *Local Authorities and Independent Museums: A Research Study* (London: Egeria), (published online Aug. 2007) <http://www.aim-museums.co.uk/images/cms/pdfs/LOCAL%20AUTHORITIES%20REPORT. pdf>, accessed 21 Aug. 2008.

Balik, V. (2002), 'Floods in Czech libraries: steps to recovery', *SCONUL Newsletter* 27, 68–70.

Balik, V. and Polisensky, J. (2004), 'The National Library of the Czech Republic and the floods of 2002', *Alexandria* 16:1, 17–24.

BBC, Call for library protection boost (published online 18 Aug. 2004) <http:// news.bbc.co.uk/1/hi/england/kent/3575616.stm>, accessed 20 Sep. 2008.

Blanco, L, et al. (2007) *Mitigating disaster: a strategic guide to risk management in heritage collections* [website], (updated 2007) <http://webworld.unesco. org/mitigating_disaster/>, accessed 25 Aug. 2008.

British Library, *Diary of Saad Eskander, Director of the Iraq National Library and Archive (covering the period November 2006 – July 2007)* [website], (updated 2007) <http://www.british-library.uk/iraqdiary.html>, accessed 14 Jul. 2008.

British Library, *Diary of Saad Eskander, Director of the Iraq National Library and Archive. Special report: 10 March 2008*, [website], (updated 2008) <http://www.british-library.uk/iraqreport.html>, accessed 17 Jul. 2008.

Cadw [Welsh Assembly Government's historic environment division], *Welcome* [website], (updated 2008) <http://www.cadw.wales.gov.uk/> accessed 24 Aug. 2008.

Carducci, G. (2004), 'Restitution of cultural property'. *Alexandria* 16:3, 171–4.

Cole, S. (2004), 'The United Kingdom and Ireland Blue Shield', *Alexandria* 16:3, 153–8.

Collections Link, *Comply with the Law* [website], (updated 2006) <http://www.collectionslink.org.uk/comply_with_the_law>, accessed 24 Aug. 2008.

Collections Link. *Raise Funds* [website], (updated c.2006) <http://www.collectionslink.org.uk/raise_funds>, accessed 24 Aug. 2008.

The Collections Trust, *Welcome to the Collections Trust* [website], (updated 2008) <http://www.collectionstrust.org.uk/>, accessed 24 Aug. 2008.

Communities and Local Government, *Communities and Local Government* [website], (updated 8 Aug. 2008) <http://www.communities.gov.uk/corporate/>, accessed 24 Aug. 2008.

Creber, J. (2003) 'Aftermath – service continuity and continuity', in Matthews, G. and Feather, J.P. (eds.) (2003), 191–211.

CyMAL. Museums Archives and Libraries Wales, *CyMAL. Museums Archives and Libraries Wales* [website], (updated c.2007) <http://new.wales.gov.uk/ topics/cultureandsport/museumsarchiveslibraries/cymalL4/?lang=en>, accessed 23 Aug. 2008.

Delehanty, R. (2006), 'Waiting for the resurrection: New Orleans – the aftermath', *Museum News* [website], (updated May. / Jun. 2006) <http://www.aam-us.org/pubs/mn/MN_MJ06_NewOrleans.cfm>, accessed 5 Aug. 2008.

DCMS, *Department for Culture, Media and Sport* [website], (updated 15 Aug. 2008) <http://www.culture.gov.uk/>, accessed 23 Aug. 2008.

Easthope, L. and Eyre, A. (2008) Planning for and Managing Emergencies: a good practice guide for higher education institutions (Bristol: The Association of University Chief Security Officers and the Higher Education Funding Council for England), (published online 2008) <http://www.aucso.org.uk/uploads/file/the%20guide%20final_1%20june%2008.pdf>, accessed 31 Jan 2009.

Edmondson, R. (2002) *General guidelines to safeguard documentary heritage*, 2nd edition, (Paris: UNESCO) [Available in Arabic, English, French, Russian, Spanish], (published online Feb. 2002) <http://portal.unesco.org/ci/en/ev.php-URL_ID=2059&URL_DO=DO_TOPIC&URL_SECTION=201.html>, accessed 22 Aug. 2008.

EmmS. *What is the Regional Emergencies & Disaster Support (REDS) Service?* [website], (updated c.2006) <http://www.emms.org.uk/reds.htm>, accessed 22 Aug. 2008.

English Heritage, *English Heritage – Stonehenge & the History of England* [website], (updated 22 Aug. 2008) <http://www.english-heritage.org.uk/>, 23 Aug. 2008.

English Heritage, *Flooding and Historic Buildings: Technical Advice Note*, (London: English Heritage), (published online 2004) <http://www.english-heritage.org.uk/upload/pdf/Flooding_and_Historic_Buildings._Technical_Advice_Note_2004.pdf>, accessed 25 Aug. 2008.

English Heritage. Research and Conservation. Heritage Protection (2008). *Heritage Protection Reform – Draft Heritage Protection Bill* [website], (updated 30 Jul. 2008) <http://www.english-heritage.org.uk/server/show/nav.8380>, accessed 21 Aug. 2008.

Feather, J. (2006), 'Managing the documentary heritage: issues for the present and future', in Gorman, G.E. and Shep, S.J. *Preservation Management for Libraries, Archives and Museums* (London: Facet Publishing), 1–18.

Feather, J. (2004), 'Introduction and principles', in Feather, J (ed.), *Managing Preservation for Libraries and Archives. Current Practice and Future Developments* (Aldershot: Ashgate Publishing Limited), 1–25.

'*The Florence Flood. News, archives and photos for the Florence flood of 1966*' [see *November 4th 2006 40th anniversary of the Florence flood*] [website], (updated 14 Jan. 2008) <http://www.florence-flood.com/>, accessed 25. Aug. 2008.

Frost, G. and Silverman, R. (2005), 'Disaster recovery in the artefact fields – Mississippi after Hurricane Katrina', *International Preservation News* 37, 35–47.

GCI, *Field Projects. Iraq Cultural Heritage Conservation Initiative* [website], (updated Dec. 2006) <http://www.getty.edu/conservation/field_projects/iraq/index.html>, accessed 14 Aug. 2008.

Goonewwardena, N. and Aho, M. (2007), 'Writing a new chapter – glocalization: creating libraries across the globe – a case study in Sri Lanka, Information Providers', in *Coping with Disaster in Asia and Oceania, Asia and Oceania Section, World Library and Information Congress, 73rd IFLA Conference and Council,* Durban, South Africa, 19–23 Aug. 2007, IFLA, (published online 2007) <http://www.ifla.org/IV/ifla73/papers/140-Goonewardena_Aho-en.pdf>, accessed 24 Aug. 2008.

Great Britain, *Civil Contingencies Act 2004 (Contingency Planning) Regulations 2005. S.I.2005 No 2042* (London: The Stationery Office Limited).

Greenwood, H. and Maynard, S. (comps.) (2006), *Digest of statistics 2006,* (Loughborough: LISU and MLA), (published online), (updated 20 Dec. 2006) <http://www.lboro.ac.uk/departments/ls/lisu/pages/publications/digest06.html>, accessed 4 Sep. 2008.

Harrop, K. et al. (2002), 'Bidding for records: local authority archives and competitive funding', *Journal of the Society Archivists* 23:1, 35–50.

Harvey, R. (1993) *Preservation in Libraries: Principles, Strategies and Practices for Librarians (Topics in Library and Information Studies)* (London, Melbourne, Munich, New York: Bowker Saur).

H-Museum, *H-Museum's Current Focus: Floods in Europe. Damage to museums, history places, archives and libraries* [website], (updated 12 Oct. 2002) <http://www.h-net.org/~museum/flood.html>, accessed 13 Jul. 2008.

Harvey, R. (2007), 'UNESCO's Memory of the World Programme', *Library Trends*, 56:1, 259–74.

HEFCE (2005), *Risk management in higher education. A guide to good practice, prepared for HEFCE by PricewaterhouseCoopers (Good Practice. Guidance February 2005/11)* (Bristol: HEFCE), (published online) <http://www.hefce.ac.uk/ pubs/hefce/2005/05_11/>, accessed 22 Aug. 2008.

Heritage Preservation, *Heritage Emergency Task Force. Hurricanes 2005* [website], (updated 2005) <http://www.heritagepreservation.org/PROGRAMS/Katrina.HTM>, accessed 24 Aug. 2008.

Heritage Preservation (2002), *Cataclysm and challenge. Impact of September 11, 2001, on Our Nation's Cultural Heritage. A report from Heritage Preservation on behalf of the Heritage Emergency National Task Force,* [Project Director Ruth Hargraves,] (Washington, DC: Heritage Preservation), (published online 2002) <http://www.heritagepreservation.org/PDFS/Cataclysm.pdf>, accessed 29 Aug. 2008.

Historic Scotland, *Historic Scotland – the official website* [website], (updated 25 Aug. 2008) <http://www.historic-scotland.gov.uk/>, accessed 25 Aug. 2008.

Hoeven, H. van der and Albada, J. van (1996), *Lost memory: libraries and archives destroyed in the twentieth century* (Paris: UNESCO), (published online Mar. 1996) <http://unesdoc.unesco.org/images/0010/001055/105557e.pdf>, accessed 22 Aug. 2008.

'Humanitarian response to the Indian Ocean earthquake 2004' *Wikipedia* [website], (updated 21 Aug. 2008) <http://en.wikipedia.org/wiki/ Humanitarian_response_to_the_2004_Indian_Ocean_earthquake#Contributing_non-governmental_organisations_.28NGOs.29>, accessed 27 Aug. 2008.

ICA, *International Council on Archives* [website], (updated 5 Sep. 2008) <http://www.ica.org/>, accessed 6 Sep. 2008.

ICCROM, *ICCROM: home page: (International Council for the Study of the Preservation and Restoration of Cultural Property)* [website], (updated 20 Aug. 2008) <http://www.iccrom.org/>, accessed 25 Aug. 2008.

ICOM, *International Council of Museums* [website], (updated n.d.), <http://icom.museum/>, accessed 6 Sep. 2008.

ICRC, *National Implementation of International Humanitarian Law: Protection of Cultural Property* [website], (updated 2008) <http://www.icrc.org/web/eng/siteeng0.nsf/htmlall/section_ihl_nat_cultural_property?opendocument>, accessed 23 Aug. 2008.

ICRC, *International Review of the Red Cross, 2004 – No. 854* [website], (updated 2004) < http://www.icrc.org/web/eng/siteeng0.nsf/html/section_review_2004_854?opendocument>, accessed 20 Sep. 2008.

ICOMOS, International Council on Monuments and Sites [website], (updated 2008) <http://www.international.icomos.org/home.htm>, accessed 20 Sep. 2008.

IFLA, *International Federation of Library Associations and Institutions* [website], (updated n.d.) <http://www.ifla.org/>, accessed 6 Sep. 2008.

IFLA PAC Regional Centre for Asia and National Diet Library (2005), *Open seminar on the documentary heritage damaged by the Indian Ocean Tsunami and the meeting of Directors of the IFLA/PAC Regional Centres in Asia and others, National Diet Library, Tokyo, 6 Dec. 2005* (Tokyo: National Diet Library), (published online Dec. 2005) <http://www.ndl.go.jp/en/iflapac/news.html>, accessed 14 Aug. 2008). [The program was as follows: Keynote address: "Disaster programs of the IFLA PAC" by Marie-Thérèse Varlamoff, Director, PAC International Focal Point, Reports of countries damaged by the Indian Ocean Tsunami given by Dady P. Rachmananta, Director of the National Library of Indonesia and by Upali Amarasiri, Director of the National Library Sri Lanka, "Restoration of soaked and muddy land ledgers in Banda Aceh, Indonesia" by Isamu Sakamoto, Paper Conservator, Director of the Tokyo Restoration & Conservation Center and "Recent activities of the IFLA/PAC Regional Centre for Asia" by Masaki Nasu, Director of the IFLA/PAC.]

'International Response to Hurricane Katrina' Wikipedia [website], (updated 11 Aug. 2008) <http://en.wikipedia.org/wiki/International_response_to_Hurricane_Katrina>, accessed 23 Aug. 2008.

Johnson, I. M. (2005), 'The impact on libraries and archives in Iraq of war and looting in 2003: a preliminary assessment of the damage and subsequent reconstruction efforts', *International Information and Library Review* 37:3, 209–71.

Jokilehto, J. (2000), 'ICCROM's involvement in risk preparedness', *Journal of the American Institute for Conservation* 39:1 [website], (updated 2000) <http://aic.stanford.edu/jaic/articles/jaic39-01-014_indx.html>, accessed 5 Aug. 2008.

Kennedy, J. (1995), 'Norfolk Record Office: an initial report', *Journal of the Society of Archivists* 16:1, 3–6.

Kidd, S. (2005), *Fire safety management in heritage buildings. Historic Scotland Technical Advice Note 28* (Edinburgh: Historic Scotland).

Koch, C. (trans. and ed.) (2003), *A Blue Shield for the protection of our cultural heritage. Proceedings of the Open Session co-organized by PAC Core Activity and the Section on National Libraries (International Preservation Issues Number 4)*, (Paris: IFLA PAC), (published online 2003) <http://www.museums.ca/media/Pdf/blueshield.pdf>, accessed 26. Aug. 2008.

Lawley, I. (2003), 'Local authority museums and the modernizing government agenda', *Museum and Society* 1:2, 75–86.

Leicester County Council. *Emergency management* [website], (updated 10 Feb. 2007) <http://www.leics.gov.uk/chief-execs/emergency_management/>, accessed 24 Aug. 2008.

LISC (NI), *Library and Information Services Council (Northern Ireland)* [website], (updated Jun. 2008) <http://www.liscni.co.uk/>, accessed 23 Aug. 2008.

Lomas, H., *Renaissance in the regions. Collections Link* [website], (updated n.d.) <http://www.collectionslink.org.uk/raise_funds/fund_overview/renaissance>, accessed 26 Aug. 2008.

London Resilience Partnership, *London Prepared* [website], (updated 2008) <http://www.londonprepared.gov.uk/>, accessed 24 Aug. 2008.

MI5, *UK Home Page* [webpage], (updated 2008) <http://www.mi5.gov.uk/>, accessed 24 Aug. 2008.

MLA, *About us* [website], (updated 2008) <http://www.mla.gov.uk/website/aboutus/>, accessed 26 Aug. 2008.

MLA. *Accreditation Scheme* [website]. (updated 2008) <http://www.mla.gov.uk/programmes/accreditation>, accessed 24 Aug. 2008.

MLA, *Programmes Designation* [website], (updated 2008) <http://www.mla.gov.uk/programmes/designation/00desig/>, accessed 24 Aug. 2008.

MLA, *Renaissance* [website], (updated 2008) <http://www.mla.gov.uk/programmes/renaissance>, accessed 21 Aug. 2008.

MLA (2008). *The designation scheme for museums, libraries and archives. Application guidance notes* (London: MLA).

MLA (2004), *Accreditation standard. The accreditation scheme for museums in the United Kingdom* (London: MLA), (published online 2004) <http://www.mla.gov.uk/resources/assets//A/accreditation_standard_pdf_5640.pdf>, accessed 30 Aug. 2008.

M25 Consortium of Academic Libraries. Disaster Management Group. *Disaster Control Plan* [website], (updated 2004) <http://www.m25lib.ac.uk/m25dcp/>, accessed 22 Aug. 2008.

Matthews, G., Smith, Y. and Knowles, G. (2004), 'The Disaster Control Plan. Where is it at?', *Library and Archival Security* 19:2, 3–24 [Published 2007].

Matthews, G. et al. (2004), *An investigation into the work of REDS (Regional Emergencies & Disaster Squad). A report to East Midlands Museums, Libraries and Archives Council (EMMLAC)* (Birmingham and Leicester, Centre for Information Research (CIRT), University of Central England in Birmingham, East Midlands Museums, Libraries and Archives Council (EMMLAC)), (published online 2004) <http://www.mlaeastmidlands.org.uk/templates/temp_cor_rep_index.rm? category=keywords_root.taxonomy.corporate.documenttype.Report&category=keywords_root.taxonomy.corporate.subject.Collections&id=589&sort_type=date&num=5&term=&submit.x=11&submit.y=13&from=6>, accessed 27 Aug. 2008.

McKinley, J. and Reynolds, P. (1999), 'Training needs of museums in Surrey: an analysis 1988/1999', *Surrey Museums* [website], (updated 21 May 1999)

<http://www.surreymuseums.free-online.co.uk/staff/train.html>, accessed 21 Aug. 2008.

The Museum of Witchcraft, *Museum of Witchcraft* [website], (updated 2004) <http://www.museumofwitchcraft.com/>, accessed 23 Aug. 2008. [Diary of impact of Boscastle floods in 2004.]

Museums Association, *Tullie House Museum reopens after gallery flood* (published online 12 Jan. 2005) <http://www.museumsassociation.org/ma/10513>, accessed 20 Sep. 2008.

Museums Galleries Scotland [formerly Scottish Museums Council], *Home* [website], (updated 19 Aug. 2008) <http://www.museumsgalleriesscotland. org.uk /index.asp>, accessed 23 Aug. 2008.

National Council of Archives (2005) *Giving value. Funding priorities for UK archives 2005–2010* (London: MLA, the National Council on Archives, TNA), (published online 2005) <http://www.ncaonline.org.uk/materials/nca_giving_ value.pdf>, accessed 4 Sep. 2008.

The National Trust (2008), *Nature's Capital: Investing in the nation's natural assets* (Swindon: The National Trust), (published online 14 Mar. 2008) http://www. nationaltrust.org.uk/main/w-natures_capital.pdf, accessed 26 Aug. 2008.

The National Trust, *The National Trust* [website], (updated 2008) <http://www. nationaltrust.org.uk/main/>, accessed 23 Aug. 2008.

NIMC. Welcome [website], (updated c.2008) <http://www.nimc.co.uk/>, accessed 24 Aug. 2008.

Norman, J. (2004), 'It's back! National Motorcycle Museum reopens year after fire', *24 Hour Museum* [website], (updated 2 Dec. 2004) <http:// www.24hourmuseum.org.uk/nwh_gfx_en/ART25094.html>, accessed 23 Aug. 2008.

NPO, *National Preservation Office* [website], (updated n.d.) <http://www.bl.uk/ npo>, accessed 23 Aug. 2008.

Paine, C. (2000), *Stewardship. Assessment of needs in the museums and galleries sector: a report for the Heritage Lottery Fund and Re:source*, (published online Jul. 2000) <http://www.hlf.org.uk/NR/ rdonlyres/6BF0726A-2004-4FD0- 8B939BCA762176E8/0/needs_stewardship. pdf>, accessed 29 Jun. 2008.

Plas, E. van der (2004), 'New fund for emergency aid to culture: cultural emergency response', *Alexandria* 18:3,159–69.

Ratcliffe, F.W. with Patterson, D. (1984), *Preservation policies and conservation in British libraries: report of the Cambridge University Library conservation project*, (Library and Information Research Reports 25) (London: The British Library).

Read, F. (1991), 'Emergency planning for museums in the East Midlands', in UKIC/RAI Restoration '91, Planning for Disasters. 18 Oct. 1991.

Re:source (2002) *Benchmarks in Collection Care for Museums, Archives and Libraries: A Self-assessment Checklist* (London: Re:source: the Council for Museums, Libraries and Archives), (published online 2002) <http://www.mla.

gov.uk/resources/assets//B/benchmarks_pdf_5910.pdf>, accessed 25 Aug. 2008.

Richardson, T. (2002) 'Fire guts Edinburgh's AI library', *The Register*, (published online 12 Dec. 2002) <http://www.theregister.co.uk/2002/12/12/fire_guts_edinburghs_ai_library/>, accessed 20 Sep. 2008.

Scottish Council on Archives, *Scottish Council on Archives* [website], (updated 2007), <http://www.archives.org.uk/sca/>, accessed 23 Aug. 2008.

Scottish Council on Archives. *About the Scottish Council on Archives* [website], (updated 2005) <http://www.archives.org.uk/sca/about.htm>, accessed 23 Aug. 2008.

Selwood, S. (ed.) (2001), *The UK Cultural Sector. Profile and Policy Issues.* (London: Policy Studies Institute).

Shaheen, M. (2007) 'Academic Institutions and Libraries of Pakistani Administered Kashmir: A Pre and Post Earthquake Analysis', in *Information Providers Coping with Disaster in Asia and Oceania, Asia and Oceania Section, World Library and Information Congress, 73rd IFLA Conference and Council*, August 2007, Durban, South Africa, IFLA, (published online Aug. 2008) <http://www.ifla.org/IV/ifla73/papers/140-Shaheen-en.pdf>, accessed 14 Jul. 2008.

Sheffield Industrial Museums Trust (2008) *Flood recovery news. Kelham Island Museum. Towards the new Kelham* [Tells the story of the recovery process] [website], (updated 24 Jul. 2008) <http://newkelham.blogspot.com/>, accessed 5 Aug. 2008.

Shimmon, R. (2005). 'The Blue Shield: the cultural Red Cross?' in: Wellheiser, J. G. and Gwinn, N. E. (eds.) (2005), 41–50.

Shimmon, R. (2004), 'The International Committee of the Blue Shield 1998- 2004: an overview', *Alexandria* 16:3, 2004, 133–41.

SLIC, *Introduction* [website], (updated 24 Jul. 2008) <http://www.slainte.org.uk/slic/slicindex.htm>, accessed 23 Aug. 2008.

Society of American Archivists, *Hurricane Katrina Recovery Information* [website], (updated 2005) <http://www.archivists.org/news/katrina.asp>, accessed 5 Aug. 2008.

Spurr, J. (2007) *Iraqi Libraries and Archives in Peril: Survival in a Time of Invasion, Chaos, and Civil Conflict, A Report* [part of the University of Chicago Oriental Institute's Lost Treasures from Iraq project.], (Chicago: University of Chicago) [website]. (updated n.d.) <http://oi.uchicago.edu/OI/IRAQ/mela/update_2007.htm>, accessed 28 Aug. 2008.

Taboroff, J. (2001), 'The World Bank and ProVention. International disaster relief and protection of cultural heritage'. *CRM [Cultural Resource Management] Online* 24:8, .30–32, (published online 2001) <http://crm.cr.nps.gov/archive/24-08/24-08-10.pdf, accessed 23 Aug. 2008.

TNA (2004), *Standard for record repositories* (Kew: The National Archives), (published online 2004) <http://www.nationalarchives.gov.uk/documents/standard2005.pdf>, accessed 25 Aug. 2008.

UCL [University College London], *Short courses from CSH* [website], (updated 2006) <http://www.ucl.ac.uk/sustainableheritage/short_courses.htm>, accessed 24 Aug. 2008.

UKIRB, *United Kingdom and Ireland Blue Shield Organisation* [website], (updated n.d.) <http://www.bl.uk/blueshield/>, accessed 24 Aug. 2008.

UK Resilience. *Civil Contingencies Act* [website], (updated 26 Aug. 2008) <http://www.ukresilience.gov.uk/preparedness/ccact.aspx>, accessed 22 Aug. 2008.

UK Resilience. *Recovery Guidance – Infrastructure Issues. Historic Environment* [website], (updated 11 Jan. 2008) <http://www.ukresilience.gov.uk/response/recovery_guidance/infrastructure_issues/listed_buildings.aspx>, accessed 6 Sep. 2008.

UK Resilience, *Welcome to UK Resilience* [website], (updated Aug. 2008) <http://www.ukresilience.gov.uk/>, accessed 20 Sep. 2008.

UNESCO, *Memory of the World* [website], (updated 2 Nov. 2007) < http://portal.unesco.org/ci/en/ev.php-URL_ID=23929&URL_DO=DO_TOPIC&URL_SECTION=201.html>, accessed 22 Aug. 2008.

UNESCO, *International Strategy for Disaster Reduction. Disaster reduction begins at school. Fact sheet,* (published online 2006) <http://www.unisdr.org/eng/public_aware/world_camp/2006-2007/pdf/Fact-sheet-en. pdf>, accessed 23 Aug. 2008.

UNESCO (2005a), *International Strategy for Disaster Reduction. 12 October 2005 International Day for Disaster Reduction* [website], (updated 2005) <http://www.unisdr.org/eng/public_aware/world_camp/2005/2005-iddr.htm>, accessed 23 Aug. 2008.

UNESCO (2005b), *Kobe report draft. Report of session 3.3, Thematic Cluster 3. Cultural Heritage Risk Management. World Conference on Disaster Reduction. 18–22 January 2005, Kobe, Hyogo, Japan,* (published online 2005) <http://www.heritagerisk.org/report-session-3-3.pdf>, accessed 29 Aug. 2008.

UNESCO (2004), *Protect cultural property in the event of armed conflict. Information kit* (Paris: UNESCO).

University Museums UK Group (2004), *University museums in the United Kingdom: a national resource for the 21st century* (University Museums UK Group), (published online 2004) <http://www.umg.org.uk/media/Text.pdf>, accessed 4 Sep. 2008.

Varlamoff, M.-T. (2004), 'De l'utilité des plans d'urgence' *Alexandria* 16:3, 143–51.

Vnouček, J. (2005), 'The Prague flood diary', in Wellheiser, J. G. and Gwinn, N. E. (eds.) (2005), 103–108.

Weinstein, A. (2006), 'After a Disaster. The National Archives as "First Preserver"' *Prologue* 38:1, (published online 2006) <http://www.archives.gov/publications/prologue/2006/spring/first-preserver.html>, accessed 5 Aug. 2008.

Wellheiser, J. G. and Gwinn, N. E. (eds.), *Preparing for the worst, planning for the best: protecting our cultural heritage from disaster. Proceedings of a conference sponsored by the IFLA Preservation and Conservation Section, the IFLA Core*

Activity for Preservation and Conservation and the Council on Library and Information Resources, Inc., with the Akademie der Wissenschaften and the Staatsbibliothek zu Berlin. Berlin, Germany, Jul 30–August 1, 2003 (Munich: K G Saur).

Wellheiser, J. and Scott, J. (2002), *An Ounce of Prevention: Integrated Disaster Planning for Archives, Libraries and Record Centres*. 2nd edition (Lanham, Maryland and London: The Scarecrow Press, Inc and Canadian Archives Foundation).

Wise, C. (2006), 'Thinking the unthinkable: disaster planning for the M25 Consortium of Academic Libraries', *SCONUL Focus* 38, 95–7, (published online 2006) <http://www.sconul.ac.uk/publications/newsletter/38/29.rtf>, accessed 22 Aug. 2008.

The World Bank. *Cultural Heritage in Sustainable Development* [website], (updated Jun. 2008] <http://web.worldbank.org/wbsite/external/topics/exturbandevelopment/extchd/0,menuPK:430436~pagePK:149018~piPK:149093~theSitePK:430430,00. html>, accessed 30 Aug. 2008.

Chapter 3
The Situation in the United Kingdom: Overview

Introduction

Data that fed into an understanding of the contemporary situation regarding disaster management in archives, libraries and museums in the UK was acquired from a variety of sources. This included the literature, organisational, institutional and news websites, personal contacts, attendance at seminars and conferences, an e-mail survey of regional museum, library and archive councils and their national counterparts, a questionnaire survey and interviews.

Previous Surveys

Ratcliffe's seminal report on the state of preservation and conservation in UK libraries in the 1980s noted that: 'There are very few libraries which have any kind of contingency plans formulated to meet emergencies, large or small' (Ratcliffe with Patterson 1984, 53). A survey of libraries and archives in England, Wales and Northern Ireland, undertaken a year later revealed there was:

> A significant number of actual incidents in any year which either threaten or affect libraries, archives and their contents ... [but that] Only a small number of institutions has any organised plan aimed at preventing such incidents and effecting recovery from them. (Tregarthen Jenkin, 1987, 35)

Tregarthen Jenkin reported that '... only 6.6 per cent of the institutions surveyed had disaster control plans in use ...' (p. 2).

In another national survey carried out in 1986, only 9 per cent of university and polytechnic libraries, which responded, replied that they had a disaster control plan (Mowat 1987, 39). By 1988, this figure had risen, with nearly 36 per cent of SCONUL (then Standing Conference of National and University Libraries) member libraries reporting they had a disaster control plan (Moon and Loveday 1989, 14).

Figures for all kinds of library were reported amongst the results of a nationwide survey of preservation undertaken in the early 1990s. That questionnaire survey revealed that 29 per cent of the 488 libraries that responded had a disaster control plan, written or otherwise (Feather, Matthews and Eden 1996). In a project focusing on disaster management, undertaken two years later, just over 20 per cent reported having a written disaster control plan (Matthews and Eden 1996, 7).

The NPO, based at the British Library, recently published *Knowing the Need* (Walker and Foster 2006), which reports the findings of preservation assessments, using a standard tool developed by the NPO, carried out in libraries and archives over the previous five years. Amongst its coverage is disaster planning. On this aspect, Walker and Foster comment:

> The fact that only 59 per cent of material is covered by a written disaster control
> plan is a great improvement on past estimates, but is still disappointing given
> the much greater awareness in recent years of the need to analyse and minimise
> risk to assets. (2006, 12)

They add that this is more disappointing if staff training is also taken into account as adequacy regarding whether the item is covered by an up-to-date, written disaster control plan, and staff are trained in its implementation, is found to be: Adequate 54 per cent, Inadequate 46 per cent (p.11).

Indeed, in another publication of the following year that, based on the above findings, outlined the state of preservation of collections in the UK, the NPO highlighted that '46% of collections have no up-to-date, written disaster control plan' (NPO 2007 3). Here, having identified 'the need', the NPO also advocated a coordinated approach of action based on evidence to meet the 'need'. With regard to disaster planning, proposed actions were identified as 'training' and 'information', with a national/regional focus that should; 'Provide resources; work towards incremental support; support and advocate effective prioritisation of effort; advocate performance measures for the care of collections; continuing needs assessment' (NPO 2007 5).

In a review of needs in museums and galleries for the Heritage Lottery Fund and Resource, Paine (2000, 27), drawing on others' reports, noted, with regard to planning response for disasters, that even in the East Midlands where an emergency manual and disaster response team had been established, disaster planning varied between museums; and that a lot of museums in Wales did not have contingency plans.

In its report on UK museum needs, ABL Cultural Consulting (2000, 13) noted:

> Figures presented in AMC mapping studies indicate variations in the number
> of museums which have produced disaster plans. There is a need for greater
> understanding of the importance of disaster planning and the production of plans
> for all museums.

The report refers to four regions covered in the study. It noted that the Southern Museums Agency found that 77 per cent of museums had identified a need for emergency planning but only 31 per cent actually had one. In the West Midlands the report states only 16 per cent had emergency plans and in the South East only 3 per cent had a disaster response plan with stocks, rehearsals and regular review. No figures were available for museums in the South West. In its matrix of need in the museum sector, the report ranks the 'need to improve disaster planning' as a number one priority, indicating that heritage assets are at risk if the need is not addressed.

At the beginning of 2004, as part of a review (Matthews et al. 2004) led by one of the book's authors of the East Midlands Museums Service (EmmS) Regional Emergencies and Disaster Squad (REDS), an e-mail was sent to the other eight Regional MLAs in England (i.e. excluding EMMLAC). This requested information about the provision of disaster management in their region, including any disaster response services or networks and training and awareness programmes. Five replied. Their responses shed light on activity in the museums domain at the time.

One regional MLA reported that: they 'have nothing set up'; another commented: they were 'Very interested to hear about this review – I've always wanted a system like REDS', adding that they would be rolling out some training in the region over the next year. Others indicated some activity in their regions, including in one, production of a template plan in 1998 that is still distributed to museums writing their own plan. Additionally, one local museums service in this region was running training with The National Trust as part of NVQ courses in disaster management. The respondent from another region advised that it did not have a regionally based emergency service, although, since 1996, they have encouraged museum members to develop plans based on the EmmS/North West Museums' Service models. This respondent added perceptively that the next phase of the Museums' Registration Scheme would require applicants to have an emergency plan in existence, so the emphasis on producing one would be heightened (Matthews et al. 2004).

UK Questionnaire Survey Method

Introduction

A questionnaire survey of UK archives, libraries and museums, the first to cover all three domains, was conducted in summer 2005. A semi-random sample of archives and libraries was used. This consisted of a random sample and a purpose-based sample approach (that incorporated geographic and institutional typology focus). This provided an approximate balance of the number of archives, libraries and museums.

Purpose of Questionnaire

The four-page questionnaire sought to elicit information that would provide an overview of disaster management activity in archives, libraries and museums in the UK. It was divided into seven sections seeking information about:

- respondent
- organisation type
- disaster control plan
- training
- in-house disaster management activities
- external arrangements
- views on disaster management
- experience of disaster(s).

Most questions asked respondents to 'tick box' as appropriate, with space for additional information or comments. Some questions used a Likert scale, to assess views. (The questionnaire sent to libraries is at Appendix A.)

The questionnaire was accompanied by a covering letter explaining the purpose of the research, with guidance on completing the questionnaire on the reverse.

Definitions

On the reverse of the letter that accompanied the questionnaire, notes providing 'Guidance in completing the questionnaire' outlined the definitions of disaster and disaster management for the purpose of the survey. These were:

Disaster
Any incident which threatens human safety and/or damages or threatens to damage or destroy, an archive's/library's/museum's buildings, collections, contents, facilities or services.

Disaster management
Planning and actions to prevent and be prepared for disasters and dealing with them effectively. These normally address four key stages: prevention, preparedness, reaction, and recovery.

It was also noted that in some institutions the term 'emergency planning' might be used in the same sense as 'disaster management'. In the questionnaire to museums, reflecting practice in the domain, the terms 'disaster management' and 'disaster control plan', were replaced by 'emergency planning' and 'emergency plan'.

Distribution and Response

Following drafting, feedback was received from the Project Advisory Panel (comprising experts in the field) and the questionnaire piloted.

In researching contact details the most comprehensive and authoritative directories identified at the time were the ARCHON website (TNA n.d.), *Museums and Galleries Yearbook 2005* (Museums Association 2005) and the *Libraries and Information Services in the United Kingdom and the Republic of Ireland 2005* (Franklin and York (comps.) 2004) directory for libraries. In total, these directories contained approximately 8000 entries.

ARCHON	Lists 2300 archives in the UK, Isle of Man and Channel Islands.
Museums and Galleries Yearbook 2005	This contains approximately 2400 entries of museums and galleries in the UK, Isle of Man and Channel Islands.
Libraries and information services in the United Kingdom and Republic of Ireland	Contains listing of 3000 libraries in the UK, Isle of Man and Channel Islands (including branches)

Surveying the total population was not feasible within the resources of the project. The original project proposal indicated an intention to conduct a 'Questionnaire survey of UK archives, museums, libraries (by post/e-mail) to all public library authorities, university libraries, local authority archives/record offices and museums (and galleries) in the UK, plus a sample of independent/ private archives, libraries and museums'. It was envisaged 'the maximum number of questionnaires, including UK and international, will be 2000' (and costings and timescale were based on this).

In order to ensure that the survey covered the full spectrum of archives/libraries/ museums and was as close as possible to the original proposal and manageable within resources and time available, the following approach was taken:

Archives	Questionnaires were sent to the national archive services for England, Northern Ireland, Scotland and Wales, all local authority archives and to a one in four sample of all other entries in ARCHON in the UK, Isle of Man and Channel Islands (these included college, school, business or company, museum, gallery, charitable, private collection, religious, and 'other' archives).
Libraries	Questionnaires were sent to all public library authorities, to the head of service in all higher education libraries and to government, national and special libraries listed in the Libraries and information services in the United Kingdom and the Republic of Ireland directory. A sample (one in four) was taken of the libraries of the colleges of the Universities of Cambridge, London and Oxford.
Museums	Questionnaires were sent to all national museums and galleries, museums and galleries with designated collections, and a one in four sample of all other museums and galleries as identified in the Museums and Galleries Yearbook 2005.

For archives and museums care was taken that proportionate geographic representation was achieved in the sample. For libraries, there was no need to ensure proportionate geographic representation as the sample was pre-selected from the Libraries and information services in the United Kingdom and Republic of Ireland mailing list.

The questionnaire was sent by post, with a note that an e-version was available on request, to named individuals, where possible, with responsibility for disaster management in the archive, library or museum.

UK Questionnaire Survey Results[1]

Questionnaires Sent and Received

Of the 1986 questionnaires sent to archives, libraries and museums in the UK, Channel Islands and Isle of Man, a response rate of 32 per cent was obtained, with 635 archives, libraries and museums returning questionnaires (see Table 3.1).

Managers[2] were asked to classify the type of archive, library or museum they worked in. Those working in libraries were asked to indicate one category only, however those in archives and museums were asked to indicate all the categories that applied. The categories available were:

---

1   Unless otherwise stated, where table percentages do not add to 100 per cent, the percentages have been rounded up or down.

2   Respondents to the questionnaire are referred to as managers. Other members of staff within the archive, library or museum are referred to as staff.

Archives	National; Local Authority; University, College or School; Business or Company; Museum; Gallery; Charitable; Private Collection; Religious; Other.
Libraries	National; Public; Higher Education; Further Education; School; Government; Industrial and Commercial; Health, Media; Prison; Professional and Learned institution; Other.
Museums	Museum; Gallery; Heritage Centre; House/Castle; National; Government Agency; Local Authority; Armed Service; University or College; National Trust; Independent; Other.

Table 3.1   Questionnaires Sent and Received

Domain	Sent	Received	% Received
Archive	656	207	32
Library	635	211	33
Museum	705	217	31
Total	1996	635	32

Questionnaires were then grouped into broad institution categories:

Table 3.2   Institution Categories

Institution category	Freq	%
National	33	5
Public/Local Authority/Government	250	39
Education	119	19
Other*	233	37
Total	635	

* The 'Other' institution category refers to any archive/library/museum that could not be classified as national, government (ether local or national) or education.

Responsibility for Disaster Management

The vast majority (96 per cent) of managers identified an individual who was responsible for disaster management in their archive/library/museum. Job titles given for the person with responsibility for disaster management include:

Archivist
Director of Library Services
Assistant Librarian
Head of Conservation
Building Manager
Head of Operations
Business Support Manager
Health and Safety Manager
Collection Care Manager
Visitor Services Manager
Curator

Disaster Control Plan

Over half (56 per cent) of managers advised that their archive/library/museum had a written disaster control plan (see Table 3.3).

The vast majority of national archives/libraries/museums (86 per cent) had a written disaster control plan. (It might have been expected that 100 per cent of National libraries would have written disaster control plans, but this category included institutions with national in their title, not just those designated as National.) This compared to 68 per cent in the Education category, 57 per cent in the Public/Local Authority/Government category and 44 per cent in the Other institution categories had written disaster control plans.

Where a disaster had been experienced in the previous five years archives/libraries/museums were more likely to have a written disaster control plan (69 per cent), compared with those that had not experienced a disaster (52 per cent).

Table 3.3   Written Disaster Control Plan

Written DCP exists	Total	Domain		
		Archive	Library	Museum
	%	%	%	%
Yes	56	50	57	61
No	23	28	26	14
In preparation	22	22	17	25

Preparation of Disaster Control Plans

The majority of disaster control plans were prepared by individuals or groups within the archive/library/museum, with no involvement from others in the institution or external consultants (see Table 3.4).

Review of Disaster Control Plans

Almost two-thirds (65 per cent) of written disaster control plans had been updated in the last 12 months (see Table 3.5).

Integration into Institution-wide Plans

Over half (55 per cent) of all written disaster control plans in archives, libraries and museums were part of wider institution plans. Library disaster control plans were more frequently integrated into the institutional plan than those of archives or museums (see Table 3.6).

Table 3.4   Disaster Control Plan Prepared by

DCP written by:	Total	Domain		
		Archive	Library	Museum
	%	%	%	%
Individual	40	36	42	40
Internal group	33	29	35	35
Institutional staff	6	10	2	6
Internal and institutional staff	13	16	13	11
External consultancy	1	2	0	1
External consultancy with internal and/or institutional staff	5	1	7	6
Other	3	6	2	1

Table 3.5   Disaster Control Plan Last Updated

DCP last updated	Total	Domain		
		Archive	Library	Museum
	%	%	%	%
In last 12 months	65	61	68	66
Between 1 and 3 years	20	22	19	19
Over 3 years	8	11	5	7
Never	6	5	8	6
Don't know	1	1	0	2

Table 3.6   Disaster Control Plan: Part of Institutional Plan

DCP part of institution plan	Total	Domain		
		Archive	Library	Museum
	%	%	%	%
Yes	55	49	67	50
No	38	44	30	40
Don't know	2	2	3	2
Not applicable	5	5	1	9

Table 3.7   Experience of Disaster

Domain	Experience of disaster			
	Had experienced a disaster		Had not experienced a disaster	
	Freq	%	Freq	%
Archive	57	29	141	71
Library	71	35	135	66
Museum	58	28	151	72
Total	186	30	427	70

Disasters – Experience

Experience of Disaster Almost a third (30 per cent) of archives, libraries and museums had experienced a disaster in the previous five years (see Table 3.7).

National museums had experienced the most disasters in the previous five years (57 per cent) and independent museums the least (16 per cent).

Types of Disaster Experienced Of the 186 (30 per cent) archives/libraries/museums where a disaster had occurred in the previous five years, 39 (21 per cent) reported more than one incident had taken place. In total, details of 225 incidents were reported. (More archives/libraries/museums could have experienced multiple disasters; managers were only asked to provide details of the most recent occurrence.) Water related disasters were the most commonly reported (68 per cent). Others were much less frequent: fire – 11 per cent, vandalism – 3 per cent, theft/break-in/burglary – 6 per cent, bomb incident/terrorist threat – 2 per cent, other (e.g. building collapse, IT, power failure, etc.) – 10 per cent.

Lessons Learned Respondents who had experienced a disaster were asked to provide three lessons they had learned that they would pass to others. The most frequent lessons learned (irrespective of whether or not they had a disaster control plan) in order (across the domains), were:

1. Awareness of building issues, e.g. maintenance, regular checks, updating plans
2. The importance of training, particularly in regard to knowledge of the disaster control plan and how to respond in a disaster
3. Availability of adequate emergency equipment in appropriate locations.

Managers in libraries also pointed out the need to maintain clear communication channels between staff and the disaster response team. Where the disaster control plan had been deemed to be ineffective, managers in archives highlighted the importance of insurance, and managers in museums drew attention to the need for awareness, vigilance and the need to know who was in charge at all times.

Existence of Disaster Control Plans

More disasters had occurred in archives, libraries and museums that had a written disaster control plan (see Table 3.8). [Note: we are unable to identify whether disaster control plans were in place before the disaster occurred, likewise we are not able to identify whether experiencing a disaster was a driver for writing a disaster control plan.]

Where a written disaster control plan existed, 44 per cent of libraries, 34 per cent of museums and 31 per cent of archives had experienced a disaster in the last five years.

Table 3.8   Disaster Control Plan/Experience of Disaster

Disaster control plan	Had experienced a disaster		Had not experienced a disaster	
	Freq	**%**	**Freq**	**%**
Written DCP	126	37	218	63
DCP in preparation	29	23	98	77
No DCP	27	20	107	80

Effectiveness of Disaster Control Plans in a Disaster

The majority (83 per cent) of managers in institutions that had experienced a disaster reported their disaster control plan was effective during the disaster (see Table 3.9).

Training

Managers' Training   Managers were asked to indicate the disaster management related training they had received and needed (see Table 3.10).

Staff Training   Managers were also asked to indicate the disaster management related training other staff in the archive/library/museum had received and, in the managers' opinion, needed (see Table 3.11).

Factors Affecting Training   The domain affected training, with managers and staff working in the museum domain receiving more training than those in other domains, and managers and staff in the archive domain the least. Managers working in archives expressed the greatest need to receive further training than those in other domains and library managers expressed the greater need for staff to receive further training. Managers working in museums indicated less need for further training either for themselves or staff.

Institutional category also affected training. Managers and staff in the Education category have received the most training and those in the Other category the least. Managers and staff in the Public/Local Authority/Government category report the most need for further training and those in the Other category the least.

The existence or not of a disaster control plan is another factor influencing training. Managers and staff in archives/libraries/museums with a disaster control plan had received the most training and those without a plan the least. Managers in

Table 3.9   Effectiveness of Disaster Control Plan in a Disaster

DCP effective in a disaster	Total		Domain					
			Archive		Library		Museum	
	Freq	%	Freq	%	Freq	%	Freq	%
Yes	104	83	28	74	38	84	38	88
No	15	12	6	16	6	13	3	7
Don't know	7	6	4	11	1	2	2	5
Total	126		38		45		43	

Table 3.10   Managers' Training

Training – managers	Received		Needs	
	%	Rank	%	Rank
Risk assessment	53	1	20	11
Health and safety	52	2	16	15
Formulating a disaster control/emergency plan	47	3	22	10
Sources of help and support	37	4	18	13
Accreditation requirements	32	5	15	16
Handling and salvaging damaged materials	31	6	31	3
Security	31	6	16	14
Effective communications in an emergency	20	8	29	4
Undertaking exercises and simulations	20	8	35	1
Providing service continuity and access	19	10	26	6
Developing a staff training programme	18	11	28	5
Selecting and training a disaster/emergency response team	16	12	31	3
Developing cooperative networks	16	12	25	7
Collection designation requirements	14	14	23	8
Insurance	13	15	20	12
Financial aspects of disaster/emergency management	9	16	35	1
Counselling	5	17	23	8

archives/libraries/museums with a disaster control plan in preparation expressed the greatest need for training.

Finally, experience of disaster also affected training. Managers in archives/libraries/museums who had experienced a disaster in the previous five years reported they had received more training than those in archives/libraries/museums who had not. Experience of disaster had little effect on the training other staff in the archive/library/museum had received, or on training needed by managers and staff.

Table 3.11   Staff Training

Training – staff	Received		Needs	
	%	**Rank**	**%**	**Rank**
Health and safety	49	1	17	13
Risk assessment	38	2	18	11
Security	31	3	13	16
Handling and salvaging damaged materials	29	4	38	1
Formulating a disaster control/emergency plan	27	5	19	10
Sources of help and support	23	6	18	11
Accreditation requirements	21	7	15	15
Undertaking exercises and simulations	19	8	34	2
Developing a staff training programme	17	9	20	8
Providing service continuity and access	16	10	26	4
Effective communications in an emergency	16	11	32	3
Insurance	15	12	13	16
Collection designation requirements	14	13	16	14
Selecting and training a disaster/emergency response team	13	14	25	5
Developing cooperative networks	12	15	20	8
Financial aspects of disaster/emergency management	9	16	25	5
Counselling	7	17	22	7

Table 3.12   In-house Disaster Management Activities

Activity	%
Regular checks of fire equipment	89
Regular checks of electrical equipment	84
Regular equipment maintenance	72
Regular IT backup and security procedures	70
Planned building maintenance	69
Installation of automatic fire detection system	65
Assessment of suitability of storage methods	61
Regular review of security measures	60
Regular formal risk assessments	60
Obtaining police and fire service advice	59
Day-to-day hazard and safety checks	59
Assessment of collections' location and display	59
Review of insurance cover	54
Updating and making floor plans available	51
Provision of emergency response equipment and materials	51
Maintenance of up-to-date lists of specialist suppliers/services	49
Obtaining other specialist advice	47
Planning for service continuity	32
Installation of automatic fire suppression system	20

In-house Disaster Management Activities

The frequency that managers indicated in-house disaster management activities were performed in their archives/libraries/museums is shown in Table 3.12.

Factors Affecting In-house Activities   The domain influenced in-house activities, with museums undertaking more in-house activities and archives the least of the three domains. The institutional category also had an influence, with National archives/libraries/museums carrying out more in-house disaster management activities than other institution categories; those in the Other category undertake the least of the four categories. Archives/libraries/museums with a written disaster control plan more frequently carry out in-house disaster management activities than those without a plan or where one is in preparation. Where there had been a disaster in the previous five years more in-house disaster management activities are conducted, compared to those archives/libraries/museums who had not had a disaster.

Insurance

Almost two-thirds of managers reported that their archive/library/museum had insured its collections (see Table 3.13).

Museums were most likely to have taken out insurance, with 74 per cent of managers in museums reporting they had insurance, compared to 66 per cent of libraries and 48 per cent of archives. Managers in 19 per cent of archives and 15 per cent of libraries did not know if they had insurance cover. Where a disaster control plan was in preparation 68 per cent of archives/libraries/museums had insurance, as did 66 per cent of those who have a written disaster control plan, whereas only 50 per cent of those without a disaster control plan were insured.

Table 3.13   Insurance

Insured	Freq	%
Yes	377	63
No	154	26
Don't know	69	12
Total	600	

Disaster Simulations/Exercises

Only 26 per cent of archives, libraries and museums had conducted a disaster simulation/exercise. There was no significant difference between domains or whether institutions had experienced a disaster in the previous five years. The remainder of managers who answered this question said their archive/library/museum had never conducted a disaster simulation/exercise. (It should be noted that 12 per cent of managers did not answer this question.)

Commercial Disaster Recovery Subscriptions

Almost a third (32 per cent) of archives/libraries/museums did not subscribe to any commercial disaster recovery company. This was the case for 47 per cent of museums, 29 per cent of archives and 19 per cent of libraries. Those without a written disaster control plan were more likely to subscribe to a disaster recovery service (42 per cent), followed by 34 per cent where a disaster control plan was in preparation and 26 per cent where there was a written disaster control plan. Archives/libraries/ museums which had experienced a disaster in the previous five year were more likely to subscribe to a disaster recovery service, only 23 per cent of those who had experienced a disaster reported they did not subscribe to any disaster recovery services compared to 36 per cent of those which had not experienced a disaster.

One disaster recovery company, Harwell Drying and Restoration Services (HDRS) (now renamed Harwell Document Recovery Services), was subscribed to by 39 per cent of archives/libraries/museums.

Formal and Informal Cooperative Networks

What managers perceived as formal or informal was not uniform. Some referred to a particular network as formal whilst others referred to the same network as informal. A third of managers said their archive/library/museum was part of at least one formal or informal network. Some examples of formal networks mentioned were:

*   Avon Universities in Cooperation (AULIC)
*   Cambridge College Libraries Forum for Disaster Planning
*   Glasgow Area Disaster Planning Network
*   Hampshire County Museum Service
*   M25 Consortium of Academic Libraries
*   North West Academic Libraries (NOWAL)
*   Regional Emergency and Disaster Support (REDS), East Midlands Museum Service
*   The Library and Information Services Council (Northern Ireland) Disaster Planning Working Group.

Accreditation Scheme

The impact of the Accreditation Scheme, introduced in 2004, is reflected by the fact that more museums reported writing a disaster control plan in 2005 than in any other year.

Attitudes to Effectiveness of Disaster Management

Managers were asked their attitude to a number of statements with regard to the effectiveness of disaster management in their archive/library/museum. They were asked to tick the option that most closely expressed their attitude to each statement, the options were: strongly disagree, disagree, neither agree nor disagree, agree and strongly agree. These options were then coded using the following scale 1 – strongly disagree, 2 – disagree, 3 – neither agree nor disagree, 4 – agree, 5 – strongly agree; and the mean calculated. In the main, scores obtained for attitudes fell within a narrow range that broadly reflected neither agreement nor disagreement with the statements. The mean scores obtained are shown in Table 3.14.

Table 3.14   Effectiveness of Disaster Management

Statement	Mean
Other service pressures leave insufficient time for disaster management	3.4
There is appropriate knowledge/expertise in house	3.0
We do not have enough staff	3.2
Existing arrangements are satisfactory	2.8
Senior management does not consider it a priority	2.5
There are not sufficient funds associated with it	3.2
Training provided is adequate	2.7
The design or upkeep of the buildings make it difficult	3.2

Highest and Lowest Scores   In the main, scores obtained for attitudes fell within a narrow range that broadly reflected neither agreement nor disagreement with the statements.

Factors Influencing Views   The possession of a disaster control plan is the most significant factor with managers in archives/libraries/museums with a disaster control plan being much more positive than those without a disaster control plan. The institution category has some influence on attitudes, those managers in the Public/Local Authority/Government category having the least positive attitude. The domain has limited influence with managers in archives having the least positive attitudes of the three domains. Experiencing a disaster does not affect attitudes.

Perceptions of Importance of Disaster Management

Managers were also asked the importance of a number of factors relating to disaster management in their archive/library/museum. They were asked to tick the option that most closely expressed the level of importance of each factor, the options were; not important, low importance, neither high nor low importance, fairly important and very important. These options were then coded using the following scale: 1 – not important, 2 – low importance, 3 – neither high nor low importance, 4 – fairly important, 5 – very important; and the mean calculated. The mean scores obtained are shown in Table 3.15.

Table 3.15   Importance of Disaster Management

Factor	Mean
Accreditation scheme[1]	3.7
Availability of equipment/supplies	3.9
Collection designation scheme[2]	3.0
Condition of building(s)	4.0
Condition of equipment	3.9
Development of regional support networks	3.3
Health and safety issues	4.2
Insurance	3.8
Liaison with civil emergency planners	3.1
Preparation of Disaster Control Plan	4.0
Review of Disaster Control Plan	4.0
Security	4.3
Terrorist threats	2.4
Training	4.0
Vandalism	3.2

Notes:

1. The Accreditation scheme applies to museums in the UK only

2. The Collection designation scheme applies to England only

Highest and Lowest Scores   Managers perceived security, health and safety, preparation and review of disaster control plans and the condition of buildings as the most important factors. Terrorist threats were perceived as the least important. In general, managers in museums consider the accreditation scheme to be fairly important.

Factors Influencing Views   The possession of a disaster control plan is the most significant influence on perceptions of importance, those managers in archives/ libraries/museums which do not have a written disaster control see disaster management as the least important. The institution category has some influence on perceptions of importance, with managers in National archives/libraries/museums tend to see disaster management as more important (e.g. terrorist threats, availability of emergency equipment and supplies) than those in other institution categories. The domain and experience of disaster had little influence on perceptions managers expressed. The location of the archive/library/museum influenced the perception of the importance of terrorist threats, with managers in Northern Ireland considering it to be more important than managers in other countries.

Perceptions of Satisfaction with Disaster Management

Finally, managers were asked how satisfied they were with a number of factors relating to disaster management in their archive/library/museum. They were asked to tick the option that most closely expressed their level of satisfaction with each factor, the options were: not satisfied, low satisfaction, neither high nor low satisfaction, fairly satisfied and very satisfield. These options were then coded using the following scale: 1 – not satisfied, 2 – low satisfaction, 3 – neither high nor low satisfaction, 4 – fairly satisfied, 5 – very satisfied; and the mean calculated. The mean scores obtained are shown in Table 3.16.

Table 3.16   Satisfaction with Disaster Management

Factor	Mean
Accreditation scheme[1]	3.4
Availability of equipment/supplies	3.4
Collection designation scheme[2]	3.0
Condition of building(s)	3.2
Condition of equipment	3.6
Development of regional support networks	3.0
Health and safety issues	3.7
Insurance	3.5
Liaison with civil emergency planners	3.0
Preparation of Disaster Control Plan	3.2
Review of Disaster Control Plan	3.2
Security	3.7
Terrorist threats	3.5
Training	3.1
Vandalism	3.5

*Note*s:

1.   The Accreditation scheme applies to museums in the UK only

2.   The Collection designation scheme applies to England only

Highest and Lowest Scores   Managers were most satisfied with health and safety issues, security and condition of equipment. In the main, perceptions of satisfaction fell within the neutral to fairly satisfied range.

Factors Influencing Views   The existence of a disaster control plan is the factor that most influenced views, in archives/libraries/museums where there was a disaster control plan managers are the most satisfied with arrangements for disaster management. Although the institution category influences perceptions of satisfaction there is no one category that is most or least satisfied with arrangements for disaster management. The domain has a limited impact on level of satisfaction, with managers in museums being most satisfied. Experiencing a disaster does not influence satisfaction with disaster management arrangements.

Survey of Regional Museum, Library and Archive Councils (MLAs) and National Equivalents

In addition to the questionnaire survey of institutions, an investigation into the work of regional MLA's and their equivalents in the devolved administrations was undertaken. The aim was to gain insight into their activities in disaster management, in particular any training initiatives, publications or guidelines being widely used. It was hoped to find out about any regional activities that individual institutions might tap into regionally.

Method

An e-mail survey was conducted of the nine regional branches of MLA in England and their equivalent bodies for Libraries, Archives and Museums within Northern Ireland, Scotland and Wales. Tailored e-mail requests were sent to named individuals whenever possible (identified from the organisation's website or provided by another contact). It was not straightforward identifying individuals with responsibility for disaster management in all MLAs. The organisations approached were asked to provide information relating to their own disaster management activities and current initiatives, if any. The regional MLAs and national equivalents contacted are shown in Table 3.17.

Fifteen out of the 16 organisations contacted responded. Additionally, the websites of all the organisations contacted were reviewed in order to obtain evidence of involvement in disaster management and possible useful sources of information.

Table 3.17   Organisations Contacted by Country

Country	Organisation
England	ALM London EEMLAC EMMLAC MLA North West MLA West Midlands NEMLAC SEMLAC SWMLAC YMLAC
Northern Ireland	Library and Information Services Council (Northern Ireland) Northern Ireland Museums Council The Public Record Office of Northern Ireland (PRONI)
Scotland	Scottish Council on Archives Scottish Libraries & Information Council Scottish Museums Council
Wales	CyMAL: Museums Archives and Libraries Wales

Findings

The email survey and website review revealed there was greater evidence of coordination of related activities in some MLAs/national equivalent organisations than others.

E-mail Survey   The variation and limitations of activities and involvement in disaster management was reflected in the e-mail survey. Responses obtained from the survey were grouped under the following headings: Disaster Control Plan, Training, Networks, Dissemination, and Accreditation.

Disaster Control Plan   Two respondents reported having a disaster control plan template, another was considering reprinting one it had published earlier, and another had a template available on its website.

Training   This was the area in which most respondents were active, with seven reporting training activities. These included running workshops (which included contracting in experts, such as HDRS to undertake them), running their own courses or using courses run by major institutions in their region.

Networks   The survey revealed a few cases of local collaboration in addition to those already known (such as REDS, M25 Consortium). There were the beginnings of some cross-regional collaboration, but no national coordination.

Dissemination   One regional MLA advised of a recent MLA publication on security, and another advertised National Preservation Office training courses.

Accreditation   The other issue along with training that received most mention was the new Accreditation scheme for museums in England, with five MLAs referring to it. They were either already offering advice and training relating to it, or were planning to do so, in response to the emergency planning requirements outlined in the scheme (see Chapter 1).

Websites   The review of regional and national equivalent websites revealed variation of information on disaster management. Few websites revealed examples of activities relating to disaster management (an example of a positive development was a website that provided a useful annotated list of training providers). This is underlined by the MLA (England) website (*The Museums, Libraries and Archives Council* 2008), which, at the time of the survey, provided little context to the subject, just links to websites. For example, under the heading 'Collections Advice Network', it provided links to two documents on its own pages, one on insurance for museums (Graham and Prideaux 2004), and under the heading 'Emergency preparedness and response services', it offered links to 12 websites, including:

- UK
    - Conservation Register
    - East Midlands Museums Service
    - UK and Ireland Blue Shield Organisation
- International
    - Conservation Online
    - Federal Emergency Management Agency
    - North East Document Conservation Center
    - US National Parks Service.

A search of the websites of the regional MLAs that did not respond to the e-mail survey revealed little activity on their part in the field of disaster management/ emergency planning, but they did provide some links to sources of information.

To keep the issue of lack of evidence of activity in perspective, it should be noted that disaster management is but one activity amongst many in the area of collection care/management that the regional and national MLAs have had to address since they came into being in 2003.

Recent Developments

It should be noted that there have been developments in the regions since the survey was undertaken. These will be referred to in Chapter 7, Planning for the future. Also, as noted in Chapter 2, it should be remembered that at the time of writing, spring 2008, MLA (England) was undergoing a restructure

...to streamline the MLA's national and regional operations in a major reorganisation ... to scale back funding to the nine separate regional MLAs and work with them to plan for their eventual replacement by a unified structure. By April 2009 smaller regional MLA teams will be better placed to work with other cultural services and a joined-up government presence in the region. The changes pave the way for the outcome of an ongoing regional review ... The move follows quickly in the wake of decisions to cut back the central MLA Council and move key operations out of London.

The combined package heralds a new era for the MLA, which is being reconfigured as a single national entity based principally in Birmingham ... and will be represented by expert teams in each English region. (*MLA Board takes radical step to sharpen delivery* 2008)

Conclusion

The chapter, through analysis of the UK questionnaire survey and survey of MLAs, has provided a contemporary overview of disaster management practice in archives, libraries and museums in the UK. (Chapter 7 includes activity that has taken place since the surveys were undertaken.) It has identified achievements and aspects where further work is required. These are addressed further in Chapter 6.

Appendix 3A: Sample Questionnaire

 Arts & Humanities
Research Council

Safeguarding heritage at risk: disaster management in United Kingdom archives, libraries and museums

A   YOUR CONTACT DETAILS

Name: _____

Job Title: _____

Name of Institution: _____

Name of Library _____

Address of Library _____

_____

Contact telephone number: _____ Website address: _____

E-mail address: _____

B   ABOUT YOUR ORGANISATION

Please indicate the type of your library [*Please tick the one most applicable*]

National	☐	Public	☐	Higher Education	☐	Further Education ☐
School	☐	Government	☐	Industrial and commercial	☐	Professional and learned ☐
Health	☐	Media	☐	Prison	☐	institution

Other [please specify] _____

C   DISASTER CONTROL PLAN

Who is responsible for disaster management in your library? [*Please specify job title/working group/committee or state 'Don't know'*] _____

Does your library have a written Disaster Control Plan?   Yes ☐   No ☐   In preparation ☐

If yes: Who put together the plan? [*Please tick one only or specify other*]

Individual from library	☐	Group/committee of library staff	☐
Institutional staff	☐	Institutional and library staff	☐
External consultancy	☐	External consultancy with library and /	☐
Don't know	☐	or institutional staff	

Other [please specify] _____

In what year was the plan first written? [*Please state 'Don't know' if appropriate*] _____

When was the plan last updated?

In the last 12 months	☐	Between 1 and 3 years ago	☐	Over 3 years ago	☐
Never	☐	Don't know	☐		

Is your plan part of a wider institutional plan?　Yes ☐　No ☐
　　　　　　　　　　　　　　　　　　　　　　　Don't know ☐　Not applicable ☐

Is your plan available on your Internet website?　Yes ☐　No ☐　Don't have one ☐

Is your plan available on your Intranet?　Yes ☐　No ☐　Don't have one ☐

D　TRAINING

State training received and training needs for yourself / other staff in your library in the following areas: [*Please tick across the four rows as appropriate*]

	Training received		Training needs	
	Yourself	Other staff	Yourself	Other staff
Sources of help and support	☐	☐	☐	☐
Formulating a Disaster Control Plan	☐	☐	☐	☐
Risk assessment	☐	☐	☐	☐
Security	☐	☐	☐	☐
Insurance	☐	☐	☐	☐
Selecting and training a Disaster Response Team	☐	☐	☐	☐
Developing a staff training programme	☐	☐	☐	☐
Handling and salvaging damaged materials	☐	☐	☐	☐
Health and safety	☐	☐	☐	☐
Providing service continuity and access	☐	☐	☐	☐
Developing cooperative networks	☐	☐	☐	☐
Effective communications in an emergency	☐	☐	☐	☐
Counselling	☐	☐	☐	☐
Financial aspects of disaster management	☐	☐	☐	☐
Undertaking exercises and simulations	☐	☐	☐	☐
Collection designation requirements	☐	☐	☐	☐
Other(s) [please specify]				
_____	☐	☐	☐	☐
_____	☐	☐	☐	☐

E　IN-HOUSE ACTIVITIES

Which of these activities does your library undertake? [*Please tick all that apply*]

Day-to-day hazard and safety checks	☐	Updating & making floor plans available	☐
Regular formal risk assessments	☐	Provision of emergency response equipment	☐
Planned building maintenance	☐	& materials	
Regular checks of fire equipment	☐	Maintenance of up-to-date lists of specialist	☐
Regular checks of electrical equipment	☐	suppliers / services	
Regular equipment maintenance	☐	Review of insurance cover	☐
Assessment of suitability of storage methods	☐	Regular IT backup & security procedures	☐
Assessment of collections' location & display	☐	Planning for service continuity	☐
Regular review of security measures	☐	Installation of automatic fire detection system	☐
Obtaining police and fire service advice	☐	Installation of automatic fire suppression	☐
Obtaining other specialist advice	☐	system	

Is your collection(s) insured?　　　　　　　Yes ☐　No ☐　Don't know ☐

If yes, when was your insurance last reviewed? [*Please specify year or state 'Never' or 'Don't know' as appropriate*]　_____

When was the most recent occasion an emergency/disaster simulation/exercise for library staff was conducted? [*Please specify year or, if no simulation/exercise, state 'Never'*]　_____

F   EXTERNAL ARRANGEMENTS

Which commercial services, if any, does your library subscribe to for disaster management support? [*Please tick all that apply*]

Belfor-Relectronic   ☐ Document SOS   ☐
Cedric Chivers   ☐ Harwell Drying and Restoration Service   ☐
Data and Archival Damage Control Centre   ☐ Riley Dunn and Wilson   ☐
None   ☐ Other(s) [*please specify*]

_____

_____

Which local, regional or national disaster management cooperative networks, if any, is your library a member of? [*Please list formal and informal or state 'None'*]

Formal:	Informal:
_____	_____
_____	_____
_____	_____

G   YOUR VIEWS

To what extent do you agree or disagree with the following statements with regard to effective disaster management in your library? [*Please tick to indicate your level of agreement or disagreement with each statement*]

	Strongly disagree	Disagree	Neither agree nor disagree	Agree	Strongly agree
'Other service pressures leave insufficient time for it'	☐	☐	☐	☐	☐
'There is appropriate knowledge / expertise in-house'	☐	☐	☐	☐	☐
'We do not have enough staff'	☐	☐	☐	☐	☐
'Existing arrangements are satisfactory'	☐	☐	☐	☐	☐
'Senior management does not consider it a priority'	☐	☐	☐	☐	☐
'There are not sufficient funds devoted to it'	☐	☐	☐	☐	☐
'Training provided is adequate'	☐	☐	☐	☐	☐
'The design or upkeep of the buildings make it difficult'	☐	☐	☐	☐	☐

Currently, how important with regard to effective disaster management in your library, are the following? [*Please tick one box for each factor to indicate how important each is to you*]

Factor	Not important	Low importance	Neither high nor low importance	Fairly important	Very important
Terrorist threats	☐	☐	☐	☐	☐
Vandalism	☐	☐	☐	☐	☐
Preparation of Disaster Control Plan	☐	☐	☐	☐	☐
Review of Disaster Control Plan	☐	☐	☐	☐	☐
Liaison with civil emergency planners	☐	☐	☐	☐	☐
Condition of building(s)	☐	☐	☐	☐	☐
Condition of equipment	☐	☐	☐	☐	☐
Availability of equipment / supplies	☐	☐	☐	☐	☐
Health and safety issues	☐	☐	☐	☐	☐
Insurance	☐	☐	☐	☐	☐
Security	☐	☐	☐	☐	☐
Training	☐	☐	☐	☐	☐
Development of regional support networks	☐	☐	☐	☐	☐
Collection designation scheme	☐	☐	☐	☐	☐

How satisfied are you with current disaster management arrangements in your library? [*Please tick one box for each factor to indicate your level of satisfaction*]

Factor	Not satisfied	Low satisfaction	Neither high nor low satisfaction	Fairly satisfied	Very satisfied
Terrorist threats	☐	☐	☐	☐	☐
Vandalism	☐	☐	☐	☐	☐
Preparation of Disaster Control Plan	☐	☐	☐	☐	☐
Review of Disaster Control Plan	☐	☐	☐	☐	☐
Liaison with civil emergency planners	☐	☐	☐	☐	☐
Condition of building(s)	☐	☐	☐	☐	☐
Condition of equipment	☐	☐	☐	☐	☐
Availability of equipment / supplies	☐	☐	☐	☐	☐
Health and safety issues	☐	☐	☐	☐	☐
Insurance	☐	☐	☐	☐	☐
Security	☐	☐	☐	☐	☐
Training	☐	☐	☐	☐	☐
Development of regional support networks	☐	☐	☐	☐	☐
Collection designation scheme	☐	☐	☐	☐	☐

H   DISASTERS

Has your library experienced an emergency/disaster in the last five years?   Yes ☐   No ☐

If yes, please give details of the most recent, e.g. type, location, cause, extent and damage:

What are the 3 main lessons you learned and would pass on to others?

1

2

3

Was your Disaster Control Plan effective?   Yes ☐   No ☐   Didn't have a plan ☐   Don't know ☐

Thank you for your time and co-operation

Please return in the SAE provided. Please address any queries to: Yvonne Smith, Liverpool John Moores University, John Foster Building, 98 Mount Pleasant, Liverpool L3 5UZ, Tel: 0151 231 3453, Email: Y.M.Smith@livjm.ac.uk

References

ABL Cultural Consulting, *UK museums needs assessment. A report by the Heritage Lottery Fund and Resource, Final report April 2002*, (London: Resource), (published online Apr. 2002) <http://www.hlf.org.uk/NR/rdonlyres/CD7DEF8A-C354-4D67-9B48-5F6AD44146CD/0/Museum_needs_report_full.PDF>, accessed 22 June 2008.

Feather, J. Matthews, G. and Eden, P. (1996), *Preservation Management. Policies and Practices in British Libraries* (Aldershot: Ashgate).

Franklin, L. and York, J. (comps.) (2004), *Libraries and Information Services in the United Kingdom and the Republic of Ireland 2005* (London: Facet Publishing).

Graham, R and Prideaux, A., *Insurance for Museums*, (London: MLA), (published online 2004) <http://www.mla.gov.uk/resources/assets//R/risk_insurance_pdf_5879.pdf>, accessed 22 June 2008. [First published 2000.]

Matthews, G. and Eden, P. (1996). 'Disaster management in British libraries. Project report with guidelines for library managers', *Library and Information Research Report 109* (London: The British Library).

Matthews, G. et al. (2004), *An investigation into the work of REDS (Regional Emergencies & Disaster Squad). A report to East Midlands Museums, Libraries and Archives Council (EMMLAC)* (Birmingham and Leicester: Centre for Information Research (CIRT), University of Central England in Birmingham, East Midlands Museums, Libraries and Archives Council (EMMLAC)), (published online 2004) <http://www.mlaeastmidlands.org.uk/templates/temp_cor_rep_index.rm? category=keywords_root.taxonomy.corporate.documenttype.Report&category=keywords_root.taxonomy.corporate.subject.Collections&id=589&sort_type=date&num=5&term=&submit.x=11&submit.y=13&from=6>, accessed 27 Aug. 2008.

McKinley, J. and Reynolds, P. (1999), 'Training needs of museums in Surrey: an analysis 1988/1999', *Surrey Museums* [website], (updated 21 May 1999) <http://www.surreymuseums.free-online.co.uk/staff/train.html>, accessed 21 Aug. 2008.

MLA, *MLA Board takes radical step to sharpen delivery*, (published online 20 Feb. 2008) <http://www.mla.gov.uk/news/press_releases/regional_reorganisation>, accessed 18 May 2008.

MLA, *The Museums, Libraries and Archives Council (MLA),* [website], (updated 2008) <http://www.mla.gov.uk/home>, accessed 21 Aug. 2008.

Moon, B. E. and Loveday, A. J. (1989). 'Progress report on preservation in universities since the Ratcliffe report', in NPO (1989), 11–17.

Mowat, I. R. M. (1987), 'Preservation problems in academic libraries', in Palmer, R. E. (ed.) (1987), 37–43.

NPO (2007), 'Knowing the need and meeting the need. The state of preservation of the UK's library and archive collections' (London: NPO), (published online) <http://www.bl.uk/npo/pdf/meeting.pdf>, accessed 11 Feb. 2009.

The Museums Association (2005), *Museums and Galleries Yearbook 2005* (London: Museums Association).

NPO (1989), *Preservation and Technology: Proceedings of a Seminar at York University, 20–21ˢᵗ July 1988* (National Preservation Office Seminar Papers 3) (London: NPO, British Library).

Paine, C., *Stewardship. Assessment of needs in the museums and galleries sector: a report*, (published online Jul. 2000) <http://www.hlf.org.uk/NR/rdonlyres/6BF0726A-2004-4FD0-8B939BCA762176E8/0/needs_stewardship.pdf>, accessed 29 Jun. 2008.

Palmer, R. E. (ed.) (1987), 'Preserving the word', *The Library Association conference proceedings*, Harrogate (London: The Library Association).

Ratcliffe, F. W. with Patterson, D. (1984), 'Preservation policies and conservation in British libraries: report of the Cambridge University Library conservation project', *Library and Information Research Reports 25* (London, The British Library).

Tregarthen Jenkin, I. (1987), 'Disaster planning and preparedness: an outline disaster control plan', *British Library Information Guide 5* (London: The British Library).

TNA, *ARCHON Directory* [website], (updated n.d.) <http://www.nationalarchives.gov.uk/archon/>, accessed 20 Aug. 2008.

Walker, A. and Foster, J. (2006), *Knowing the need: A report on the emerging picture of preservation need in libraries and archives in the UK* (London: NPO), (published online Feb. 2006) <http://www.bl.uk/services/npo/pdf/knowing.pdf>, accessed 18 May 2008.

Chapter 4
The Worldwide Situation: Overview

Introduction

The chapter begins with an outline of the aim of the international survey aspect of the research and describes how it was undertaken. Findings, based on analysis of responses, the literature and organisational websites, and conference attendance, are then presented under key themes that emerged from this element of the research. These begin with an overview of general sources of information, guidance and advice available from international associations and examples of these (English language) from other countries. This is followed by an outline of select models of, or approaches to, disaster management in different countries with examples of activities and initiatives, followed by an insight into regional or local networks and the kind of activities they pursue. Training has a key role to play and an example of a major international programme is included. The chapter ends with consideration of issues arising from analysis of the international survey.

International Survey

The aim of the international survey aspect of the research was to gain insight into international and regional activities in disaster management, and into national activities within other countries, to identify any activities that might have relevance to the situation in the United Kingdom and the development of disaster management there.

The following methods were used in the survey: literature search and review (including Internet); e-mail requests to international associations, institutions and individuals; visits to various countries and interviews with key individuals; telephone interviews, and attendance at conferences and meetings outside the UK.

Literature Search and Review

The literature search revealed accounts of activities and developments on an international and national basis. Websites of international associations and national organisations were also searched. Findings of both these aspects of the literature search provided information that contributed to the selection of international associations, national institutions and individuals outside the UK for inclusion in the survey.

There is considerable literature on the topic (see, for example, for English-language items, Kulczak and Lennertz 1999; and Matthews 2003) which has grown since the 1970s. More recently, on an international basis, with the rapid growth in the use of the Internet and the opportunities it provides for the dissemination of news of major disasters, it has become difficult to keep track of information appearing on websites and e-discussion lists in particular.

In addition to information about disaster management, approaches to it, developments and initiatives, the literature search revealed many accounts of disasters, their aftermath and subsequent activities and initiatives throughout the world (see examples outlined later in this chapter, and in Chapter 8). Websites of international associations and national organisations offer considerable information as well as the printed literature. In the aftermath of the Indian Ocean tsunami and Hurricane Katrina, there was a massive increase in information and communication about disasters and their management in the relevant professional literature and websites, and also in the news media in general, which impacted on research methods.

Through the literature review, previous international surveys were identified. The methods used in these and response rates achieved contributed to the decision as to how to undertake the international survey. Within the constraints of the project, it was not deemed feasible to undertake a major survey of institutions worldwide similar to that undertaken of institutions in the UK earlier in the project. Designing a survey tool suitable for the varied kinds of respondents, administering distribution, 'chaser' and analysis of a survey of that kind and scale would not be possible within the resources available.

Major surveys identified in the literature review included:

International Federation of Library Associations and Institutions, *Survey on Disaster Planning in National Libraries* (Varlamoff and Plassard 2004). In February 2004, the IFLA PAC office sent a questionnaire survey to 177 national libraries to find out how many libraries had a disaster plan. Responses were received from 73 national libraries (41 per cent). Thirty-nine of these, about 53 per cent, reported they had a disaster plan.

International Council of Museums, Museums Emergency Programme (ICOM MEP) *Prevention and Recovery in Emergency Situations*. In 1999, ICOM sent a questionnaire requesting information about disasters to its national committees. It received replies from about 40 countries (Menegazzi 2003). Under its MEP, ICOM in 2003 undertook a questionnaire survey of 'some 2000 museum professionals' with a

> view to identifying people who had had direct involvement in a disaster affecting a museum, and to collecting information on museums which have already experienced disasters (either human or natural), about existing institutions/ associations operating in the field of emergency preparedness and response, and about the programmes and activities already organised or planned in this field.
> (ICOM MEP *Module 1 Surveys*)

One hundred and seventy five responses were received. Polley (2003) outlines how the American Association of Museums (AAM) response to the ICOM request was put together. As part of the information gathering process for a reply a one-page survey was sent to 2893 institutional members of AAM (796 were returned (28 per cent)).

Heritage Preservation (2005a), *A Public Trust at Risk*: The Heritage Health Index Report on the State of America's Collections. Information on disaster management is included in the Index, published in December 2005, a project of Heritage Preservation, in partnership with the Institute of Museum and Library Services, a federal agency.

The literature search also revealed several recent, key conferences that in addition to providing relevant information, also indicated organisations and individuals for inclusion in the e-mail survey. These conferences included:

ICOM MEP, International Symposium of *Cultural Heritage Disaster Preparedness and Response*, 23–27 November 2003, Salar Jung Museum, Hyderabad, India (Meengazzi (ed.) 2004).

IFLA PAC, the IFLA Core Activity for Preservation and Conservation and the Council on Library and Information Resources, Inc., with the Akademie der Wissenschaften and the Staatsbibliothek zu Berlin, *Preparing for the Worst, Planning for the Best: Protecting Our Cultural Heritage from Disaster*, 30 July 2003–1 August 2003 (Wellheiser, J G and Gwinn, N E (eds.) 2005).

UNESCO, World Conference on Disaster Reduction. *Cultural Heritage Risk Management*, 18–22 January 2005, Kobe, Hyogo, Japan (Session 3.3 Cultural Heritage Risk Management) (UNESCO 2005).

Canadian Museums Association (CMA), *Cultural Property Protection Conference*, 16 January 2006, Ottawa, Canada (CMA 2006).

E-mail Survey

A selective list of relevant organisations and institutions was compiled and approached (via named individuals where possible) in a targeted manner. This involved taking a mixed 'cascade' and 'snowball' approach (e.g. starting with worldwide organisations, down to regional and national, and taking up contacts suggested by respondents). This provided a manageable approach within the confines (e.g. time, funding) of the project, to achieve an insight into worldwide disaster management activities relating primarily to archives, libraries and museums. This approach also permitted the research team to demonstrate sensitivity in selecting and timing approaches to organisations and individuals in the aftermath of major natural disasters across the world during the period of the research.

Whilst many institutions were known from previous work and the literature, the list was initially formalised by reference to 'links' pages on the major international organisations' (e.g. ICA, ICOM, IFLA) websites, and others with an emphasis specifically related to preservation and/or disaster management (for example

CoOL). Lists available via these were also consulted for relevant organisations (e.g. Institute for Museum and Library Services (US)).

Tailored e-mail requests were sent to named individuals (identified from website), with responsibility for preservation or disaster management. Those approached were asked to provide information about:

- their body's/institution's disaster management strategy
- models of operation
- funding
- key issues currently faced
- networking
- examples of good practice
- guidance/advice/support offered
- training
- contacts/collaboration outside the cultural heritage sector
- new/recommended publications
- surveys
- future plans.

These were tailored appropriately to acknowledge recent activities/ achievements/initiatives.

Those to whom the request was sent thus included: international organisations, regional branches/centres; other regional bodies, national organisations, individual institutions/individuals, and national co-operative networks. Anonymity of responses was assured.

Response   Of the 115 international institutions and organisations contacted, 44 (38 per cent) responded (see Table 4.1).

There was a good response in terms of representation of archives, libraries and museums. It is not straightforward to categorise in this way as some respondents cover archives, libraries and museums, others two or one, and others have broader coverage but include them along with other components of the cultural heritage. Geographically, response was worldwide in coverage, e.g. ICOM; regions were covered too, e.g. Africa, Asia, the Caribbean, Latin America; and national, with input from individual countries around the world, e.g. Australia, Benin, Brazil, Canada, Chile, Croatia, Kenya, the Netherlands, New Zealand, Russia, Sweden, Turkey, United States. Where there was no response, information was in some cases available on institutions' websites.

Conference Attendance

The project head attended *The 3-Ds of preservation: disasters, displays, digitization* symposium, co-sponsored by the Bibliothèque nationale de France and the IFLA PAC & IFLA Section on Preservation and Conservation, Bibliothèque nationale

Table 4.1   Breakdown by Institution Type

Institution Type	Number Contacted	Number of Replies	Number of information/ contacts offered
International Organisations	9	4	4
Regional Branches of International Organisations	30	10	9
National Organisations	39	16	15
Individuals	31	13	13
Network Groups	6	1	1
Total	**115**	**44**	**42**

de France, Paris, 8–10 March, 2006. Papers from around the world on disaster management were presented (Koch (ed.) 2006) and opportunities were taken to speak informally with contacts made via the e-mail survey (e.g. with contacts from Chile, Sweden and the US). The participant also attended a tour of the basement of the building to learn about and see countermeasures in place should the River Seine flood.

The same team member was invited to attend *Capturing Katrina: Collections – Recovery Experiences* and *Future Directions in Safeguarding Document Collections*, Library of Congress, Washington DC, 20–21 April 2006 (Preservation Directorate 2006). Here, he was able to sit in on the recording of oral histories of 'first responders' who had gone to assess salvage requirements in the aftermath of Hurricane Katrina, and then to attend a meeting of key players from across the cultural heritage sector at which they discussed future strategy.

Interviews

Interviews with 14 international practitioners (ten institutions) took place. Interviewees had a variety of backgrounds including conservators (in archives, galleries, museums), consultant, director of national heritage organisation, librarian, museum educator, programme manager of international organisation. Countries covered included the Netherlands, Sri Lanka, and US.

Findings

Guidance and Advice

International   ICA, ICOM and IFLA are involved in a wide range of activities related to disaster management. Pre- and post-incident information about these, including publications, is available on their websites. They have produced guidance on various aspects of disaster management. For example, the ICA Committee on Disaster Prevention (ICA/PDP) compiled guidelines on prevention and control in archives to assist archivists implement a disaster management policy and strategy (ICA 1997). IFLA through its Preservation and Conservation Section offers *Selected resources on disaster management* on its website and its Core Activity on Preservation and Conservation (IFLA PAC 2008) has recently produced a short manual on preparedness and planning available in English, French and Spanish (McIlwaine 2006). ICOM, through its *Museums Emergency Programme* (MEP), provides information and support for preparedness and response in emergency situations; it also facilitates provision of external support to countries or regions affected by disaster. For example, as well as providing general information such as useful tools, details of training and conferences, links to other sources, part of the ICOM website also gives updates on catastrophes around the world, how others can help and details of a disaster relief fund (ICOM *Disaster Relief for Museums*).

Effective communication of activities and support is essential for their promotion. The international associations make use of a range of methods to communicate and disseminate guidance and advice about disaster management, internationally and through regional networks. Newsletters, bulletins, guidance notes and briefings, bibliographies and conferences, seminars, practical workshops and training events, and lists of contacts are commonly used. Interestingly, one survey respondent (from a national museum), referred specifically to the usefulness of newsletters:

> To help raise the profile of preventive conservation within such a large organisation, a monthly newsletter containing information on current topics of interest is produced. As this news-sheet is no more than one page, a supplement that covers specific topics in greater detail is also produced.
>
> I have had considerable success with this form of communication because it is easy to produce, always current, and not too wordy meaning people are more likely to read it and pass it on to others. I began the newsletter 3 years ago with a circulation of 20 people and now have almost 100 people on the current mailing list.

Websites increasingly carry publications, including newsletters, advice, announcements of events and links to other sources. (See for example, AFRICOM,

ICA *Regional Branches*, and IFLA PAC *IFLA Core Activity on Preservation and Conservation. Regional Centres.*) This medium also permits access to photographic and moving images of the impact of disasters and methods, for example, of handling and salvaging damaged materials. As with websites in general, some are easier to navigate and use than others, are updated more frequently, contain a wider range of information, indicate authority of information more clearly.

Activity is also undertaken at regional level where it can be directed at local circumstances. ICA regional branches, ICOM regional organisations and IFLA PAC regional centres are active throughout the world. An event which exemplifies such activity was an open seminar on the documentary heritage damaged by the Indian Ocean Tsunami and the meeting of the Directors of the IFLA/PAC Regional Centres in Asia and others (IFLA PAC Asia and National Diet Library 2005). As well as papers on the situation and damage and recovery in the countries affected and future developments, there was an overview of IFLA PAC's programmes. This included sessions at IFLA annual conference and their publication, a pre-conference on the subject, survey on disaster planning in national libraries, a manual on disaster planning, workshops on disaster planning, networking, relief and disaster partnership.

Advice and support can take many forms – information, equipment, supplies, finance, conservation expertise, etc., particularly in the aftermath of a major region-wide incident. The ICOM through its MEP provides information and support for preparedness and response in emergency situations; it also facilitates provision of external support to countries or regions affected by disaster. UNESCO, too, provides much information through its *UNESCO Libraries Portal* and its *UNESCO Archives Portal*, which, for example, on its *Disaster Preparedness and Recovery* pages, provides links to over 20 resources from around the world.

National   National institutions produce guidance which is relevant beyond their own walls and, indeed, their staff with specialist expertise and experience are often called upon before, during and after major incidents for telephone and on the spot advice.

In Australia, the Australia Heritage Council has produced guidelines for devising a disaster plan specifically for small museums (Söderlund 2000); the National Archives of Australia has published a disaster preparedness manual (National Archives of Australia 2000); and the National Library of Australia has made its disaster plan available on its website (National Library of Australia *Collection Disaster Plan*).

The Museum of New Zealand Te Papa has produced three concise guides to aspect of disaster management: preventive conservation, emergency procedures, and minimising disaster (Te Papa National Services 2001a, 2001b, 2001c).

The Canadian Conservation Institute (CCI) has published two useful guides to emergency planning for cultural institutions (CCI 1995a and 1995b). Speakers' presentations from the CMA (2006) *Cultural Property Protection Conference* are available on the conference website and provide up to date information and advice on risk management, cultural property protection, museum security, and case studies.

In the US, Heritage Preservation, supported by a National Endowment for the Humanities award, responded to a need recognised post-Katrina by producing a field guide to emergency response, providing step-by-step advice on what to do immediately after a disaster (Heritage Preservation 2006). The guide comes with an instructional DVD. This is in addition to Heritage Preservation's well-known *Emergency Response and Salvage Wheel* (2005b), available in various languages. Also, as result of lessons learned following Hurricane Katrina, Heritage Preservation has made available online a guide to finding federal aid for disaster response and recovery (Heritage Preservation *Guide to Navigating Federal Emergency Management Agency and Small Business Administration Disaster Aid for Cultural Institutions*).

Further examples of guidance and advice may also be found following references in the following section.

Models of Operation

The research has revealed various national approaches to disaster management. Economic, legal, political, social and technological contexts can all influence models adopted in different countries. Some have a strong central focus, others encourage a regional approach supported by the centre, while in other instances, there is no formal central coordination and regional and local networks are established almost haphazardly. Some have developed with civil emergency planning.

Most formal developments seem to be in developed countries. The international non-governmental agencies operate there but also play a key role in supporting and developing good practice in developing countries. Others have commented on the situation in developing countries, noting that these countries

> ... have long-standing traditions of intangible and tangible cultural heritage, their needs have not been satisfied, they have large population growth and low economic development. In government budgetary allocations, culture is the least priority. As cost-effective allocation of resources is required for heritage protection, no measures are available for risk prevention and preparedness and emergency response. In this scenario, preparedness for the protection of cultural property will not have a place in the national planning process, being deemed of lesser importance and not a priority.
>
> For these reasons, no risk preparedness plans are drawn up; or, if plans are prepared, no financial allocations and trained personnel for the implementation of these plans are available. Museums in developing countries are poorly equipped for preventive care and protection and are poorly managed. There is no culture of awareness of risk preparedness amongst museum staff ...

Man-made disasters through armed conflict are on a different scale, bringing terror, fear for survival, loss of life and mental distress. It is very difficult to have pre-planned strategies; actions must be intelligent and situation-based ...

Over the last decade there has been a notable increase in awareness and preparedness for natural hazards and man-made disasters. A consensus has emerged about what constitute disaster preparedness and the vital role of planning. Individual institutions have prepared emergency plans with great enthusiasm. Valuable professional inputs from international and local experts have enriched these plans. But the reality found in developing countries is that there is no consistency in updating the plans an keeping them alive. Risk preparedness plans are invariably forgotten with time because of changing priorities or a lack of enthusiasm from management. (De Silva 2004, 3–4)

Ngulube (2005) reports that a study he undertook '... demonstrated that disaster preparedness and security of records and archives did not form a significant part of the preservation activities of [public] archival institutions in South Africa' (p.15). Furthermore, '... far too many archives in the ESARBICA [East and Southern Africa Regional Branch of the International Council on Archives] region have neither a disaster-preparedness nor a security plan in place. In fact, too many archivists in the region have not even given serious thought or effort to the development of either of these plans' (p.16). He adds that the remarks on disaster management made in this study could be generalised to many countries in Africa' (p.16), which is supported by surveys of others (for example, Akussah and Fossu 2001 [academic libraries in Ghana], Hlabaangani and Mnjama 2008 [information centres, Botswana], Ngulube and Magazi 2006 [public libraries of KwaZulu-Natal]).

Examples of approaches that have been identified are provided below. References to the literature and websites offer sources of further information than space permits here.

Chile   To develop and facilitate disaster prevention in Chile, the National Library (Biblioteca Nacional de Chile) has been working closely with the ICBS locally. The national library, building on previous experience, became the regional IFLA PAC centre regional headquarters in 2003 and set up a national Blue Shield Committee. Planned activities included developing a work plan that could also be used by other institutions. Work on a Blue Shield Plan is planned in collaboration with the National Archive and the National Centre for Conservation and Restoration (Cruzat 2004). ICOM and the Directorate of Libraries, Archives and Museums in Chile are represented on the committee.

The Library also works with the Joint Committee for Hygiene and Safety '... whose existence has been required by Chilean law since 1968 for the private sector, ensures workers' safety and well-being, with particular emphasis on prevention' (Cruzat 2006, 23). Emergency guidelines were prepared following recommendations of the National Preparedness Institute, the Chilean Fire Department, the police, the Civil Defence Corps, and the Centre for Conservation and Restoration (Cruzat 2006). Among a range of activities and achievements is the Chilean Blue Shield Committee's agreement with ONEMI, the National Emergency Office, part of the Interior Ministry:

> One of the interesting aspects of our agreement with ONEMI is related to the regional and national reach of the institution. This will allow us to expand upon the work we have done with government support and personnel experienced in this area. Chile is a rather earth-quake prone country, and ONEMI is internationally recognised for its response both to earthquakes and other types of emergencies.

> Heritage preservation is among the objectives of ONEMI, but the organization has not yet developed upon this goal. So it is set to benefit from its agreement with us as well. (Cruzat 2006, 26)

Regional activities and a countrywide network are planned so that experience and expertise from the centre is cascaded elsewhere.

Switzerland   In Switzerland civil emergency planning is well established, and the cultural heritage is embedded in this (see, Federal Office for Civil Protection *Protection of Cultural Property*), reflecting strong commitment on behalf of national government. Its website offers considerable advice, with regard, for example, to organisation and responsibility nationally and in the cantons, protective measures for cultural property, guidelines for the preparation of a disaster plan, and a journal. The civil protection system in Switzerland was revisited in 2000 in the context of post cold war Europe and contemporary hazards; a 'new' civil protection concept was determined in 2001, which included cultural property, its organisation, protective measures and legal basis.

A recent local initiative further illustrates activity: launched by the Vaud Cantonal Archives on 23 March 2004, the Consortium for the Preservation of Documentary Patrimony in case of Disaster (COSADOCA *About Us*) arises from an agreement concluded between: the Vaud Cantonal Archives, the Cantonal University Library (Dorigny), the Main Library of the Ecole polytechnique fédérale de Lausanne (EPFL) and the University of Lausanne. Its objective is the implementation of an inter-institutional collaboration for the rescue of documentary patrimony in case of disaster at the western Lausanne locations (Dorigny and EPFL). 'Beyond the mutualisation of the material resources, COSADOCA provides a common discussion board for public institutions, whose partial or total closure in case of natural damage and disasters would bring harm to the proper functioning of the educational networks. It offers the opportunity to voice opinions in front of the authorities and to value the conservation and patrimonial missions as well as the spreading of knowledge to related institutions. COSADOCA is also an organ of practical and technical information for any institution confronted with a small or large disaster' (COSADOCA *Consortium for the Preservation of Documentary Patrimony in Case of Disaster*). For further information about COSADOCA, its operation and civil protection, see a presentation by Meystre (2005).

A mid-term conference of the IFLA PAC and the University of Lausanne in March 2008, considered current disaster management issues and a day of practical training at a local civil protection facility (Université de Lausanne 2008).

The Netherlands   The Netherlands Institute for Cultural Heritage (NICH) (NICH *Netherlands Institute for Cultural Heritage*) provides national coordination, but with a strong regional and local element. It has recently developed a regional network approach to dealing with 'calamities'. The Institute supports groups collectively on a regional basis to compile their own disaster plan and create a disaster network locally. Work to this end is project based and involves the emergency services. The NICH has also produced two texts on the Dutch Regional Approach to Safety and Security for Cultural Heritage Collections (NICH *Research and Consultancy. Calamities*). NICH have been working on developing a strategy for disaster management based on local networks. This strategy is becoming very popular in the Netherlands. A paper on this subject was presented at the 2003 IFLA conference in Berlin (Peek 2005).

United States   In 1995, the Heritage Emergency National Task Force (2008), a partnership of 41 national service organisations and federal agencies was created to protect cultural heritage from the damaging effects of natural disasters and other emergencies. It is co-sponsored by Heritage Preservation and the Federal Emergency Management Agency (FEMA) (2008). During 2003–04, the innovative *Alliance for Response* (Heritage Emergency National Task Force. *Alliance for Response*) initiative brought cultural heritage leaders and emergency responders together through a series of forums in Boston, Cincinnati, Dallas, and New York City. Each forum increased awareness of the need to protect cultural and historic resources, strengthened local partnerships, and led to new planning and mitigation efforts. Further regional forums have taken place since then and the initiative has reached more than 600 institutions in 15 cities. New local networks have formed in some areas.

The Heritage Emergency National Task Group has also established web pages relating to hurricanes, *Hurricanes 2005* offers archived reports on damage and response, activities of the Task Force, and links to a range of resources for cultural institutions (Heritage Emergency National Task Force *Hurricanes 2005*).

In 2002, Heritage Preservation (2002) published a report, Cataclysm and challenge. Impact of September 11, 2001, on Our Nation's Cultural Heritage. In this,

> The Task Force wanted not only to assess the condition of their collections following September 11, but also to evaluate how prepared the institutions had

been to deal with any type of emergency. We hope to document emergency management efforts that proved most beneficial as well as identify resources needed to cope more effectively with future disasters ... The report concludes with a series of recommendations ... (Heritage Preservation 2002, 1)

Heritage Preservation, in partnership with the Institute of Museum and Library Services, a federal agency, recently undertook a comprehensive survey of the preservation of cultural heritage organisations across the US. The survey covered all kinds and sizes of cultural heritage organisation including small and large institutions. The findings were published in *Heritage Health Index* (Heritage Preservation 2005a), a report of the first comprehensive survey to assess the condition and preservation needs of collections in archives, historical societies, libraries, museums and scientific research organisations across the US. Emergency planning was included in the broad scope of the survey. A major finding is that: '80 per cent of U.S. collecting institutions do not have an emergency plan that includes collections, with staff trained to carry it out' (Heritage Preservation, 2005a, Summary report, 8). The results have considerable significance for planning and advocacy.

A recent initiative, Risk Evaluation and Planning Program, developed by Heritage Preservation and funded by the Institute of Museum and Library Services, aims to develop good practice at local level (Heritage Preservation 2008). This is a pilot programme for implementation in 2008 – museums can apply for funds to enable an evaluation of man-made and natural risks (two-day site visit and report) and assistance in creating or updating an emergency plan.

In 2006, The Council of State Archivists (CoSA) 'developed its Framework for Emergency Preparedness ... as a central focus of Phase One of its Emergency Preparedness Initiative' (CoSA *Framework for Emergency Preparedness*). All state archives and records management programmes undertook an assessment as part of the implementation of the framework. The assessment aimed to identify disaster preparedness strengths and weaknesses. One of the findings is that most state archives have '... an emergency preparedness and recovery plan in place for the principal archival facility. However, in many cases, the plans are reviewed infrequently, drills are not regularly practised, and Continuity of Operations (COOP) planning is inadequately addressed' (CoSA 2006a and 2006b). As with the Heritage Health Index, it provides the basis for advocacy and strategy development.

Other   Proceedings of international conferences can be a useful source about developments, initiatives and aspirations of countries throughout the world. An excellent example of this is ICOM's *International symposium on cultural heritage disaster preparedness and response* held in Hyderabad, India in 2003 (Menegazzi (ed.) 2004). 'Country contributions' include Argentina, Benin, Bhuta, Brazil, Bundi, Congo, Costa Rica, India, Italy, Kenya, Liberia, Madagascar, Malaysia, The Netherlands, Peru, Puerto Rico, Sri Lanka, St Kitts and Nevis, Sweden, Trinidad and Tobago, Turkey, the United States, Venezuela.

Regional Networks

Reasons for cooperation with regard to disaster management are clearly illustrated by Davis and Kern (2003, 117–41) with examples from the US.

> A cooperative network is one of the most efficient strategies for maximizing library strengths *before* a disaster occurs, Networks vastly improve each library's ability to *respond* to and *recover* from disaster, while saving members time, money and effort. Once a network is activated, benefits can multiply across the board. (Davis and Kern, 118)

More detail about the advantages of such networks is provided by Matthews (2005) who outlines and considers how they might function and what advantages they might bring.

Some networks have been formed as a direct result of hazards in their region, to improve risk reduction and reaction and involve a range of organisations. Davis above refers to this with regard to California and the frequency with which earthquakes occur there.

Another such example is CARDIN, the Caribbean Disaster Information Network, which '... seeks to provide a new and dynamic approach to accessing and disseminating disaster related information in a manner that adequately prepares and minimizes the effect of disasters in the Caribbean Region'. It has recently developed a virtual library offering full text documents, presentations, maps, audio and video clips (CARDIN *About Us*). (For further information on CARDIN, also see Lashley 2003.) In collaboration with the Latin American Centre for Disaster Medicine, CARDIN organised a three day workshop on disaster information management in Cuba in November 2006 (IFLA PAC 2006) 'The main objective of this workshop is to strengthen the institutional capacities of the disaster information units in the Caribbean countries...'.

In the same region, CARBICA, the Caribbean Branch of the ICA, also known as the Caribbean Archives Association, is one of thirteen branches that operate under the aegis of the ICA. An example of recent activity is that which followed Grenada's experience with Hurricane Ivan and a plan to involve all islands in the region in mitigation and response.

> On September 7, 2004, Grenada was hit by a Category 4 hurricane. Not only was over 90 per cent of the housing stock destroyed but the country's rich archival heritage located in various parts of the island experienced serious trauma. For several weeks after the hurricane, some of Grenada's scattered archives laid exposed to the elements, some sat over several inches of water while others sat soaking in broken-down buildings. Through CARBICA's intervention, arrangements were made for a complete assessment of the damages. The assessment was undertaken by Mrs Yulu Klein during the period December 13–17, 2004, three months after the passage of Hurricane Ivan. Her report

assessed the damage to the records and archives, made recommendations for their rehabilitation and proposals for improvements to mitigate such damaging effects in the future.

Annually, every island in the Caribbean region is threatened with or experiences the devastating effects of a hurricane. The damage to Grenada's scattered archival collection underscores the need for vulnerable islands like ours to take decisive action to secure our collections as well as effect disaster preparedness plans that would hasten the recovery of damaged archives.

It is easy, however, to recognize what needs to the done. More importantly though, is enforcing what have to be done and by whom. The necessary skills and structures to accomplish some are varied across the region. Being cognizant of this fact, CARBICA through CARTAS, the Caribbean Archives Taskforce for Disaster Protection, proposes the development of a broad-based hazard mitigation and response strategy for the protection of records and archives, by providing technical assistance to all countries in the region. Every member island in the region is therefore urged to actively participate in this project when it comes on stream. (CARBICA 2006)

It is interesting to note in a previous issue of CARBICA News that the Society of American Archivists found the funding to undertake the report (CARBICA 2005).

A presentation by the Project Leader, at the ICA Congress in 2008, provides an update on CARTAS and presents it as a case study model and identifies what makes it different (Griffith Klein 2008). She also mentions other sources of information, for example, the Caribbean Disaster Emergency Response Agency (CDERA), and Cultural Heritage Without Borders.

Australia   DISACT ('DISaster ACT'), a disaster recovery resource for public collections in the ACT [Australian Capital Territory] region, was established by cultural and scientific collecting institutions in Canberra to improve disaster preparedness and provide local mutual assistance in the event of emergencies affecting public collections. DISACT sponsors disaster recovery training, conducts quarterly DISACT Network meetings and has a website resource. The website offers details of events, meetings, training, resources, links and importantly informs not only what DISACT can but what it can not do (DISACT *DISACT – ACT Public Collections Disaster Recovery*). A member of DISACT advised the authors in e-mail correspondence:

In Canberra, we have a group called DisACT that meets every 3 months. The group is made up of representatives from the major cultural institutions as well as others responsible for small museums, galleries, government department archives and libraries. At our meetings we discuss various aspects and share experiences of disaster management e.g. coping with water leaks, malfunctioning air conditioning, etc. DisACT has a Memorandum of Understanding, signed by the heads of the major federal cultural institutions ... affirming that their institutions will provide support if it is needed at a fellow institution. There is also an unofficial understanding that members provide advice and sometimes assistance to smaller institutions when their collections are damaged. DisACT also sponsors a two day training session on 'Disaster Recovery' twice a year. This is open to anyone. DisACT also has a website with information on disaster recovery http://www.cpbr.gov.au/disact/. This includes a list of suppliers who can provide services during an emergency. The website also hosts a discussion list for DisACT members.

A rationale for DISACT and networks in general is provided by Hughes (Strategy to Increase Cooperation for Disaster Preparedness: some Australian examples for saving resources and raising awareness).

Another well known collaborative group in Australia is CAVAL Collaborative Solutions (CAVAL), a consortium owned by Australian universities, which has a Risk Management Group (CAVAL *Risk Management Group*). Established in 1986, the group aims to raise

> ... awareness of the need to plan ahead in order to better cope with a disaster in the library and lending assistance in recovery from disasters. Its main objectives are
> * to create a forum for information exchange between member libraries.
> * to establish and maintain disaster response plan procedures.
> * to help institutions set up their own risk management/disaster response plan.
> * to support Risk Management Training.
> * to encourage libraries to establish risk management practices taking into account their individual preservation needs.
> * to keep member institutions abreast of current developments.

(CAVAL Risk Management Group)

The group website provides a generic disaster response and recovery plan that can be used as a basis for developing a disaster plan (CAVAL *Risk Management Group*).

The Australian Heritage Collections Council's mission is to promote excellence in the management, care and provision of access to Australia's heritage collections so that together, they reflect Australia's cultural and natural diversity. The Council is a collaboration between the Commonwealth, State and Territory governments and the museums sector, and comprises people working in a wide range of cultural heritage institutions across the breadth of urban and regional Australia.

reCollections is an important component of the Council's National Conservation and Preservation Strategy for Australia's Heritage Collections. It offers information on many aspects of 'counter-disaster planning' (Heritage Collections Council *Recollections. Managing Collections. Counter-Disaster Planning*).

US   There is a considerable number of networks in the US. Two of the best known are mentioned briefly here. For details of others see Chapter 8.

California Preservation Program As stated above, network groups have been established to offer mutual assistance with regard to earthquake, flood and fire to which the state is prone. One such example is the California Preservation Program, which includes disaster assistance among its services. Its website (California Preservation Program Emergency Preparedness and Response) provides details of local area networks, training workshops, tools for emergency preparedness and response, including a generic disaster plan workbook, library disaster plan template, disaster resources, disaster plan exercise, and a pocket response plan for collections.

Northeast Document Conservation Center NEDCC's 'mission is to improve the conservation efforts of libraries, archives, historical organizations, museums, and other repositories; to provide the highest quality services to institutions without in-house conservation facilities or those that seek specialized expertise; and to provide leadership in the preservation and conservation fields' (NEDCC About NEDCC. Introduction). It began in the early 1970s when six State libraries in New England agreed to cooperate to address the problem of paper deterioration. With regard to disaster management, it offers, for example, 24/7 telephone assistance, sources of additional information, dPlan – disaster control plan template, a series of emergency management leaflets, courses and workshops (NEDCC *dPlan*™. *The Online Disaster-Planning Tool*).

Training

Many of the organisations mentioned in this chapter offer training of various kinds – their websites should be consulted for details.

Training is vital for effective disaster management – respondents and interviewees constantly reminded the authors of this. Some have also described recent developments in training, in particular longer training sessions followed by a period of monitoring while skills develop. Here trainees are encouraged to return to their own organisations and develop plans, networks and collaborations within their own region, creating local awareness and sharing of experience and expertise. They are also encouraged to include staff at all levels in in-house activity related to disaster management in order to develop a sense of ownership for disaster management within their own institution/organisation. They may in some instances be visited at intervals by trainers to review progress.

In this area, ICOM, the GCI and ICCROM have developed an initiative of particular note for museums, with this approach very much at its heart. The *Teamwork for Integrated Emergency Management* (TIEM) Course was first implemented in 2005–2006 in South, Southeast and East Asia. Its aim is

> to focus on risk assessment and emergency preparedness and response for museums and other cultural institutions. The course reflects a capacity building approach to emergency management by combining training workshops with practical experience gained over an extended period of time. The course guides participating institutions through the processes of undertaking risk assessment and implementing emergency plans and strategies that are suitable for their own institutions, taking into account local contexts, traditions, and methods (ICOM MEP Module 4).

A MEP online bibliography was created by the GCI as an additional resource (GCI *Project Bibliographies*). For further and updated information, see the ICOM website.

Another initiative, *Preservation Education Curriculum: an Introduction to Preservation*, provided by NEDCC (development funded by the Institute of Museum and Library Services) supports educators at Library and Information Schools. 'It encompasses issues for libraries, archives, museums, and collections-holding institutions of all kinds', and includes a session on Disaster Planning with appropriate resources provided (NEDCC *Preservation Education Curriculum*).

Issues

Information Overload

Söderlund, introducing guidelines for small museums she had produced commented: 'These guidelines would not have been possible without the enthusiastic response of the museum community around the world. Following requests for information, I was inundated with information, suggestions, sample plans and guidelines … As there is a wealth of information regarding disaster preparedness available, there were many sources to consult while writing this guide' (Söderlund 2000, 1). The authors, based on their experience of this project, would echo these comments, and would add that since 2000 there has been even more information available via the Internet. Indeed, major disasters such as 11 September 2001, the Indian Ocean tsunami, and Hurricane Katrina have all contributed to the literature and information available via the Internet and elsewhere.

For some, there seems overall to be too much information – to make a start or to know what to use. Comments from some of our interviewees illustrate this. For example,

There's volumes on the Internet but it's all the same stuff. You can read it for weeks but won't get any further. (International conservation expert)

Did web search. Didn't read anything in depth. When I browsed documents they were good but as to their application in our own context, I didn't see that. (Professional body)

I think it's actually sort of mediating the information ... it was actually just sort of picking the half a dozen sites that would give them the kind of basic information they needed to get started but they were in danger of you know, just sort of typing stuff into Google and getting so many hits back that they just couldn't actually navigate what was there and authentic and reliable, a professionally respected site. So a lot of [consultants'] work is actually pointing people, getting them started, pointing them in the direction of the right place to look. (National MLA)

... So much new stuff comes out we're going to have to pick and choose to give people right information... there's only so much they [people in post-disaster location] can absorb, they're still shocked. There's a limited amount of information clearly presented that will empower them to act. Too much information – too many 'it depends', 'ifs', 'maybes', just paralyses people. (International museum and library)

... we wonder where to get this information, if it's available – you need a website, I repeat, there are 15,000 websites out there that have bits of disaster recovery, but not the one that I wanted, whatever that might be. (International gallery)

Templates

Many institutions or agencies provide templates of disaster control plans that provide a framework of headings/activities and prompts for institutions to complete to use to devise their own plans. There appear to be mixed views on their effectiveness, with some concerned that they do not encourage ownership, with perhaps just one person ticking boxes and thinking the job is done. Others produce templates to be used within a framework of support, training and ongoing liaison and review, and based on an institution specific risk assessment. Indeed, internationally there appears to be more of a shift by major organisations and collaborative networks from solely providing templates to create plans, to developing formal systems of training and collaboration for writing plans, with systematic development and monitoring by the training provider once the trainee returns to their institution to implement disaster management systems.

In the US, there are many examples of templates with accompanying support and advice. For example, as mentioned above, the California Preservation Program website offers a range of guidance and advice for libraries and archives on emergency preparedness and response and training tools, to go with its template. It also advertises programs and workshops. Amongst these is an archived webcast *Ten things you need to know before disaster strikes* (Page 2006).

Also mentioned above, NEDCC has recently produced dPlan™: The Online Disaster Planning Tool (NEDCC *dPlan™: The Online Disaster Planning Tool*), a tool that aims to help institutions simplify the process of writing a disaster plan specific to them. It is possible that a 'lite' version of the plan may be developed for those who want less of an in-depth plan.

Developments such as dPlan™ reflects the positive attitude to the use of templates. Others have told us they 'Prefer to direct enquirers to find information themselves and then we review', and

> [we] Advise to do background reading rather than use a template" ... because "Sometimes the documents are done dryly, they're almost academic. So many people cut and paste from the Internet, some have the same mistake in. (Commercial recovery service)

Another interviewee, when asked about this, pointed to a bookcase and indicated several examples of templates and guidance from different parts of the world, commenting that common elements can be found in these but some are so detailed and lengthy that were too complex, particularly for small institutions. She was thus aware that producing a template was 'not an easy task'.

Language

With disasters happening all over the world, there is much information and guidance relating to disaster management available in languages other than English. Brinkman (2004, 12) attests to the significance of this:

> Have you heard about the experience of Chinese museums with floods? ... Has any native English speaker read all the reports on the floods in Germany and the Czech Republic written in German and Czech? Does any body know about an important meeting on emergencies in the Netherlands, a meeting held in Dutch only?

He went on to say

> ... a great deal of information is already available, but not always in the language of the country of a given museum. Who, except those of you who speak Japanese, have learned about the recommendations, written in Japanese, after the Kobe earthquake? Have Japanese museum professional been able to carefully go through the outcome of the meeting on emergencies in Draguignan, produced in French? (Brinkman 2004, 13)

Websites of organisations whose language is not English, do provide some documents in English and international associations translate into several languages. The significance of international conferences in this context is underlined, especially if translation is available and/or proceedings in more than one language are published.

People

The impact of major disasters on staff of cultural heritage institutions must be kept in mind too, as they live in the midst of the aftermath of the disaster and their personal lives will be affected. If they have suffered personal loss, had their homes destroyed, their children's schools washed away, for example, how might this impact on their role in the recovery of archive, library or museum services? With regard to the population in general and trying to get back to a normal way of life, archivists in particular raised the issue of vital records with regard to disaster planning. These are documents essential for the operation of all aspects of everyday life and include, for example, business, legal, medical and financial records. On a personal level, lack of birth and death certificates, property deeds, insurance documentation, for example, can complicate attempts to return to normal.

Conservators   Salvage and recovery of items post disaster was frequently an issue for those on the scene without conservation expertise. Already, perhaps in shock, they were unsure as to what to do with different types of material and needed expert advice from experienced conservators either from the public or private sector. The sector needs to determine whether it has sufficient expertise of this kind. Attention also needs to be paid to appropriate storage for artefacts, items and collections.

Ongoing training for experienced conservators is required too. An initiative in 2007 that addressed this was one led by the AIC (2008) funded by a grant from the Institute for Museums and Library Services. Through a four-and-a-half-day workshop, offered in three locations, for conservators and professionals in archives, libraries and museums, the aim was to produce '60 collections emergency response team members trained to assess damage and initiate salvage of cultural collections after a disaster has occurred' (AIC 2007a). Out of this has developed the American Institute for Conservation – Collections Emergency Response Team (AIC-CERT). 'The mission of AIC-CERT is to respond to the needs of cultural institutions during emergencies and disasters through coordinated efforts with first responders, state agencies, vendors and the public …'; the 2007 advanced training program has now 'resulted in a force of 60 "rapid responders" trained to assess damage and initiate salvage of cultural collections after a disaster has occurred'. (AIC c.2007b). They will be of particular benefit to cultural institutions run by volunteers or a single staff member. Such initiatives respond to a need for rapid response teams with expertise, equipment and funds to be dispatched to disaster scenes that became evident after recent events (see Frost 2006 and Silverman

2006). (The AIC website offers links to information about various aspects of dealing with disasters [AIC *Disaster Response and Recovery*].)

Conclusion

Much advice and guidance on disaster management is available for archives, libraries and museums. The Internet has facilitated worldwide dissemination of this. International assistance is often forthcoming in the aftermath of catastrophic region-wide disasters. There are also examples of schemes where experts from developed countries are assisting those in developing countries to advance disaster management practice in prevention and preparedness, through, for example, support in devising disaster control plans in line with local circumstances, and undertaking training. There is a range of approaches and levels of activity in different countries – affected by different factors such as political motivation, financial support and appropriate experience and expertise. Catastrophic, region–wide disasters have massive impact and human safety and reinstatement of the infrastructure rightly take priority over archives, libraries and museums in such cases. They may, therefore, have to 'go it alone' for a while. Responses from national governments and international agencies will vary – increasingly the institutions in the cultural heritage sector are forming collaborative regional networks to provide mutual support and sharing of resources pre- and post-disaster. Whilst the nature and constraints of the study have precluded in-depth, country-wide coverage worldwide, it is hoped that the 'snapshot' offered in this chapter provides an insight to the kind of issues faced and activities undertaken in different contexts – and offers lessons and motivation to others.

References

AFRICOM, *International Council of African Museums* [website], (updated Aug. 2008) <http://www.africom.museum/>, accessed 13 Aug. 2008.

AIC, *Welcome to AIC* [website], (updated Aug. 2008) <http://aic.stanford.edu/>, accessed 23 Aug. 2008.

AIC (2007a), *AIC Collections Emergency Response Training* (Washington: AIC), (published online c.2007) <http://aic.stanford.edu/education/workshops/documents/certdes.pdf>, accessed 7 Aug. 2008.

AIC (c.2007b), *Rapid Response Team for Cultural Institutions* (Washington DC: American Institute for Conservation, Collections Emergency Response Team), (published online c.2007) <http://aic.stanford.edu/news/AIC-CERT.pdf>, accessed 7 Aug. 2008.

AIC, *Disaster Response and Recovery* [website], (updated c.2005) <http://aic.stanford.edu/library/online/disaster/index.html>, accessed 7 Aug. 2008.

Akussah, H. and Fosu, V. (2001), 'Disaster management in academic libraries in Ghana', *African Journal of Library, Archives and Information Science* 11:1, 1–16.

California Preservation Program, *Emergency Preparedness and Response* [website], (updated Feb. 2008) <http://calpreservation.org/ disasters/index. html>. accessed 6 Aug. 2008.

CARDIN, *About Us* [website], (updated 2 Dec. 2005) <http://www.mona.uwi.edu/ cardin/about.asp>, accessed 2 Aug. 2008.

CARBICA (2008), 'Grenada: rescue plan for the records', *CARBICA News* 7, (published online Aug. 2005) <http://www.carbica.com/newsletters/news_august_2005.htm>, accessed 6 Aug. 2008.

CARBICA (2006), 'Grenada's experience with hurricane Ivan and the Cartas project', *CARBICA News* 8, (published online Sep. 2006) <http://www.carbica. com/newsletters/news_september_2006.htm>, accessed 6 Aug. 2008.

CAVAL, *Risk Management Group* [website], (updated 1 Jul. 2008) <http://www. caval.edu.au/riskman.html>, accessed 6 Aug. 2008.

CCI (1995a), 'Emergency Preparedness for Cultural Institutions', *CCI Notes* 14:1 (Ottawa: Canadian Conservation Institute).

CCI (1995b), 'Emergency Preparedness for Cultural Institutions: Identifying and Reducing Hazards', *CCI Notes* 14:2 (Ottawa: Canadian Conservation Institute).

CDERA, *Caribbean Disaster Emergency Response Agency (CDERA)* [website], (updated Aug. 2008), <http://www.cdera.org/>, accessed 6 Aug. 2008.

CMA (2006), *Cultural Property Protection Conference 2006*, Ottawa, 16 Jan. 2006 [website], (updated 2006), <http://www.museums.ca/protection/en/ presentations.html>, accessed 6 Aug. 2008.

CoOL, *Disaster preparedness and response* [website], (updated 26 Mar. 2008) <http://palimpsest.stanford.edu/bytopic/disasters/>, accessed 14 Aug. 2008.

CoSA, *Framework for Emergency Preparedness* [website], (updated 11 Feb.2007) <http://www.statearchivists.org/prepare/framework/index.htm>, accessed 6 Sep. 2008.

CoSA, (2006a), *Safeguarding a Nation's Identity. A report to the President, Congress, Governors, and State Legislators of the United States. Executive summary. Council of State Archivists Emergency Preparedness Initiative, Securing our nation's essential records* (Iowa City: Council of State Archivists), (published online 2006) <http://www.statearchivists.org/prepare/2006EPI_ rpt_Summary.pdf> (executive summary) and, accessed 6 Aug. 2008.

CoSA (2006b), *Safeguarding a Nation's Identity. The readiness of state archives to protect the records that identify who we are, secure our rights, and tell our story as a nation. A Report to the President, Congress, Governors, and State Legislatures of the United States* (Iowa City: Council of State Archivists), (published online Feb. 2007) <http://www.statearchivists.org/prepare/ epireport_all.pdf>, accessed 6 Jun. 2008.

COSADOCA, *About Us* [website], (updated 11 Mar. 2008) <http://www.cosadoca. ch/en/consortium/>, accessed 9 May 2008).

COSADOCA, *Consortium for the Preservation of Documentary Patrimony in Case of Disaster* [website], (updated 11 Jul. 2008) <http://www.cosadoca.ch/ en/>, accessed 14 Aug. 2008.

Cruzat, X. A. (2006), 'The never ending challenge: disasters and preservation in Chile', in Koch, C. (ed.) (2006), 22–29.

Cruzat, X. (2004), 'National Library of Chile – disaster prevention', in World Library and Information Congress', in *70ᵗʰ IFLA General Conference and Council* [Summary], Buenos Aires, 22–27 Aug. 2004, IFLA, (published online Aug. 2004) <http://www.ifla.org/IV/ifla70/papers/087e_trans-Cruzat.pdf>, accessed 14 Aug. 2008.

Cultural Heritage Without Borders, *Cultural Heritage without Borders/Kosovo Welcome to the Swedish Foundation for "Cultural Heritage without Borders" Local office in Prishtina, Kosovo* [website], (updated 22 Jul. 2004) <http:// www.chwb.org/kosovo/english/home.htm>, accessed 6 Aug. 2008.

Davis, S. and Kern, K. (2003) 'Co-operative activity', in Matthews, G. and Feather, J (eds.), 117–41.

De Silva, N. (2004), 'Preparedness and response for cultural heritage disasters in developing countries', in Menegazzi, C. (ed.). (2004), 223–226.

DISACT, *DISACT – ACT Public Collections Disaster Recovery* [website], (updated 25 Feb. 2008) <http://www.anbg.gov.au/disact/index.html>, accessed 14 Aug. 2008.

The Federal Office for Civil Protection [Switzerland], 'Protection of Cultural Property' [website], (updated 9 Jul. 2008) <http://www.bevoelkerungsschutz. admin.ch/internet/bs/en/home/themen/kgs.html>, accessed 21 Aug. 2008.

FEMA, *Federal Emergency Management Agency* [website], (updated 2008) <http://www.fema.gov/>, accessed 29 Aug. 2008.

Frost, G. (2006), 'Lessons from Katrina: recovery of cultural collections', *Archival Products News* 13:2, 1–4.

GCI, *The Getty Conservation Institute* [website], (updated Spring 2008) <http:// www.getty.edu/conservation/>, accessed 14 Aug. 2008.

GCI, *Project Bibliographies* [website], (updated c.2007) <http://gcibibs.getty.edu/ asp/>, accessed 13 Aug. 2008.

Griffith Klein, Y, (2008), 'Caribbean Archives Task Force for Disaster Preparedness: if we unwrap it, would we find a model inside?' in *16ᵗʰ International Congress on Archives 2008, Archives, Governance and Development: Mapping Future Society*, National Archives of Malaysia, Kuala Lumpur, Malaysia, 21–27 Jul. 2008 (ICA), (published online 2008) <http://www.kualalumpur2008.ica.org/ sites/kl2008/files/079_GRIFFITHKLEIN_Disasters%20and%20Disaster%20 Mitigation.ppt#1>, accessed 6 Aug. 2008.

Heritage Collections Council, *reCollections:. Managing Collections. Counter-Disaster Planning* [website], (updated 2000) <http://archive.amol.org.au/ recollections/4/6/index.htm>, accessed 6 Aug. 2008.

Heritage Emergency National Task Force, *Heritage Emergency National Task Force* [website], (updated 2008) <http://www.heritagepreservation.org/PROGRAMS/TASKFER.HTM>, accessed 29 Aug. 2008.

Heritage Emergency National Task Force, *Alliance for Response* [website]. (updated 2005) <http://www.heritagepreservation.org/PROGRAMS/AFRmain.HTM>, accessed 14 Aug. 2008.

Heritage Emergency National Task Force, *Hurricanes Katrina* [website], (updated 2005) <http://www.heritagepreservation.org/PROGRAMS/Katrina.HTM>, accessed 14 Aug. 2008.

Heritage Preservation (2008), *Heritage Preservation's Risk Evaluation and Planning Program At-a-Glance,* (published online 2008) <http://www.heritage preservation.org/REPP/REPP%20Info%20Sheet.pdf>, accessed 6 Aug. 2008.

Heritage Preservation (2006), *Field guide to emergency response* [with instructional DVD] (Washington, D.C: Heritage Preservation).

Heritage Preservation (2005a). *A public trust at risk: the Heritage Health Index report on the state of America's collections. A project of Heritage Preservation and the Institute of Museum and Library Services* (Washington, D.C.: Heritage Preservation), (published online 2005) Summary report <http://www.heritagepreservation.org/HHI/summary.html>, accessed 29 Aug. 2008; Full report <http://www.heritagepreservation.org/HHI/full.html>, accessed 29 Aug. 2008.

Heritage Preservation (2005b) *Emergency Response and Salvage Wheel*, rev. edition (Washington DC: Heritage Preservation).

Heritage Preservation, *Guide to Navigating Federal Emergency Management Agency and Small Business Administration Disaster Aid for Cultural Institutions* [website], (updated c.2005) <http://www.heritagepreservation.org/federal/index.html>, accessed 3 Aug. 2008.

Heritage Preservation (2002), *Cataclysm and challenge. Impact of September 11, 2001, on Our Nation's Cultural Heritage. A report from Heritage Preservation on behalf of the Heritage Emergency National Task Force, Project Director Ruth Hargraves* (Washington, DC: Heritage Preservation), (published online 2002) <http://www.heritagepreservation.org/PDFS/Cataclysm.pdf>, accessed 29 Aug. 2008.

Hlabaangani, K. and Mnjama, N. (2008), 'Disaster preparedness in information centres in Gaborne, Botswana', *African Journal of Library, Archives and Information Science* 18:1, 63–74.

Hughes, J, A., *Strategy to Increase Cooperation for Disaster Preparedness: some Australian examples for saving resources and raising awareness* [website], (updated 12 Aug. 2005) <http://www.anbg.gov.au/disact/hughes-2003.html>, accessed 28 Aug. 2008.

ICA, *International Council of Archives* [website], (updated Jul. 2008) <http://www.ica.org/>, accessed 24 Aug. 2008.

ICA, *Regional Branches* [website], (updated 2008) <http://www.ica.org/en/branches>, accessed 31 Aug. 2008.

ICA/PDP (1997), *Guidelines on Disaster Prevention and Control in Archives. (ICA Studies 11)* (ICA: Paris), (published online 12 May. 2006) <http://www. ica.org/biblio.php?pdocid=452>, accessed 31 Aug. 2008.

ICBS, *The International Committee of the Blue Shield (ICBS)* [website], (updated 6 Nov. 2006) <http://www.ifla.org/blueshield.htm>, accessed 14 Aug. 2008.

ICCROM, *ICCROM – home page: The official website of ICCROM (International Centre for the Study of the Preservation and Restoration of Cultural Property)* [website], (updated 1 Aug. 2008) <http://www.iccrom.org/index.shtml>, accessed 14 Aug. 2008.

ICOM, *Disaster relief for museums* [website], (updated 4 Aug. 2008) <http://icom. museum/disaster_relief/>, accessed 31 Aug. 2008.

ICOM, *International Council of Museums* [website], (updated n.d.) <http://icom. museum/>, accessed 31 Aug. 2008.

ICOM MEP. *Preparedness and response in emergency situations* [website], (updated 17 Sep. 2007) <http://icom.museum/mep.html>, accessed 13 Aug. 2008.

ICOM MEP, *Module 1 Surveys* [website], (updated 11 Jul. 2005) <http://icom. museum/mep_module1.html>, accessed 30 Aug. 2008.

ICOM MEP, *Module 4. Education Initiative. Teamwork for Integrated Emergency Management Course* [website], (updated 9 Jul. 2008) <http://icom.museum/ mep_module4.html>, accessed 6 August 2008.

ICRC, *International Committee for the Red Cross (ICRC) – Home English* [website], (updated Aug. 2008) <http://www.icrc.org/eng>, accessed 24 Aug. 2008.

IFLA, *International Federation of Library Associations and Institutions* [website], updated 2008) <http://www.ifla.org/>, accessed 19 Sep. 2008.

IFLA PAC, *IFLA Core Activity on Preservation and Conservation. PAC. Regional Centres* [website], (updated 8 Jan. 2008) <http://www.ifla.org/ VI/4/reg-cent.htm>, accessed 1 Sep. 2008.

IFLA PAC (2006), 'Workshop on Disaster Information Management', *International Preservation News* 39, 36.

IFLA PAC ASIA and National Diet Library (2005*), Open seminar on the documentary heritage damaged by the Indian Ocean Tsunami and the meeting of Directors of the IFLA/PAC Regional Centres in Asia and others*, National Diet Library, Tokyo, 6 Dec. 2005 (Tokyo: National Diet Library) [website], (updated c.2005) <http://www.ndl.go.jp/en/iflapac/news.html>, accessed 14 Aug. 2008.

Koch, C. (ed.) (2006), *The 3-D's of Preservation: Disasters, Displays, Digitization. Proceedings of the international symposium, organised by The Bibliothèque Nationale de France in collaboration with IFLA, Paris, 8–10 March 2006* (Paris: IFLA-PAC), (published online 2006) <http://www.ifla.org/VI/4/news/ ipi7-en.pdf>, Accessed 31 Aug. 2008.

Kulczak, D. and Lennertz, L. (1999), 'A Decade of disaster: a selected bibliography of disaster literature, 1985–1995'. *Library and Archival Security* 15:1, 7–66.

Lashley, B. (2003), 'Co-operative Disaster Planning for Libraries: a Model', *International Preservation News* 31, 26–33, <http://www.ifla.org/VI/4/news/ipnn31.pdf>, accessed 31 Aug. 2008.

Matthews, G. (2005), 'Disaster Management: Sharing Experience, Working Together Across the Sector', *Journal of Librarianship and Information Science* 37:2, 63–74.

Matthews, G. (2003), 'A Guide to sources of information', in Matthews, G. and Feather, J (eds.), 213–28.

Matthews, G. and Feather, J. (eds.) (2003), *Disaster Management for Libraries and Archives* (Aldershot: Ashgate).

McIlwaine, J. (2006), *IFLA Disaster Preparedness and Planning. A Brief Manual.* (International. Preservation Issues Number 6) (Paris: IFLA PAC), (published online 2006) <http://www.ifla.org/VI/4/news/ipi6-en.pdf>, accessed 31 Aug. 2008.

Menegazzi, C. (ed.) (2004), *Cultural Heritage Disaster Preparedness and Response. International Symposium Proceedings. Salar Jung Museum, 23–27 November 2003, Hyderabad, India.* (Paris: International Council of Museums), (published online 2004) <http://icom.museum/disaster_preparedness_book/index.html>, accessed 31 Aug. 2008.

Menegazzi, C. (2003), *ICOM Museums Emergency Programme: Prevention and Recovery in Emergency Situations, ICOMOS. Museums at Risk. Thematic Reports* [website], (updated 30 Jun. 2003) <http://www.international.icomos.org/ risk/2001/icom2001.htm>, accessed 29 Aug. 2008.

Meystre, M. (2005), *Civil Protection Organisation, Western Lausanne Region, ORPC-ORL Fires: handling and treatment of burned documents. Training day 29th November 2005, Cosadoca, Centre of Civil Protection, Gollion,* (published online 2005) <http://www.cosadoca.ch/en/docs/actualites/20051129-orpc-rol.pdf>, accessed 9 May 2008.

National Library of Australia, *Collection Disaster Plan* [website], (updated n.d.) <http://www.nla.gov.au/policy/disaster/>, accessed 3 Aug. 2008.

National Archives of Australia (2000), *Disaster Preparedness Manual for Commonwealth Agencies*, (Canberra: National Archives of Australia), (published online 2000) <http://www.naa.gov.au/images/disaster%20manual_tcm2-4789.pdf>, accessed 14 Aug. 2008.

NEDCC, *Northeast Document Conservation Centre* [website], (updated 2008), <http://www.nedcc.org/home.php>, accessed 6 Sep. 2008.

NEDCC, *dPlan™: The Online Disaster-Planning Tool* [website], (updated 2006) <http://www.dplan.org/aboutdplan.asp>, accessed 31 Aug. 2008. http://icom.museum/mep_module1.html.

NEDCC, About *NEDCC. Introduction* [website], (updated n.d.) <http://www.nedcc.org/about/introduction.php>, accessed 2 Aug. 2008.

NEDCC, *Preservation Education Curriculum* [see Class 12 Disaster Planning] [website], (updated n.d.) <http://www.nedcc.org/curriculum/lesson.introduction.php>, accessed 6 August 2008.

NICH, *Netherlands Institute for Cultural Heritage* [website], (updated 2008) <http://www.icn.nl/Dir003/ICN/CMT/Homepage.nsf/index2.html?readform>, accessed 19 Sep. 2008.

NICH, *Research and Consultancy. Calamities* [website], (updated n.d.) <http://www.icn.nl/Dir003/ICN/CMT/Homepage.nsf/HFS?Readform&menu=600>, accessed 19 Sep. 2008.

Ngulube, P. (2005), 'Disaster and security management in public archival institutions in ESARBICA region', *African Journal of Library, Archives and Information Science* 15:1, 15–23.

Ngulube, P. and Magazi, L. (2006), 'A stitch in time saves nine: emergency preparedness in public libraries of KwaZulu-Natal, South Africa', *Innovation* 32, 110–24.

Page, J. (2006), 'Ten things you need to know before disaster strikes' [webcast], (Infopeople) <http://infopeople.org/training/webcasts/webcast_data/196/index.html>, accessed 6 Aug. 2008.

Peek, M. (2005), 'Setting up emergency plans: a regional approach for Dutch cultural heritage', in Wellheiser, J. G. and Gwynn, N. E, 33–7.

Plas, E. van der (2004), 'New fund for emergency aid to culture: cultural emergency response', *Alexandria* 16:3, 159–69.

Polley, A. (2003), *ICOM Museums Emergency Programme The Effect of Natural and Anthropogenic Disasters on Museums and other Cultural Resources.* (published online 30 Jun. 2003) <http://www.international.icomos.org/risk/2001/icom2001.htm>, accessed 31 Aug. 2008.

Preservation Directorate, the Federal Library and Information Center Committee, and the American Folklife Center, Library of Congress (2006) *Draft of notes (4/25/06), "Future Directions in Safeguarding Document Collections", sponsored by the Preservation Directorate, the Federal Library and Information Center Committee, and the American Folklife Center, Library of Congress, Jefferson Building Room 119, 21 April 2006, Washington D.C., Library of Congress.*

Silverman, R. (2006), 'Towards a national disaster response protocol', in Koch, C. (ed.).(2006), 44–55.

Söderlund, K. (2000), *Be prepared: guidelines for small museums for writing a disaster preparedness plan. Canberra: Commonwealth of Australia on behalf of Heritage Collections Council. A Heritage Collections Council Project undertaken by Söderlund Consulting Pty Ltd.,* (Canberra: Heritage Collections Council) *(*published online 2000) <http://sector.amol.org.au/__data/page/44/beprep.pdf>, accessed 13 Jul. 2008.

Te Papa National Services (2001a). *Resource Guides. Emergency Procedures* (Wellington: Museum of New Zealand Te Papa Tongarewa), (published online Jun. 2001) <http://www.tepapa.govt.nz/NR/rdonlyres/3ECB70FF-7948-4E26-B976-E6F09CFBDF06/0/Emergency.pdf#Page=3>, accessed 31 Aug. 2008.

Te Papa National Services (2001b), *Resource Guides. Preventive conservation* (Wellington: Museum of New Zealand Te Papa Tongarewa), (published online

Jun. 2001) <http://www.tepapa.govt.nz/NR/rdonlyres/017BFB88-80F4-4F1F-AE08-79C94A25CC5A/0/Conservation.pdf#Page=2>, accessed 31 Aug. 2008.

Te Papa National Services (2001c). *Resource Guides. Minimising disaster* (Wellington: Museum of New Zealand Te Papa Tongarewa), (published online Jun. 2001) <http://www.tepapa.govt.nz/NR/rdonlyres/961F6489-3130-47DB-B53F-BE5C94475C48/0/MinDisaster.pdf#Page=2>, accessed 31 Aug. 2008.

UNESCO, *In focus. Tsunami in South Asia* [website], (updated 2008) <http://portal.unesco.org/ci/en/ev.php-URL_ID=17830&URL_DO=DO_TOPIC&URL_SECTION=201.html>, accessed 31 Aug. 2008.

UNESCO (2005), *KOBE REPORT draft. Report of Session 3.3, Thematic Cluster 3. Cultural Heritage Risk Management. World Conference on Disaster Reduction. 18–22 January 2005, Kobe, Hyogo, Japan*, (published online 2005) <http://www.unisdr.org/wcdr/thematic-sessions/thematic-reports/report-session-3-3.pdf>, accessed 31 Aug. 2008.

UNESCO, *UNESCO Archives Portal: Resources: Preservation and Conservation: Disaster Preparedness and Recovery'* [website], (updated c.2005) <http://www.unesco.org/webworld/portal_archives/pages/Resources/Preservation_and_Conservation/Disaster_Preparedness_and_Recovery/index.shtml>, accessed 31 Aug. 2008.

UNESCO, *UNESCO Libraries Portal*, [website], (updated c.2005) <http://www.unesco.org/cgi-bin/webworld/portal_bib2/cgi/page.cgi?d=1>, accessed 31 Aug. 2008.

Université de Lausanne, *Salvage in case of disaster in library and archives. Mid-term conference of the IFLA PAC section and core activity* [and COSADOCA], University of Lausanne Amphimax 350 – Switzerland, 26 – 28th March 2008 [website], (updated 2008) <https://www2.unil.ch/iflapac08/traiterPresentation.do>, accessed 31 Aug. 2008.

Varlamoff, M.-T. and Plassard, M.-F., *Survey on disaster planning in national libraries*. World Library and Information Conference: 70th IFLA General Conference and Council, 22–27 August 2004, Buenos Aires, Argentina, (published online 2004) http://www.ifla.org/IV/ifla70/papers/142e_trans-Varlamoff_Plassard.pdf. accessed 28 Aug. 2008.

Wellheiser, J. G. and Gwinn, N. E. (eds.) (2005), *Preparing for the worst, planning for the best: protecting our cultural heritage from disaster. Proceedings of a conference sponsored by the IFLA Preservation and Conservation Section, the IFLA Core Activity for Preservation and Conservation and the Council on Library and Information Resources, Inc., with the Akademie der Wissenschaften and the Staatsbibliothek zu Berlin. Berlin, Germany, Jul 30–August 1, 2003, IFLA Publications 111* (München: K G Saur).

Chapter 5

The Disaster Control Plan

Introduction

There is much already written relating to the disaster control plan (in its entirety or to aspects of it): theory, guidance and advice; see, for example: Alire 2000; Anderson and McIntyre 1985; Ashman 1995; Doig 1997; Dorge and Jones 1999; EmmS 2001; ICA/PDP 1997; Kahn 1998; Matthews and Eden 1996; Matthews and Feather 2003; McIlwaine 2006; Short-Traxler 2005; Society of Archivists, Scottish Region, Disaster Preparedness Working Group 1996; TNA 2004; UKIRB n.d.; Wellheiser and Scott 2002. A bibliography of disaster literature, 1985–1995, gives details of over 40 titles under the heading, *Plans and planning manuals* (Kulczak and Lennertz 1999). Many disaster control plans and templates are available via the Internet (see links, for example on CoOL (2008) and M25, Disaster Management Working Group (M25 Consortium of Academic Libraries 2005) websites).

Significance of the Disaster Control Plan

Mansell has summed up succinctly the rationale for a disaster control plan, and, indeed, why disaster planning is significant:

> … not the least of which are that they:
>
> provide a framework for people to work within.
>
> require people to focus and think through potential problems and solutions in advance.
>
> provide clear procedures and clarify people's roles and responsibilities.
>
> There is consensus that a good plan makes an incident much easier to manage and helps individuals to make decisions quickly and assess situations effectively and efficiently. Plans minimize risk, maximise the speed of recovery and help the organization get back into business quickly. The development of a DCP is positive evidence of a duty of care for objects, collections and staff; it shows disaster control planning forms part of the risk management and overall operation of the entity. (Mansell 2003, 14)

If it is to be effective, the plan must be more than words on paper, it should be a framework for action. The Disaster/Emergency planning pages on the NPO'S (UK) website underline this by advising that disaster control planning will:

- Enable action to be taken to mitigate harm from identified risks
- Identify the need for resources to react to, and recover from an incident
- Enable training to be identified and undertaken
- Identify sources of expertise and assistance in the event of an incident
- Necessitate increased internal co-operation …
  (NPO n.d.)

There certainly seem to be advantages in having a disaster control plan in place – 83 per cent of managers in institutions that had experienced a disaster reported in response to our questionnaire that their disaster control plan was effective during the disaster (see Table 3.9).

There are also examples from the literature where those who have experienced disasters and their aftermath speak positively about the disaster control plan. Following the catastrophic events of 11 September 2001, for example, Heritage Preservation reported:

Although the events of September 11 were caused by an unprecedented act of terror, we found that standard, proven emergency management plans and responses turned out to be the most effective way of dealing with the disaster. (Heritage Preservation 2002, 20)

Following a flood at a repository of the University of Sussex, for example, the University Librarian commented:

Above all, I am convinced disaster planning is absolutely essential – and not much use when something as bad as this happens … In the end you just cope. (Shorley 2004, 47)

This was qualified by a colleague:

The second lesson is the value of having a written disaster plan. Although the plan had no direct effect on the outcome of the disaster, the reading and discussions that accompanied it were invaluable in helping us react to the flood. We already knew where to begin. (Howes 2003, 186)

At a meeting attended by many who had experienced the aftermath of Hurricane Katrina it was noted: 'Disaster plans provide a chance of recovery: no plan, no chance' (Preservation Directorate … 2006).

Comments respondents provided to the questionnaire request for three lessons learned after experiencing a disaster that they would pass on to others underline these sentiments, too. For example:

An effective disaster control plan would have saved more of the material. (Museum archive)

Disaster plan was reasonably effective, although they can never be perfect. (Local Authority archive)

The plan gives a good framework but you have to think on your feet. (Higher Education library)

Important to have a disaster control plan and trained staff. Important to update it regularly. (Higher Education library)

You need to block off a chunk of time to write/review plan and think scenarios through – it's quicker than doing it piecemeal. (Public library)

Plan for the long term – refurbishment/rebuilds take time. (Public library)

The better the plan, the smaller the damage. (Professional or Learned Institution library)

Have a plan. Make it known. Put it to the test. (Museum)

Emergency manual invaluable. (Local Authority museum)

Familiarity among staff in the emergency plan breeds a great deal of confidence. (National museum)

Content of Disaster Control Plans

In the UK and elsewhere, disaster control planning has moved forward (for a brief overview, see Matthews, Smith and Knowles 2004, 9–12) but there is no room for complacency. With recent major region-wide incidents, natural and man-wide, awareness is high. Initiatives and advice abound – there has been an increase in the number of institutions who have developed disaster control plans. What can be learned from the content of disaster control plans that might be of use to others?

Disaster Control Plan Analysis

Along with the data gained about disaster control plans from the questionnaire survey, an investigation into a sample of disaster control plans and their contents was undertaken. The objectives were to:

*   assess the structure and content of plans
*   identify areas of weakness or good practice in plans
*   identify new ideas and emerging trends.

It was hoped that the results of this exercise would contribute to good practice and the development of guidance for professionals writing DCPs.

Method

Three hundred and fifty institutions reported in the questionnaire survey that they had a written disaster control plan. From this group, a sample of 130 was selected (37 per cent) and a copy of their DCP requested for review (see Table 5.1). Factors taken into consideration in selecting the sample, included:

*   Domain
*   Institution type
*   Geographical location
*   Who wrote the plan
*   Experience of Disaster

The total number of plans received for review and analysis was 37, four of which were recovered from Internet websites. Table 5.2 shows the breakdown of returns in terms of domain and geographical location.

In order to review the structure and content of the disaster control plans, an analysis framework was devised. The 'traditional' four headings of Prevention, Preparedness, Reaction, and Recovery formed the main framework. Each heading was broken down into further sub-headings (see Disaster Control Plan Analysis Framework section, below).

The framework was developed from the arrangement of guidelines in Matthews's and Eden's *Disaster Management In British Libraries* (1996), based on research into practice in the mid 1990s, and the M25 Disaster Management Working Group template (itself developed in part from Matthews's and Eden's guidelines) that had been updated in 2004 (M25 Consortium of Academic Libraries 2005). Although these represent comprehensive coverage of the various components of a disaster control plan, a review of current literature including guidelines and templates available through the Internet was incorporated to identify any new trends and inclusions that may have appeared in recent years following, for example, terrorist attacks and natural disasters internationally and within the UK. In this way, a

Table 5.1   Disaster Control Plans Sample Selected for Review

	Written DCP Frequency	Sample Frequency	Sample %
Domain			
Archives	101	35	27
Libraries	119	46	35
Museums	130	49	38
Total	350	130	
Institution Type			
National	28	14	11
Pub/La/Gov	140	50	38
Education	81	28	22
Other	101	38	29
Total	350	130	
Country			
England	285	75	58
Scotland	38	29	22
Wales	17	16	12
Northern Ireland	5	5	4
Channel Islands	5	5	4
Total	350	130	
Experience of Disaster			
Archives	31	10	32
Libraries	52	20	39
Museums	43	20	47
Total	126	50	40
Written by			
Individual	134	50	39
Internal Group	112	38	30
Staff	20	4	3
Staff – internal and institutional	45	19	15
External consultant	3	3	2
External consultant and staff	16	4	3
Other	9	5	4
Missing	11	7	5
Total	350	130	

Table 5.2   Disaster Control Plans Received

Country	Received			Total Received
	Archives	**Libraries**	**Museums**	
England	8	9	6	23
Wales	0	2	1	3
Scotland	3	3	2	8
Northern Ireland	1	0	1	2
Channel Islands	1	0	0	1
Total	13	14	10	37

categorised list, or framework, of topics and activities that a disaster control plan might address was produced.

Disaster Control Plan Analysis Framework

The framework which was used for the analysis follows below. For those creating or updating a plan, it may serve as a useful checklist. (*Italic type* – denotes additions to Matthews's and Eden's guidelines as identified in the review of M25 guidelines and additional sources.)

Prevention
- Advice, expertise and services (identification of key people with relevant experience/knowledge)
- Risk assessment
- Building maintenance/*checklist*
- *Equipment maintenance/checklist*
- Security measures/maintenance
- Collections (location/risks/storage/handling)
- Communication (how can staff prevent disaster, report incidents?)
- Prevention of:
  - Fire Hazard
  - Flood Damage
  - Infestation
  - *Housekeeping guidelines, daily use*

- Training (aware of dangers/possible situations/*handling collections/stock/ information given to contractors*)
- Health and Safety
- Procedures Manual
- IT
- Finance (availability in event of disaster)
- Public relations

Preparedness
- Written plan of action (draw from key people with relevant experience/ knowledge)
- *Portable 'reaction' section of plan*
- *Update the plan and inventories regularly*
- *Test the plan*
- How to raise the alarm
- Who to call (Disaster Reaction Team in place)
- Building maintenance (fire equipment/floor plans available showing location of equipment and mains switches, etc./knowledgeable staff in control/display floor plans of exit routs and assembly points)
- Evacuation procedures
- Emergency equipment and details of suppliers (purchased and stored in convenient location)
- Salvage priorities
- *Accommodation for salvage operation*
- Collections (inventory of holdings and their locations)
- Insurance
- Emergency ordering and invoicing procedures
- Training
- Health and safety
- Procedures manual
- IT preparedness
- Finance (availability in event of disaster)
- Public relations

Reaction
- Procedures for initial action
- Communication (contact details)
- Initial assessment of situation
- Advice, expertise and services (conservation needs and decision-making, etc., contact details)
- Guidelines for Disaster Reaction Team
- Disaster report form
- Collections (procedures for salvage of collections/material, priority list for salvage)

- Building (shut down systems/use dehumidifier if necessary)
- Security maintenance (rope off area if necessary, only authorised personnel on scene)
- Collections (location/risks/storage/handling)
- Training
- Bombs (dealing with bomb threats/suspicious packages)
- Health and safety
- Human resources (staff involved in the response team/report writing)
- Service continuity and access (inform users of what has happened, have temporary arrangements in place in case of disaster)
- IT (emergency backup)
- Finance (availability in event of disaster)
- Public relations

Recovery
- Advice, expertise and services (conservation teams and salvage experts needed)
- Buildings (removal of stock/collection and cleaning of area/restoration of area)
- Collections (area needed for treatment, drying etc., temporary storage for undamaged)
- *Conservation (procedures in-house and contacting expert conservation teams)*
- Handling (check environmental conditions/conditions of objects on returning to area)
- Communication (with emergency services, keep staff informed of developments)
- Communication (with consumers, pre-booked groups, etc.)
- Security maintenance (rope off area if necessary, only authorised personnel on scene)
- Training (review disaster and reaction and incorporate lessons in future training events)
- Insurance (claim)
- Health and safety
- Human resources (make counselling available, continued reports and follow up plans/revision of DCP)
- Service continuity and access (inform users of what has happened, have temporary arrangements in place in case of disaster)
- IT (emergency backup)
- Finance (availability in event of disaster)
- Public relations
- *Recording of disaster and writing of official report*
- Learning and revision of plan

Additions/updates made reflect activity between the publication of Matthews's and Eden's guidelines in 1996 and the M25 review in 2004. For example, Prevention, *Equipment maintenance* – as more institutions obtained equipment and stored it, the need for maintenance and checking for past 'use by date' became apparent as incidents occurred and equipment was put to use. Preparedness, *Portable reaction plan* – well developed and established plans were encompassed in large documents which it was realised (through training and experience) would be too unwieldy for use in a real incident. Thus, concise easy to understand and use versions were put together and made widely available. *Test the plan* – similarly, the experience of activating plans and guidance on this in the literature (for example, Muir and Shenton 2002) underlined the need for regular updating and testing of plans to keep them effective. *Accommodation for salvage operation* – actual incidents and dealing with them emphasised the need for space and accommodation for handling, sorting and storing items in the aftermath of a disaster. Reaction, *Bombs* – an increase in the threat of terrorist attacks raised the need for guidance on how to deal with them, and this became available on civil emergency planning websites. Recovery, *Recording of disaster* – as accounts of recording (taking photographs, video-recording) the disaster and its impact were disseminated, usefulness, for example, in dealing with insurers and loss adjusters, and reviewing practices, became apparent. It was facilitated over this period by the availability of 'throw away' cameras and developments in digital photography.

Analysis

Disaster control plans received were checked against the analysis framework. The frequency with which individual aspects appeared within the plans received was noted.

High Representation

Those aspects that appeared most frequently are listed in Table 5.3.

Low Representation

Those aspects that appeared least frequently are listed in Table 5.4.

Limitations of analysis

It is possible that aspects with 'low representation', whilst not included in the disaster control plan, may be included in other institutional policies and documents, for security or training, for example. Indeed, some aspects of the disaster control

Table 5.3   Highest Representation of Features Within DCPs

Stage of DCP	Heading	Frequency of representation
Preparedness	Written plan of action	36
Prevention	Procedural manual	36
Preparedness	Who to call in a disaster situation	35
Preparedness	Building Maintenance – knowledgeable staff in control	35
Reaction	Communication – contact details	35
Preparedness	How to raise the alarm	34
Reaction	Advice – decision making	34
Reaction	Initial assessment of situation	33
Recovery	Advice – expertise and services	32
Preparedness	Emergency equipment – where stored	32
Reaction	Collection – handling	32
Reaction	Procedures for initial reaction	32
Recovery	Building maintenance – removal of stock/collections	32
Prevention	Advice – experts	31
Reaction	Guidelines – collection salvage procedures	31
Reaction	Guidelines – for disaster reaction team	31
Reaction	Advice – services	31
Recovery	Communication – with staff	31
Prevention	Collections – risks identified	30
Preparedness	Emergency equipment – what has been purchased	30
Reaction	Collections – handling guidelines	30
Recovery	Collections – conservation procedures for stock/objects	29
Recovery	Communication with emergency services	29
Preparedness	Health and safety matters	27
Reaction	Building maintenance – equipment (dehumidifiers)	26

plan were not submitted for analysis on the grounds of security. Eleven institutions removed pages before sending for this reason.

Likewise, in some instances sections do not exist as the plan focuses on the recovery stage only. To see if this were the case, five institutions whose plan had no prevention section were contacted for more information where an explanation of this was not given with the original submission. The reasons given for not including a prevention section were:

Table 5.4   Lowest Representation of Features within DCPs

Stage within DCP	Heading	Frequency of representation
Prevention	Training – information given to contractors	3
Preparedness	Testing of the plan	4
Prevention	Training – All staff in handling and collection care	4
Prevention	Finances (availability in event of disaster)	5
Prevention	Collections – handling	5
Preparedness	Procedures – threat by telephone, package, chemicals etc.	8
Preparedness	Portable 'reaction' section of plan	8
Prevention	Public relations	8
Preparedness	Financial issues	8
Reaction	Bomb threats & suspect packages	9
Prevention	Daily housekeeping guidelines	9
Preparedness	Collections – inventories of holdings	9

We do not have a separate plan as such. Over recent years we have carried out risk assessments of various parts of the Library system … This has resulted in a major relocation and refurbishment of a new off site store … removal of library stock from parts of our sub-basement areas. (Higher Education library)

We have a separate IT Recovery plan, there is also an extensive University disaster plan. (Higher Education library)

The templates that the [gallery named] sites use to formulate their BCP (normally a paper one) are only available for staff. (Gallery)

For security reasons, sections of the plan where deleted before submission; names and numbers, priority lists and collection inventories. (Local Authority archive)

> Disaster prevention is one area that we haven't really tackled yet. There are informal procedures for checking basements, gutters etc., especially in the event of heavy rain ... but as far as I am aware, there is no formal maintenance schedule. (Higher Education library)

Top Three Lessons

Respondents to the questionnaire who advised they had experienced a disaster were asked to give up to three lessons they would pass on to others. For those who had a disaster control plan and reported it had been effective in a disaster, the top three lessons learnt, across all domains, were:

1. Training (all staff need to know about the plan and response needed)
2. Building issues (maintenance/checks/plans)
3. Emergency equipment (good stock/appropriate location)

Their importance fluctuates slightly between Domains:

Archives:

1. Training
2. Building issues
3. Emergency equipment

Libraries:

1. Training
2. Emergency equipment
3. Communication (between staff/disaster response teams)
4. (Building issues came fourth.)

Museums:
1. Building issues
2. Training
3. Emergency equipment

Those who had experienced a disaster but did not have a disaster control plan agreed that building maintenance was important but ultimately had learnt different lessons, highlighting the following (across the domains) as their top three lessons learnt:

1. Building maintenance
2. Storage of collections (how/where/inspected regularly)
3. Keeping independent control of the plan within a wider institutional plan.

For those who had experienced a disaster and reported they had a disaster control plan, but reported it had been ineffective during the disaster, the following (across the domains) were identified as their top three lessons learnt:

1. Training
2. Building issues
3. Storage arrangements (location/risks)

Other lessons that respondents suggested in general (in no rank order) included:

> Constant awareness and vigilance
> Get advice
> Have IT back-up system
> Know who is in charge in the event of a disaster, at all times
> Quick action
> Update the plan and contact lists

Differences Between Archives, Libraries and Museums

Archives

Archive plans balance a full, comprehensive plan with the need for usability within the 'reaction' section (in the event of an incident). They favour the use of flow charts to indicate actions to take. If an archive had insurance, this was usually indicated and cover explained within the plan at the time. Of the archives surveyed, 45 per cent subscribed to HDRS (for details of the services offered by HDRS see their website (HDRS n.d.)).

Libraries

Library plans were fuller and more comprehensive, including the four stages of Prevention, Preparedness, Reaction and Recovery. Of the libraries in the sample, 86 per cent subscribed to HDRS.

Museums

Museum plans focus on prevention relating to collection care, they also address reaction and recovery, but preparedness may be documented elsewhere. Emphasis was often placed to directing the Disaster Reaction Team, and checklists were favoured within plans. If a museum is insured, this was often not mentioned within the plan. HDRS was subscribed to by 33 per cent of the museums in the sample.

Interesting Features in Disaster Control Plans

Interesting features noted in the disaster control plans analysed included:

Archives

An archive provided floor plans that indicated the housing of priority salvage material and where mains switches, fire exits, fire extinguishers, etc, were located. The DCP also contained easy to navigate flow charts identifying whom to call in the event of the disaster and salvage priorities for each location. It looked at practical issues that would arise in the case of a recovery programme, such as the medical background of those who may assist in the recovery operation. There is also a reminder that photocopier toner and batteries within computers are carcinogens.

The DCP for a Local Authority archive reminded staff of the need to wear gloves at all times when handling fire damaged items, in order to protect staff from skin irritation and advised that some chemicals deposited by fire may be carcinogenic. The plan importantly reminded the team to deal with wet documents first as they will break down more quickly than dry/fire damaged items. An Appendix contained a blank template for recording movement of objects and labels with a blank space to write in the crate number as movement occurs.

Another Local Authority archive service produced a 'Disaster Handbook'. This took the form of an A5 booklet with eye-catching coloured front cover. The back cover contained an index facilitating easy navigation in a crisis. To aid retrieval, the staff contact list and pager number were in a vivid colour.

Libraries

A university library outlined the HDRS 'Priority User Scheme' in its plan, stating clearly the services provided through subscription should they be needed in an incident. Designated Disaster Teams members are named and equipment supplies listed.

Under Reaction, a Special library has devoted two pages to dealing with a telephone bomb threat. One page is devoted to dealing with suspicious objects and packages e.g. letter bombs, and additional information relating to vandalism issues and theft. A section is included on what to do in the event of lone working.

Another university library had used the title 'Plan and Manual' as within the general manual is a 'reaction plan' to be followed in the event of an incident; this emphasises that there are separate uses for these sections.

The library of a government department provides a handout to staff titled 'Procedures in the Event of a Disaster in the ... Library'. This offers practical advice from the point of call out, such as – what to wear, what to bring (including a reminder of not forgetting your own house keys!), who will be responsible for which tasks and how to salvage materials. It provides the HDRS hotline number.

A university library produced an action flow chart containing the basics of what to do if disaster occurs including: reporting an incident, assessment, emergency response, service continuity, prevention of further damage, and recovery of damaged items. A checklist is included for the Disaster Co-ordinator, with two sections: ongoing tasks and tasks during times of disaster. The ongoing tasks include maintaining the contacts list and ensuring disaster kit contents are replenished.

The disaster plan of a public central library is divided into three sections: action checklist for first three hours; checklist for next twenty-four hours; and action checklist for the next month.

Museums

A heritage and museum service had a 'Disaster Plan' which outlined how three teams were to be set up in the event of a disaster: the first to assess, make decisions and direct, the second to secure areas and eliminate hazards, and the third to establish a temporary operational base for administration.

In another plan, produced by a museum and art gallery, the roles specified for the disaster management team were – co-ordination, requisition, documentation, salvage and security. Ideal qualities are stated, along with the responsibility each will have in the event of a disaster. A flow chart of responsibility is given, together with a call out tree. The plan also contains a 'Disaster Scenarios' table, which highlights disasters that could occur and their possible causes, how they can be prevented and what the impact would be if they did occur – this could be used as a prevention checklist.

A plan produced by a museum trust contained details of stockpiled equipment, together with a summary of holdings on adjacent sites as back up should the sites own stockpile fail. This plan also contained a section listing problems and vulnerable areas at each site, with a summary of previous problems and what might be done to alleviate them.

Presentation and Usability

The plans were also ranked with regard to presentation and usability. Whilst this was a desk exercise (i.e. there was no attempt to follow instructions and put them into action), advice and feedback from questionnaire respondents and interviewees relating to this was born in mind. Criteria used were:

- Portable/user friendly size
- Clear, concise action instructions
- How to assess immediate situation/damage
- Who to call
- Disaster Response Team instructions

- Salvage/handling instructions
- Use of flow charts/check lists/floor plans

Features noted in the top ten ranked plans are shown in Table 5.6.

'Reasons' for No Plan

Introduction

Respondents to the questionnaire were invited to provide any additional information they wished. Some used this opportunity to explain why they did not have a written disaster control plan. Whist many of the issues raised are not perhaps surprising, they underline the reasons outlined anecdotally by speakers and participants in conferences on the subject, and in the literature. They outline areas institutions need to address if they are to plan effectively for disaster, and underline the challenges faced by those who wish to do this in the context of disinterest or apathy on the part of senior management.

Common Issues

The issues raised can be categorised:

- Staffing levels
- Lack of expertise
- Senior management support
- Service provision priority; or other priorities
- Funding
- Time
- Disaster control plan not considered necessary
- Shared premises

Some respondents refer to more than one issue, suggesting that a combination of factors prevents them devising a written disaster control plan.

Extracts from respondents provided below illustrate the factors that deter them from producing a plan. Whilst they are listed below by domain, each domain gives similar reasons.

Archives

> The complement of 3–5 staff besides the College Archivist is a relatively new situation and priority has necessarily been given to service issues ... (Local Authority archive)

Table 5.5   Top Ranked Plans

Rank	Institution	Features of plan
1	National museum and gallery	Portable, user-friendly action plan presented in a 'flip chart' style. A small booklet for each member of staff on emergency procedures accompanied the plan. Emergency guidelines provided, as was plan of building.
2	Government Department library	Plan contained clear action checklist. Portable disaster instruction leaflets provided for each member of staff.
3	Local Authority archive	A clear, concise and portable A5 booklet, with colour coded sections and action checklists.
4	National museum	Good handling guidelines and short action plan in the form of a flip chart.
5	National archive	Clear guidelines listed for fire and flood. Good use of floor plans to indicate potential problem areas, mains and salvage priorities.
6	College library	Clear action points to follow and the use of flow charts. The plan contained concise, necessary information.
7	National museum and gallery	A single sheet of action instructions placed on relevant doors throughout the building.
8	Local Authority records office	Bound A4 document, with concise guidelines to follow in the event of a disaster. Salvage priorities and techniques provided.
9	Museum archive	An A4 document with clear instructions for fire/flood and the salvage team, use of flow charts.
10	Museum archive	Contained 'valuables' checklists as well as action instructions. Different checklists for separate disaster roles: 'Dealing with the immediate disaster', 'Summoning help' and 'Assessing the damage'.

I was given the job of drawing up the disaster plan in 2000. However, having completed the plan my supervisor just left it in their in-tray and ignored it. As a result it has never been implemented. (Local Authority archive)

… While the company provides the best possible storage, with no money to spend on a leaking building and one over-stretched part-time member of staff, it's unlikely things will move forward. (Business/Company archive)

There is a lack of senior support for the work, despite my stressing the importance of DCP. Without such support, progress is limited. (Local Authority Archive)

We are a … club with a part-time archivist (professionally qualified) working on the whole collection of which the archive is a small part and takes approximately

150 hours per annum. Most of which is spent identifying and cataloguing records. It [disaster management] is not a high priority within the organisation, nor is funding available. I did attend a Disaster Training Day (SE museums) several years ago so am aware of issues. Just unable to implement. (Private Collection archive)

... a private collection ... [with] national and international recognition ... housed at a private residence ... there is a chronic shortage of funds ... (Local Authority archive)

... time is at a premium to concentrate to write it ... (Local Authority archive)

...In brief, financial constraints prevent any realisation of being free from risk ... (Private Collection archive)

We are a tiny archives service, and in attempting to achieve the impossible we do not always succeed. ... We have had a disaster plan in preparation for some time ... but have never finished it ... (Local Authority archive)

We have considered writing a disaster plan but have never found time to do so. (Local Authority archive)

Disaster planning and training ARE important to us, but priority has to be given to documenting and boxing our large collection .. important, but not immediate priority ... Initial assessment suggests relative low risks. (Gallery archive)

We are all volunteers, no grant aid ... to help in this area ... (Museum archive)

We can just survive provides that nobody is sick or takes leave ... In a situation like this, disaster planning is a complete joke. (Local Authority archive)

We do not have any trained archival staff ... There is no time to do anything beyond dealing with enquiries and regularly checking atmospheric conditions. (Educational Institution archive)

We are hoping to move to new premises within the next three years so much of my time is currently occupied with planning and packaging. I'm also only working part-time ... so I have less time to allocate; review of our DCP has therefore dropped in our list of priorities ... (Local Authority archive)

We are a very small archive, with only two (full-time) members of staff ... and there are huge pressures on staff time as a result. This is perhaps why disaster planning has not been as high up on the list of priorities as it should have been in the past. (Archive)

1. We do not have enough staff to mount a credible rescue plan. 2. Have tried in the past to organise a regional response team through the Regional conservation network without success. Why? Lack of interest, no support from above, too complicated with health and safety issues and staff insurance. 3. Also tried to organise something with related units with County Hall – libraries – but it got bogged down in the bureaucracy of our hierarchical 'command and control' structure. (Local Authority archive)

That we have an archive at all is fortunate rather than planning. We have a volunteer archivist … we can only give very limited funds … little or no thought is given to their [records] preservation. Time, money, resources will probably prohibit this in future. (Educational Institution archive)

Libraries

We had discussions with the University security people here and they do not consider the Library to be a high risk area of the University. We have separate planning for electronic security … We do not have resources to do much in the way of simulation, etc. and would like to do this. However, because staff are struggling with workloads it is difficult to give this priority. (Higher Education library)

… Financial and human resources are extremely limited and I'm not sure that standard disaster management plans for libraries accommodate the small independent library with very different management, staffing and storage facilities to those in public and academic libraries. We try to model our plans on other similar institutions. (Independent subscription library)

… public library had no emergency plan because the member of staff responsible for putting it together was on long-term sick leave and no one else had picked this up. (Public library)

We are a small (2000 students) institution. I instigated the production of a disaster plan when the then librarian considered it unnecessary. We do not have any special collections, some areas of stock would be difficult to replace but none of the stock is particularly valuable. The Institute has a disaster plan. (Higher Education library)

Despite repeated request for additional funding for disaster management support, disaster planning is not considered important by the senior management team. (Government library)

The collection is located inside a security controlled [government] building with no public access. We do not consider the risk high but should a disaster take place and the collection become damaged in some way, it is likely a replacement policy would take effect. All of the documents of significant historical value have been transferred to the Public Record s Office ... (Government library)

As far as time is concerned, it is not that anyone disagrees with devoting substantial time to it as a valuable investment, it's just that we are so overloaded with other tasks that have to be accomplished within a time limit, and so those that may not become necessary sometimes are pushed into a lower place on the priority table. (Higher Education library)

Museums

Ours is a tiny one room Museum, open 5 days a week, Easter to September and staffed entirely by volunteers. Emergency planning is not something we need to consider other than evacuating the building and ensuring electronics are in good condition. (Museum)

The building and its permanent fixtures/machinery are the museum collection. Following a major disaster ... the collection could not be replicated except in replica form, perhaps from photographs/drawings. ... When it's gone, it's gone. Our main concerns therefore are to keep the internal/external machinery in good working order, a guard against fire risk. (Independent museum)

As a small museum entirely staffed by volunteers our resources are limited. We have support from ... Council. We try to comply with security, insurance, etc. requirements. (Independent museum and gallery)

Our situation is complicated by the fact that we share a site with another county council department. We do not have autonomy in the decisions about emergency planning that affect the site and over the years this has become a lower and lower priority. It has become difficult to maintain a good balance of knowledge across the site, to ensure all staff know what to do and that exercises are a regular event. Staff changes and financial pressures also have some bearing on this. (Local Authority house/castle)

We developed an emergency plan within the museum in 1995 – reviewed up to 1998. But as we fit within a larger building our plan was useless, except for local spills, as the college did not accept it. Some more interest recently but it has not resulted in any corporate action, only in terms of IT continuity. (Museum)

Conclusion

Analysis of disaster control plans, responses to the UK questionnaire, and the literature has underlined the significance of the plan to effective disaster management. The contents of the disaster control plan have been reviewed. These activities have confirmed that the basic principles of the disaster control plan are established. The importance of training in relation to the disaster control plan has been stressed. Advice on improving plans is offered. Not all institutions have disaster control plans – a summary of reasons for this is provided.

The plan on its own will not deal with disasters – people need to know what to do with it, what their roles are in particular stages or aspects – they need to be trained. It needs to be based on an institution or building and collections specific risk assessment. There is a need for testing, reviewing, updating. Otherwise it will be a file sitting on a shelf:

> If people don't own their plan, invest in it, it won't work (US museum and library).

References

Alire, C. (ed.) (2000), *Library Disaster Planning and Recovery Handbook* (New York: Neal-Schuman Publishers).

Anderson, H. and McIntyre, J. E. (1985), *Planning Manual for Disaster Control in Scottish Libraries and Record Offices* (Edinburgh: National Library of Scotland).

Ashman, J. (1995), *Disaster Planning for Library and Information Services* (London: Aslib).

CoOL, *Conservation OnLine* [website], (updated 30 Jul. 2008) <http://palimpsest.stanford.edu/>, accessed 19 Aug. 2008.

Doig, J. (1997), 'Disaster Recovery for Archives, Libraries and Records Management Systems in Australia and New Zealand', *Topics in Australasian Library and Information Studies, Number 12* (Riverine Wagga Wagga, New South Wales: Centre for Information Studies, Charles Sturt University).

Dorge, V. and Jones, S. (comps.) (1997), *Building an Emergency Plan. A Guide for Museums and Other Cultural Institutions*, (Los Angeles, California), (published online 1999) <http://www.getty.edu/conservation/publications/pdf_publications/emergency_plan.pdf>, accessed 14 Aug. 2006.

EmmS (2001), *The EmmS Emergency Manual for historic buildings and collections* (Nottingham: East Midlands Museums Service). [Available as an interactive CD Rom from [website] <www.emms.org.uk>, accessed 14 Aug 2006.]

HDRS, *Document Recovery after Fire, Flood and Explosion* [website], (updated n.d.) <http://www.hdrs.co.uk/>, accessed 18 Aug. 2008.

Heritage Preservation (2002), *Cataclysm and challenge. Impact of September 11, 2001, on Our Nation's Cultural Heritage. A report from Heritage Preservation on behalf of the Heritage Emergency National Task Force, Project Director Ruth Hargraves* (Washington, DC: Heritage Preservation), (published online 2002) <http://www.heritagepreservation.org/PDFS/Cataclysm.pdf>, accessed 29 Aug. 2008.

Howes, R. (2003), 'After the disaster: drawing up the insurance claim', *Aslib Proceedings* 5:3, 181–7.

ICA/PDP (1997), *Guidelines on disaster prevention and control in archives. (ICA Studies 11)*, (Paris: International Council of Archives), (published online Dec. 1997) <http://www.ica.org/sites/default/files/Study11E%20Final.pdf>, accessed 14 Aug. 2006.

Kahn, M. (1998), *Disaster Response and Planning for Libraries* (Chicago: American Library Association).

Kulczak, D. and Lennertz, L. (1999), 'A Decade of Disaster: A Selected Bibliography of Disaster Literature, 1985–1995', *Library and Archival Security* 15:1, 7–66.

M25 Consortium of Academic Libraries, Disaster Management Working Group (2005) *M25 Disaster Control Plan* [website], (updated 2005) <http://www.m25lib.ac.uk//content/blogcategory/87/204/>, accessed 14 Aug. 2006.

Mansell, H. (2003). 'The disaster control plan', in Matthews, G. and Feather, J. (eds.), 13–40.

Matthews, G. and Eden, P. (1996), 'Disaster management in British Libraries. Project report with guidelines for library managers', *Library and Information Research* Report 109 (London: The British Library).

Matthews, G. and Feather, J.P. (eds.) (2003), *Disaster Management for Libraries and Archives* (Aldershot: Ashgate).

Matthews, G., Smith, Y. and Knowles, G. (2004), 'The disaster control plan: where is it at?' *Library and Archival Security* 19:2, 3–23.

McIlwaine, J. (2006), *IFLA Disaster Preparedness and Planning. A Brief Manual.* (International Preservation Issues Number 6), (Paris: IFLA PAC), (published online 2006) <http://www.ifla.org/VI/4/news/ipi6-en.pdf>, accessed 14 Aug. 2006.

Muir, A. and Shenton S. (2002), 'If the worst happens: the use and effectiveness of disaster plans in libraries and archives', *Library Management* 23:3,115–23.

NPO, *National Preservation Office – Disaster/Emergency Planning* [website], (updated n.d.) <http://www.bl.uk/services/npo/disaster.html>, accessed 14 Aug. 2006.

Preservation Directorate, the Federal Library and Information Center Committee, and the American Folklife Center, Library of Congress (2006), *Draft of notes (4/25/06). 'Future Directions in Safeguarding Document Collections', sponsored by the Preservation Directorate, the Federal Library and Information Center Committee, and the American Folklife Center, Library of Congress, Jefferson Building Room 119, April 21, 2006.*

Short-Traxler, K. (2005), 'Developing an emergency control plan for Oxford University Libraries', *SCONUL Focus* 35, 45–51.

Shorley, D (2004), 'Disaster planning: "in the end you just cope"', *Library + Information Update* 2:3, 46–7.

Society of Archivists, Scottish Region, Disaster Preparedness Working Group (1996), *Disaster preparedness: guidelines for archives and libraries* (London: Society of Archivists).

TNA (2004), *Protecting archives and manuscripts against disasters*, (published online Jun. 2004) <http://www.nationalarchives.gov.uk/ documents/memo6. pdf>, accessed 18 Aug. 2008.

UKIRB, *United Kingdom and Ireland BLUE SHIELD Organisation* [website], (updated n.d.) <http://www.bl.uk/services/npo/blueshield/overview.html>, accessed 14 Aug. 2006.

Wellheiser, J. and Scott, J. (2002), *An Ounce of Prevention: Integrated Disaster Planning for Archives, Libraries and Record Centres*, 2nd edition (Lanham, Maryland: The Scarecrow Press Inc. and Canadian Archives Foundation).

Chapter 6
Findings: Key Themes

Introduction

Analysis of the literature review, UK questionnaire survey, international e-mail survey and attendance at conferences, identified key topics relating to disaster management/ emergency planning in archives, libraries and museums. Some of these have been mentioned in previous chapters. Further information and opinion about these issues was sought through a series of interviews with a range of stakeholders, thus enriching the picture achieved by the other methods. The words and views of experienced practitioners are thus used to illustrate the major findings of the project. (Quotations are anonymised but the type of institution is indicated. Where two types of institution are indicated a joint interview took place.) They are augmented where appropriate by 'additional comments' from respondents to the UK questionnaire survey. They are presented under thematic headings that represent the key aspects of disaster management revealed by analysis of the project's findings. They contain potential lessons for others.

Given the sensitive nature of some of the issues addressed in the research, all questionnaire and e-mail respondents and interviewees were assured of confidentiality – that they and their institutional affiliation would not be disclosed in any reports of the research. Whilst this does not permit acknowledgment of their assistance and insights, the authors are indebted to all who so generously gave of their time, experience and expertise.

With regard to the themes, the chapter begins with the broad topic of Disaster Management, then moves on to the central feature of this, the Disaster Control Plan. Financial aspects are addressed next, followed by issues relating to Buildings. Next, the impact of Disasters is considered, followed by Training, and then one of the key aspects for training, Salvage and conservation, which leads on to human aspects, Staff. The chapter ends by looking at Sustainability of disaster management activities, and the related topic that institutions are beginning to address, Business/service continuity.

Disaster Management

Senior Management Support

To succeed activity must have the support and 'clout' of senior management:

> What's needed is buy-in at the highest possible level in the organization … In theory a disaster plan is everyone's responsibility but in practice it ends up falling

on the conservation/preservation side of the house, which traditionally tends not to be of the highest grade in organisational terms, and therefore don't have the weight to make things happen. (National record office/National museum)

There may need to be some persuasion, a case made, to convince management, but this can be achieved in various ways, for example:

Can have a plan but training shows it's being taken seriously. Did an exercise at X last week – floor by floor risk assessment. Get 'head' people around the table to something like this, even for an hour, it makes them aware and has an impact on them. (Commercial disaster management service)

Even when they are supportive, it helps to keep them aware of the significance of disaster management:

On the one hand senior management are very supportive of the emergency plan. They were the ones who pushed for X to prioritise it. She reckoned she had spent about 160 hours putting the plan together, and that was just the basic plan. It didn't include the maintenance, it didn't include anything to do with salvage. They were prepared to commit that extra time, and they are certainly prepared for me to continue that work and lead the team. I have done a programme of training with all the departments within the museum to tell them that there is an emergency response plan, what it does, how we anticipate it will work, how they participate, what it does do and what it doesn't do. And I do a basic exercise with them so that they get a feel of how an emergency might shape up and what is involved. I did that first of all with the management team and they all made hugely supportive noises and said this is a very good thing and we are very glad that there is one. (Local Authority museum)

In some instances, senior management takes a lead itself:

Now, our senior manager, the chief executive is now the disaster plan manager, the head of preservation is the assistant disaster plan manager, our head of corporate services is the premises manager. So these are senior management figures who are there to support the plan … They understood that emergency planning was important and particularly with the evidence of what had happened with the leak in our archives they could see that … (Independent museum)

Other external factors may influence senior management:

Museums – easy now because required. [Disaster at] Historic houses (eg Uppark), and Norwich and archives have persuaded people they need a plan. Have the scare story – people ask – look what happened here – do *we* need a plan? … The Civil Contingencies Act applies to local authorities and has been taken on board by universities. Training at University of XXX came from top down. Damage to a building and impact it could have on University emphasised the need. (Commercial disaster management service)

There are varying levels of support though:

But on the 'we will put lots of cash into it so we are up to speed' or even 'we will commit time to let you go and talk to other museums in the hub and see if we can get anything more useful put together', etc. then no – nothing at all. (Local Authority museum)

Integration

It is also vital that archive, library and museum plans fit with those of the broader, 'parent' organisation (if there is one) and any arrangements they may have with external agencies. Buildings and collections with special needs should also be incorporated.

I think in all aspects, why we do it reasonably well is that the whole principle of emergency planning is built into our work, we're always aware of the problems. Certain aspects, like health and safety aspects, building aspects are dealt with on a monthly basis in monthly meetings. So we are aware, the training is pretty good, all the conservators, warder staff for instance have regular fire training, regular health and safety training, regular disaster training so that everybody throughout the institution is pretty well aware of what to do under the circumstances. (National museum and gallery)

Focus on the reality of the situation where you are going to be implementing. Need information on what to do right away – liaising with other authorities, like estates, security, finance, insurance. Even museums have a structure beyond. Overcome any potential hurdles in advance, otherwise it's just a piece of paper. Can't think of everything – too many permutations, but try to cover. Focus on how user friendly the document is. Content is important – so is how it is used. Shouldn't just sit on a shelf with review in 3 years. (Commercial disaster management service)

So we've got representations from each site and we've had – is it seven now? Seven plus the X archive. And the X archive is a little bit different because they have very specialist needs, being film, so they have their own very detailed disaster plan which is separate from the library's plan because they have very different storage requirements, against fire and so on, from what we have. It happens to be that the film archive is managed by the X library, it's part of us, but it has its own building, with its own special requirements. (University library)

Size of Institution

The size and type of institution will affect disaster management and the approach taken to it, particularly in small institutions with limited resources, human, financial and technical, for example.

> Ours is an independent special collection in a listed building in a major city centre. Financial and human resources are extremely limited and I'm not sure that standard disaster management plans for libraries accommodate the small independent library with very different management, staffing, and storage facilities to those in public and academic libraries. We try to model our plans on those formulated by other similar institutions. (Subscription library)

> … this a very small museum, entirely independent but housed in a listed building. All staff are volunteers and some of them in their 'first flush of youth. I am sure there are plenty of other institutions like this one who do not fit any particularly logical 'mould'. (Independent museum)

> This museum is run by trustees and volunteer staff with a variety of experience in fields other than museum administration. Most are over retirement age. All activities depend on the availability and enthusiasm of the volunteers. When required, specialist information is sought from our Curatorial Advisor. In the event of an emergency, whoever is available would deal as well as possible with the problem. We do not have enough people involved to designate a specific individual for a particular responsibility. We all have basic skills in first aid and understanding of what to do in the event of a fire or civil disturbance. (Independent museum)

> We are a small museum whose staff are all part-time volunteers. We have the confidence we can prepare an emergency plan thanks to training via the museum's area infrastructure and through our professional skills from our jobs outside museum work. However we do expect that as the plan approaches completion, we will need specific advice and training in respect of emergency response techniques and the handling and salvaging of damaged materials. Small museums like ourselves, we believe, have fewer problems in developing emergency plans (as our needs are simpler) but will require more advice and assistance from the outside if a disaster does take place as we have fewer resources and less specialist knowledge. (Independent museum)

> I think some formal network would be useful, because certainly the level of conservation knowledge and expertise of staffing varies a lot within the archive service and for example [county] have a very big conservation centre with a lot of resources but not all of us have. Some repositories are tiny and it is mainly librarians responsible for trying to run an archive service as well as a local

studies library, with no background and I think the networking idea if it could become a bit more developed could be very useful for them. Particularly for the 'smalls', there are a lot of very small archive services around. (Local Authority library service/record office)

... one of the things about being in the small authority is that, you know, even though we have links with [individuals], or have links with the museum, and I have links with the record office, what we don't know is how we compare, you know. It would be interesting to know where we are in terms of our development for emergency planning response because I think we're doing alright, but you might well say because you've spoken to a number of people 'Well no actually, you're not but you're actually doing ok.' You know, because that's quite useful benchmarking for a similar size. You know, I wouldn't expect to be up there with the national museums for example. You know, we just can't. We haven't got the collections that they have, we haven't got the staffing in place but equally that doesn't mean that we shouldn't have something in place. So, and it's always quite nice to know, you know, if it did turn out that we were doing ok. That's quite nice to know as well. (Public library)

Disaster Control Plan

(See also Chapter 5)

The approach taken to devise and maintain a disaster control plan will also indicate levels of management support. The disaster control plan is at the heart of effective disaster management. The findings highlight certain factors that should be born in mind when contemplating putting together a plan.

Approach

Who should compile the plan?   As noted above, management support is essential, as is involving more than one person (if the size of the institution permits this):

[It's] crucial to have the support of Departmental Heads and other Council staff. Disaster plans should always be a joint effort, composed by a small team and not left to one person. Training and awareness raising is essential ... (Local Authority archive)

Teams help provide a range of experience and expertise so that the plan does not have one particular focus:

[A common weakness] is not covering anything other than stock because they tend to be written by archivists and conservators, and that is their major concern. (Commercial disaster management service)

It is important to be proactive:

> You have to be one step ahead of the game and draw matters to the attention of your organisation before the emergency happens because sooner or later, if it can happen, it will. Don't be bullied into accepting things that are dangerously sub-standard. I had to argue for shelves to be raised above ground level, the shelf fitters thought this wasn't necessary. I won and made myself very unpopular, but was proved right when a pipe leaked and the ground floor flooded. I think that what I am saying is that disaster management isn't everything, disaster avoidance and mitigation is a big part of all of this. Physical disaster is not the only blow an archive can suffer. Withdrawal of funding could be devastating and result in the destruction of a collection. In a small 'one man band' such as mine, it would be a disaster for the archive if I were to suddenly disappear from the scene. It is important for organisations with archives to address these issues before they occur. (Charity archive)

And, to have appropriate experience and expertise, or to get relevant training:

> Probably where my involvement came from was when I came to work for X they realised that because of my role in the fire brigade I had experience in disaster planning and training, taking part in exercises and all these sorts of things so they, really, made use of the skills that I brought with me because there was no one else [with them] at the time. I don't know where the original disaster plan originated from – I've got a funny feeling what happened was a previous employee brought it with him from where he was working and I think he just changed the names which wasn't bad. It was put into a good document but you could tell that it didn't quite fit in with what we were doing which is why I decided to rewrite it and make sure it fitted our requirements … But because I'd had a fair bit of experience in training and that sort of thing, that's why I ran this big training exercise which went down very well and which probably again, helped to highlight the need for it. (National gallery)

> So I went to courses, I did lots of literature searches, semi self taught, and when I mentioned reinventing the wheel really what you need to do is to put emergency planning knowledge into the context of your organisation and that can be the difficult bit in that where one does tend to start reinventing the wheel to some extent because it has to work for your organization, so you start looking at others and find necessarily that standard procedures at the time, which obviously you need to know about and take into account, they actually have to fit your organisation situation. (National museum)

Concise and Flexible Throughout the project respondents and interviewees stressed that while the disaster control plan should be comprehensive, it should be concise, or brief, to the point versions of key aspects (e.g. reaction) should be available. It should also be written in a way that helps staff take a flexible approach to dealing with a variety of potential incidents.

> … it needs to be slim and easy to quickly glance through and follow … Ours is reactive really. (University archive)

> … whilst she acknowledged the 4 stages: Prevention, Preparedness, Reaction and Recovery – plans often have too much Prevention and Preparedness in them which in the case of an event will need to have been done. Don't want to wade through this material when an incident occurs – want clear, accessible information on what to do when something happens. (Public library service/record office)

> In my part the emergency planning for the collections is very, very small in terms of a written document. I don't believe in these huge written documents. I've been involved in writing some, both in the US and here, and my experience is nobody reads them, nobody gets any benefit from them. So our written document for the collections is only about four pages long and what we try and establish is training, a very short document that everybody is required to read, and on every store room door there is an emergency procedures list. (National museum and gallery)

> When we were doing it, when we were going through the initial operation we looked at as many things as we could, and so we looked at all the standard disaster plans, we went to conferences we went to this, that and the other and we looked very hard at the [US] model for instance. There's a X disaster plan system, which is very, very intense. It was horribly thick and we looked at people like the X and everybody's, and in the end we just thought that a very short, very simple system suited us best because we were trying to teach a large number of people a very small amount of information and there seemed no point at all in trying to make it too complex. And so it was a positive decision to go simple if you like, based on the fact that we'd read all these other disaster manuals, which were volumes and volumes and volumes of material and this suited us best. (National museum and gallery)

> We began with one document and it was getting bigger and bigger and getting, I thought, more and more unwieldy, so in the end we decided to split it into two parts, one was as it were the management documents and we called that the 'Control Plan' in which we set out the background to the plan, the overall roles, the preparation and prevention element of the plan and the service continuity. And the second bit which was a much smaller document was called the 'Reaction Plan' and that was intended to be the published plan, the plan that we made available. Every department in this building, every service point in this building should have a copy of this 'Reaction' plan. All the team leaders who may be Duty Officers on a Saturday or a weekend have a copy of the plan. All the managers have copies at home. Only a limited number of people have copies with home telephone numbers printed. (Public library service/record office)

> Originally when I first came here, if the fire brigade were called, we used
> to give them the plan to the building, which was a document about 2 inches
> thick and then given to the chief fire officer, you know, absolutely ridiculous.
> So now we do it, as I say, we try and do it mostly by training so the people
> automatically know what to do and don't do anything silly. (National museum
> and gallery)

> So it was very interesting at the seminar about emergency planning – that was
> a useful exercise for me to listen to what other people are doing, although some
> seemed far too complicated – I don't think they should be doing that at all. And
> then we had emergency response training as part of our collection care training
> for the X region … we wanted to keep it as simple as possible as we were
> looking at multiple sites and the areas we're looking at are so big, so it was quite
> useful to have that reinforced and have other people from the region say "that is
> a sensible useful idea". (Local Authority museum)

> [You] can't have a fixed plan, it has to be flexible. Can't do anything and water
> goes down anyway. Know where the water turn off valves are. Look to mitigate
> and prevent. In a natural disaster you can't do anything until you're in a position
> to retrieve … need to secure building, e.g. temporary roof, have to make structure
> safe. (National heritage organisation)

Priority or 'Grab' Lists   If there is sufficient time before the building needs to be
evacuated or once it is possible to enter the building post-incident, what should be
made safe or removed first? Some institutions determine lists of object to be given
priority. There seem to be mixed views on such practice.

For

> I have asked people to generate a top ten list. In the very early stages when the
> museum first started to put in place an Emergency Plan they started to look at
> what objects did they most want. For this site, they started to look at it gallery
> by gallery, which is just too big and there is no way it would work if the whole
> museum was ablaze. I try to think – the whole museum is ablaze and the fire
> service comes to you and says we have got ten minutes when you or they can go
> in and what do you want – and you can't do it like that. So I have asked every
> site for a top ten, loosely (they can go up to about fifteen but I want this to be a
> very small list so even if they can be protected by the fire service with blankets,
> or protected with hoses, we want these to be removed). I've got all of these lists
> now and I am going to put all this onto a card with all the information that is
> needed – with photographs, and where to find the objects and so on, so that I
> can give this to the fire service. This is something that I am very aware off so
> the museum's not allowed to burn down until I have finished this off [!]. (Local
> Authority museum)

Priority salvage lists, yes. They're all different too. We gave them general guidelines, 1, 2 and 3, but we didn't mandate, in any way, how they had to make these selections. Because the priorities of their collection needs and so forth … these could be the most valuable things in your collection monetarily, they could be the materials you feel you would need if you needed to set up a place outside the [institution], all of the things can contribute to it being a level 1 priority, but we didn't give them any more structure than that, because every library is different. (International museum)

Against

No, we did at one time look at the idea of using the kind of Blue Shield system but to be honest it doesn't tend to work in a museum situation very well. It's mainly because the disasters are either going to be small, in which case we can deal with them, or the security staff looking for instance for some of the pictures … the last thing we want is them trying to pull them off the wall. So, again, under those circumstances, our warder staff are told that wherever possible to protect in situ and not try and remove, and don't let the fire services try and do it either. (National museum and gallery)

Priority collections? No, we didn't want to be too specific for security reasons, we did walk them through the stores, but we didn't want to be too specific because they wouldn't remember and would have to look at the plan in the event. So that was the main thing, they would call in at the porter's lodge and the porters knew where the plan was and would hand it over, that was the most important thing of all. (University archive)

No. I mean we're in a strange position where we have continually rotating exhibitions, so we never have the same things on show. (National museum)

I know X have a plan, it itemises which works are to be saved. We did talk about that, but nobody wanted to say, let the XX collection burn and we'll save the lenders. Everyone has a different view, it was never resolved … The priorities would shift … Constantly having to reassess, and we've got no criteria really to assess. Value might be the most obvious. But you might have something valuable, but not a flammable as something a little bit cheaper. Well, I just save what I like best. (National museum)

Some interviewees haven't addressed this but would consider it:

We've got an inventory in that we've got a database of the objects. I don't think we've prioritised what would be the most important thing to grab first … we've just had valuations done of the special collections, that would automatically make that list of items over £500, although that's probably too long to take them all as priorities, it is something we perhaps need to develop a bit more, it has been at the back of our minds that we would … (University library)

Equipment and Supplies   Part of the disaster control plan should address emergency equipment and supplies that will be needed in the immediate aftermath of an incident. For example, it should provide lists of such equipment and supplies and locations of where these are located. The UK questionnaire survey found that 51 per cent of managers reported emergency response equipment and materials were provided. This provision occurred mostly in archives/libraries/museums in the National institution category (76 per cent), in local authority archives (70 per cent) and museums (69 per cent). Supplies need to regularly reviewed. This and other related issues are illustrated by the following comments:

Sustainability is a bit of an issue in terms of how we replace and replenish the supplies in the regional trailers, and what people are being encouraged to do is kind of recycle things really, in terms of, you know, the acid free tissue paper in a trailer, if a trailer's located at a particular property and they want to order, or they need to use some, they're encouraged to use that and then buy some and put it in the trailer. We also have, another big thing for us is kind of building projects, actually re-wiring projects or installing, updating fire detection systems for properties, and for that we provide a lot of kind of protection, actually, floor protection, packing materials if collections have to be moved out, and some of that material after it's been used for that will be put in the emergency salvage store, really, sort of so that the materials are kind of like re-used, or are there to be re-used in the event of an emergency. (National heritage organisation)

… issues such as are torch batteries still live, are safety helmets not past sell by date? And, after the debriefing following 7th July [terrorist attacks in London], knee-pads were ordered after the amount of very tired knees from bending down. (National library)

The fans are around the building already, they were actually stored in the disaster cupboard, or on the disaster cupboard at one point, but they kept being 'whipped' [stolen]. (University archive)

The kit is in two places on site, so the first one is actually within the security office so that's sort of there and part of the site. The second one is down the other end of the site so we tried to actually split it should there be an incident. We're very much aware that you don't want your box in the building that you can't actually get into. (Independent museum)

Sustainability   Some institutions have been undertaking effective disaster control planning for some time and have well developed plans with procedures for regular review, training and other activities. But this is not the end of it. Individuals from such institutions were very much aware of the need to maintain this and the effort required to do so.

> We have a disaster plan, it's in its 10th edition, since 2004 we've updated it pretty much every year. I guess we kind of build on that, ever since we've had the disaster plan, we should call it emergency manual, we've done training and we've had a group. So I wouldn't say it's particularly high profile, but equally I think it's well embedded, and that's probably the strength of it and the fact that we do it and manage to go through it on a fairly regular basis, I wouldn't say it's a perfect plan by any means, but at least people are familiar with it. (University library)

> Clearly, emergency planning is just something that is never finished, it's just never, and if you think it's finished then you're making a big mistake. You're never going to be at the position where you don't have to think about it again. The problem of course is making the time in people's jobs to make it happen, to keep documents up to date, to make sure that the fire brigade are taken to the next building on the list within a reasonable amount of time. You have to be very pragmatic ... make sure [procedures] work to their optimum and also are really efficient in terms of how they work, i.e. they don't take lots of staff time to keep the systems up to date, that's a priority that should be a really nice, smooth process. And then where difficulties occur we need to learn from them and make the incremental improvements that are necessary. (National museum)

> ... this sustainability issue. I don't know that we're really necessarily addressing this but certainly in terms of, well it's not directly related exactly, but in terms of climate change I'm meant to be coming up with draft policies for, mitigation really for, collections at properties in terms of climate change, part of which will be to, ... consult with colleagues really, so it won't just be my work by any means really by the time it comes out. But part of that will be linking up with others. (National heritage organisation)

Testing   One activity that can identify issues relating to sustainability is testing the plan and assessing how it works or doesn't work. (See also Training – simulations and exercises below.)

> This is probably a statement of the obvious, but actually there is no way of knowing if our plan is adequate until/unless a disaster strikes, and then we will have to find out the hard way. As far as time is concerned, it is not that anyone disagrees with devoting substantial time to it as a valuable investment, it is just that we are so overloaded with other tasks that have to be accomplished within a time limit, and so those that may not become necessary sometimes are pushed into a lower place on the priority table. (University library)

Archives, Libraries and Museums – Specific Requirements   Many of the principles involved are applicable to archives, libraries and museums but there are factors specific to each. These often relate to the different nature of items/objects in their collections

> There's a uniformity of object type in an archive, ok, there are some non-paper, non-parchment or non-photo materials but a very small minority. Whereas in museums you're dealing with painting collections, insect collections, the broadest range, what we need to do is develop training, knowledge, skills in how to deal with a disaster situation as it might affect different categories of object types. That's something that needs to be done as well. (National record office/National museum)

> ... sometimes we'll paginate, so there'll be a file of say a hundred pieces of paper, a hundred letters, and if it's a high priority collection we will paginate so it will go from one to one hundred, but we're doing less of that because the bulk, the quantity of material, we can't spend our time doing that. That makes it difficult. If you've got a file of a hundred letters, in a folder, the folder is labelled, but then you've got to go in and dry them, it's all that keeping control that is very tricky. Books are not such a problem in some ways, because you can fan them out and things but they're still together. We've got more difficult issues in terms of the binding if they get wet. It's the nature of material here that makes it more difficult to think how you'd manage it, other than lots of interweaving. You'd have to effectively keep them together and try and dry them in that way. (University archive)

> but their needs are very different from dealing with books and so on, because film has different requirements, and increasingly they're storing a lot of it digitally now (University library)

> Libraries, possibly because they've been thinking about it more have an advantage that materials are homogenous, i.e. books, whereas museums' items have different considerations. Libraries are further ahead, and better networked. (International conservation expert)

> Well I think in terms of the library, libraries are different. Book stock can be replaced, you know, as soon as you're insurance kicks in, we're not talking about things that need to have the same level of protection like, unique material, which is what we're looking at for the museum and archive collection. If a library was to burn to the ground, it would be awful, but there are other sites in the town that would, we've got 12 other library's that would kick in that we'd work on. We have, but the material that you've got, the books, the shelving, the furniture, the PC's, is all replaceable. (Public library)

> I'm trying to think of an enquiry ... One of them, it was about protecting large objects, things like mill engines, coal winding engines, this kind of thing, which

are vast ... the advice would be tailored to that particular object because they're so peculiar. (National MLA)

A factor which has recently impacted on development of plans in museums in England has been the MLA Accreditation scheme. A new revised version of the previous Registration Scheme came into effect at the end of 2004 (see Chapter 2). The criteria for this include emergency planning. As one interviewee noted:

Museums now have to have one but are starting from a low basis ... yes, nationals and big ones will have a plan, but beyond that level it is much more fragmented and there is not much expertise. (Commercial disaster management service)

The UK questionnaire survey asked respondents to advise in which year they had first devised a disaster control plan. The year in which the greatest number of plans was compiled was 2005, the year following the new Accreditation scheme. (It should be noted that the questionnaire survey was completed with four months of the year remaining.)

The museum will face accreditation in 2007. An emergency plan will be in place before then but staff resources mean that it will take some time to develop one. There is little or no external funding to purchase emergency collections rescuing equipment and as an independent, budget restrictions play a large part. For the immediate short term, the curator and collections assistant have attended training on disaster planning and will develop an interim plan. (Independent museum)

As Museum Curator I am leading the process to create our disaster plan ... this has been particularly driven by the requirements of the new MLA Accreditation scheme ... (Professional and learned institution)

As a small independent museum, run entirely by volunteers, disaster planning has not had a high priority. However, one staff member has been on extended relevant training and together with others has recently produced a plan acceptable to the Trustees. We are mindful of the need for it as we come to apply for Accreditation next spring. (Independent museum)

Templates/Models

Some are in favour of generic templates or models of disaster control plans that can be customised for use in specific institutions; others are less convinced of their usefulness.

For

I just feel at the moment there needs to be a model of disaster control. People are taking it seriously. There needs to be regular training, walk rounds, that's what we need to introduce, business continuity, planning … its invaluable, it reminds me about things. (National library)

The simplest model that I've seen so far has been X's … That in itself is simplification … I remember when we were starting to do the record office one years ago, and similarly the one in the X Museum, they can be quite unwieldy documents, and that can actually be off-putting and potentially confusing. I think that those kinds of things need to go through a series of iterations to get to something that people can readily understand and buy into. The most recent on that X sent to me, seem to just encapsulate everything. (National record office/ National museum)

The model, when we started doing this back in '89 or whatever it was, the model was John McIntyre's [Anderson and McIntyre 1985] I think everyone referred to it, and round about that time there seemed to be a flurry of activity and disaster in museum publications and so on, and it all boils down to the same thing … I quite liked the simple, succinct, concise approach that X had adopted. (National record office/National museum)

Once you've got a template, I think each template probably covers the same thing the emphasis might be different whether you're doing a library and archives or a museum and the people you'll contact might be different because you might be looking to look at well, we're looking at painting and objects we need to contact them. (Public library)

… at the moment because the museum plan is out of date. The archive plan is up and running. We use the East Midlands emergency planning CD which we found, although it is extensive really, we generally sort of cherry pick the more important points of it, so it has that list of contacts of who to phone, we've got the telephone tree, what the plumber is, the electrician, where the stopcock is now so that if the water floods, and those are basics. (Independent museum)

The plan we've got now was developed from a common pattern or a common plan. Now, it has been left to each unit to review it every 12 months to make sure it is still up to date. We can still call on advice if necessary from conservators in X, without whom we would be in some difficulty. (Local Authority archive)

Against

Not really at all in terms of disaster management consultancy. Prefer to direct enquirers to find information themselves and then we review. Quite often we review disaster control plans. (Commercial disaster management service)

Sometimes the documents are done dryly, almost academic. So many people cut and paste from the Internet, some have the same mistake in. Have seen this – 3 disaster control plans each with same error in … (Commercial disaster management service)

Advise to do background reading rather than use a template. (Commercial disaster management service)

There are so many guides out there. She has tried to collect plans from different parts of the world from NGOs and small organisations, municipal and state. We can find common elements in all documents and then specificate. She then went to a small book case and produced examples, commenting [about one] that for some even this is too complex and the language is too detailed, not clear; something more simple could be done … (International organisation)

… she asked me if I knew of a step by step plan. I can see why there isn't one – one size doesn't fit all – you need to know your institution. So X can have their coloured charts, and know their level of emergency, but it wouldn't work for us. People do need a bit more information about what needs to be included in the emergency response plan. It may not be a template. My experience has been with people that they may not even know where to start. They say, what goes in it? If nothing else we need to get that aspect of museum practice published on emergency planning. (Local Authority museum)

Financial Aspects

Only 9 per cent of managers who responded (to the UK questionnaire survey) reported that they had received training in financial aspects of disaster/emergency management. In terms of ranking, this was the next to lowest of 17 training topics listed. 35 per cent of those managers who responded reported financial aspects of disaster/emergency management as a training need, making it the most common cited (i.e. ranked first of the 17 topics).

Costs

What routine aspects of disaster management incur costs? Major building alterations, installation of fire detection and suppression systems, for example, will involve large-scale expenditure, perhaps only feasible in national or large publicly funded or specialist independent organisations. Routine activities such as training and purchase of equipment of supplies, relevant to all institutions, have associated costs, a mix of internal and external. Exercises and simulations can be expensive. Insurance cover must also be taken into account. Costs must also be measured against risks:

> It just has to be kind of relative to the risk, so that firstly what you want to do is minimise the risk, and I know you can't say there won't ever be a fire ... You've got to have your plans as much as possible. Nobody could say we'll spend two weeks a year on disaster planning, because probably in relation to the risks, it wouldn't be seen as cost effective. It's trying to get that balance. (University library)

Training

> Our training courses are all free and it's kind of a mixture that we have a, sort of an in-house program if you like that we decide that there is sufficient interest for us to put these training courses on. But we also reserve part of the budget to respond to requests from individual institutions and organisations so if somebody came to us this year and said we really want a training course on some aspect of disaster management then we would be able to go in and deliver that to just a single institution or if it was a broader interest we might ask if they would open it out to their neighbours ... But if there is specialized training, our training is not specialized, it's fairly general I suppose but we would, through our grant scheme, be able to fund people to go on specialized courses. Which I think is quite a valuable thing for us to do because it is difficult for smaller authorities and independent museums to actually find £500 to go to such-and-such a conference. (National MLA)

> And I wouldn't have done the X course if work hadn't paid, because it cost £400. (Local Authority museum)

> What we can't do, and again this is a finance thing, is we couldn't get everyone involved [in an exercise on a Saturday or Sunday] because it would cost us a lot of money in overtime right throughout. What we do here is involve as many people as we can; we have to be careful how we do it ... I suppose to a certain degree I am really reliant on the money being available to do what I want to do. I am limited to do what I can do with personnel and that's the big expense. If I have an exercise outside of normal working hours then I have to be really careful about the cost of that, and this sort of exercise really would have to be run outside of the normal office hours. It wouldn't be possible, otherwise. The amount of staff that we have really only allows us to lend four week days to do what we're supposed to do. As part of loan agreements for artworks we are told that we must have certain levels of security in every aspect. So to try and

get people away from galleries during the working week for training, that'd be difficult. And we normally try and do it when there's a quiet spell perhaps between exhibitions. (National gallery)

We need to do more of that, that's what we want to do. We had planned to do a major mock disaster, have it filmed as well, involve colleagues, professional archives, ourselves, fire services, police, everything, it was going to cost a lot of money but we felt it was worth it, but again, the management structure … (National library)

Yeah, as part of my budget I include the training aspect of it in my training budget and I have a budget for the equipment as well. When it moves into the Business Continuity side of it, I'm not 100% certain how that's going to work out because that all depends really on who is tasked with leading that part of it. If it's me it may be that my budget may have to be increased to cover the additional … Well perhaps not equipment so much but the training requirements and the testing of the plan, you know. Because if we have to bring the consultants back in to check what we've done then, you know, you know what consultants are like, they never come cheap. (National gallery)

What we need to do under business costings is planning, set it out in the business plan, … a mock exercise this year. It will cost £37,000 … a mock exercise, with our colleagues from the national archives, from the [national] museums, from the national galleries and what we're going to do is we're going to film it, and we're going to learn. (National library)

Equipment and Supplies   Initial set-up costs for stores of equipment can then be followed by replacement of items used or past their 'sell by' date.

[Disaster equipment lockers] Usual things, you find that somebody will take a pair of pliers or a screwdriver or something else and not return it but generally it's safe. I don't really normally have to spend an awful lot of money. But when I first started doing this, I did, I spent a fortune in the first year because it hadn't been done for a few years and then there were a lot of things that were missing but since then it's really been quite small … (National gallery)

Insurance   In the UK questionnaire survey 63 per cent of managers reported that their archive/library/museum had insured their collections and 54 per cent advised they reviewed their insurance cover. (It should be noted that a government indemnity scheme covers many national institutions.) It is important to speak with institutional finance officers to check on cover and with insurers and loss adjusters about valuation and advice on cover.

> One of the problems in the past was always, if we get it valued and it costs a fortune, will we be able to afford to insure it? Equally I think it's important to know what your stuff's worth, even if you take that decision, you've taken it on the basis that you know what the risks are. Or you might say that we can't afford to insure the whole collection, but you might insure the fifty most valuable items. I've honestly no idea because this is the discussion ... if I'm honest I don't think the library, I don't know what the insurance will come out at, but I don't think we could afford it from our revenue budget. It's these hard decisions, isn't it? How do you choose, which is all to do with the risk assessment, but I think the first thing is to look at the value? And to be fair to the [institution], they have paid for that for us, we haven't had to ... although I said it comes from our own budget, we haven't had to do that. (University library)

> Particularly with archives, there's sometimes a problem with valuation of stock we've provided worst case scenario costings, e.g. if every box was damaged by water and sewage, what would it cost? Gives them a ball park figure to think about, e.g. will cost £1 million to dry and sanitise so we'll insure for £10 million .. Generally should have all perils and business disruption/continuity ... Doing it without talking to people within the council who will deal with your claim is daft (e.g. insurance/finance section if nothing in place, have to start to explain why you're getting freezers in because paper deteriorates. Often a failure – too insular – look for key others. (Commercial disaster management service)

> we make case that it's worth looking at insurance cover and have contingencies in place if no cover. Loss adjusters are there as intermediaries between you and insurer. Involve them from the outset. (Commercial disaster management service)

> Also, the issue about insurance and so on cropped up in some discussions we had about whether members of staff from one organisation can work on another organisation's premises without cover, you know, legal thorns like that. (National record office/National museum)

Funding

How are costs for disaster management funded? We found no examples of a discreet budget for this, with revenue expenditure often coming from a preservation or conservation heading, or one for training.

> It just comes out of the existing budget for maintenance or equipment. (Public library service/record office)

No [separate fund], it's a shoestring. I think this year we're going to have zero budgets all around which means we've just got to buy everything. I've been fortunate up to know in that I've had a £xx,000 safety budget and what I've done is just taken bits out of it, most of which has been agreed – laptops, for example. But there isn't a separate budget as such ... [If something specific required], I'd have to go to the deputy director and say, 'look, I really feel that we need xyz', and if he agrees, then he would find the fund for it. (National museum)

But on a day to day basis it is a bit of a nightmare really. It is not something that has been tackled and it is not something that the museum has a will to tackle as there are so many other budgetary pressures. At the moment we are under pressure to save and possibly cut money from the museum's budget, so it can be spent in other areas, I think mainly the library has overspent, and as a department we are quite under funded. We do what we can but it is not at all ideal. (Local Authority museum)

We don't have a separate budget. On the whole it tends to be funded by our divisional budget in terms of the keeper's budget and my budget. We'd sought money for our events in the past and I have tried to get a budget in the past but I have to admit I haven't tried in the last few years and I think that it's probably time for me to try again. (National museum)

There's just a revenue budget, so for example every year we check the contents of disaster boxes and if someone's nicked or used a load of stuff it comes out of money ... for supplying books ... I think we're fairly lucky, because in a big library there's usually a little bit of flexibility, five hundred pounds won't make a huge difference one way or the other. And training and so on is all part of the overall training budget. (University library)

The supplies for the disaster cupboards and their maintenance comes out of my conservation budget. I suppose that is one issue in that it originally came out of a central administration budget, which now can no longer fund it. Therefore, rather half heartedly, it comes out of mine. And we are under quite strong budgetary pressure and therefore other things had to go in order to maintain the disaster cupboards but we think that they're pretty important and therefore we do continue. (National museum and gallery)

[Work relating to disaster management] comes out of core funding really, because ... it's not particularly expensive now we've got the disaster plan, we've got disaster supplies which only amounted to a few hundred pounds and that sort of money was found from core funding, and then we had training last year, but again that was just a few hundred pounds. It's not actually an expensive thing, other than my time I suppose. [Emergency recovery company subscription comes out of this funding too.] (University archive)

We don't get anything extra. We work on the basis that we have key people in place who have responsibility for building and collections, and we have it in our action plan that emergency response is important, that we're doing the plan, and that if something did happen other things that, say for example, if I was responsible for dealing with it then some of my other jobs would have to [wait] … it would be a priority. And everything would have just to go back really. But we don't have anything extra. And I suppose you could say that the record office one that we have we pay for as part of service level agreement. So we pay a sum of money direct to [county council], every year, and part of that is that we're covered by their emergencies fund. So you could say that the borough funds it in that way. (Public library)

And we have been looking at the issue of disaster kits and having some equipment available. So where there was a little of money found a couple of years ago, so most of the community museums have some kind of disaster kit (polythene, gloves, basic hand tools) but not a lot else. We do not have quantities of absorbent material, we don't have hard hats, we don't have safety boots, we don't have high-res jackets. Where that will come from I don't really know! (Local Authority museum)

I think relatively speaking a lot of the equipment that's needed is fairly low cost so a lot of places, particularly if they've got local authority funding will probably have budgets to cope with that level of expenditure anyway. And it's just with the museums, particularly the ones [that] are independent, totally voluntary run, they don't have any budgets at all never mind for things they might never need to use. We do take a slightly different approach to those kinds of museums and we would, we might raise eyebrows if the local authority was coming to us asking for money for Tyvek® suits, but we wouldn't for an independent voluntary run organisation. (National MLA)

Training, comes out of either our security budget or out of a Human Resources (HR) training budget. Mostly out of an HR training budget. And that's fairly healthy and therefore we know we can do reasonably decent things. (National museum and gallery)

Bids for internal or external funding to support one-off activities, for example, training exercise or establishment of a disaster kit or box, are common. Large-scale initiatives will require bids for capital funding.

Oh, bits and pieces. When it started we had money from the Getty Conservation Institute and money out of the Heritage Preservation General fund … since then it's been sort of patched together with foundation and federal grants and usually projects. (International museum)

... definitely room for improvement, communication with maintenance and having a good building schedule, more control over what's going on with the building is definitely what we could do with. But I think what we do well, is that we do have, good systems like fire suppression etc, because we're quite well funded in that way. The boss here is quite good at getting grant funding for particular building things like, for example, the roof has just been redone in here, that kind of thing. (University archive) [This institution has fire suppression system, very sensitive smoke detection system and flood detectors.]

And there are capital bids that people can put forward. We were talking about improving the water tank, and how capacity didn't last as long as they thought when the water went off. There was discussion about asking for capital funding to enlarge the capacity – in a forward planning sense. (National museum)

I think we foresee problems from a service manager level certainly. Then again, from a corporate level, you've got to be really safe here, but from a funding level from [national government], they agreed to the £xx million being spent on the upgrade of the building. And the reason for this upgrade is for fire safety and guarding against disasters. (National library)

In terms of resourcing post-incident actions, some institutions have procedures in place for urgent contingency expenditure.

Well I have discussed this with our finance person. In the event of an emergency we have permission to spend on the directorate code, which is the main museum budget. And if we spend all the money that is something the council will just have to deal with. Presumably as the Council have their own emergency plan there is some sort of contingency money to deal with that. (Local Authority museum)

I think there is a contingency budget, if there was something major happened – there is some contingency funding available. But if it was something like the local alert that I want to sign up to, I look in my budget, and see if I can afford it under the security heading. (National museum)

The requirements of the Accreditation scheme in England have helped some make a case for funding to support the development of disaster management.

It's just funded through the curatorial budget. We don't have a core funding aspect so it's very ad hoc, hit and miss. We were luck enough that last year, because accreditation insists that you have an emergency plan, I was able to say to my bosses well look, we need a plan, we need to be able to provide a stock pile of tissue papers, bungees, hats – the box, the emergency box – we haven't got that and we need to put money towards it, so that money was put aside that once, but if we need to renew that then we have to do a balance between that and basic curatorial issues. (Independent museum)

Buildings

Maintenance

In the UK questionnaire survey, it was revealed that planned building maintenance is carried out in two-thirds of archives/libraries/museums. National institutions are the most likely to schedule building maintenance, and those institutions without a disaster control plan, the least. With regard to the importance of condition of building(s) to effective disaster management, most respondents felt this was 'fairly important' or 'important'. Issues reported included the age, design, structure of the building and the need for regular maintenance of the building(s), facilities and infrastructure.

> I think that's probably the major key issue actually, managing our buildings, the maintenance of them, the equipment within the buildings such as aged air conditioning systems, which can fail and leak and as a result of those things some more floods can occur. (National museum)

> Myself, and we have a sort of Operations Manager, between us we would do risk assessments on the building. But I would say that actually maintenance and upkeep of our buildings is the difficult one because we have a very small maintenance budget, and looking at even simple things like blocked drains and gutters is probably a step that we're not doing yet. We're not doing the prevention aspect. (Independent museum)

> Because of the problems with our building and its services, the library sustains minor 'emergencies' (effectively water leaks) every few months. Fortunately these are generally contained very quickly and have recently caused limited damage, mainly because of the experienced staff who deal with them promptly. These recurrent problems have in fact acted as training opportunities for staff, especially new staff, and encourage all to be alert to the danger of a major threat. (University library)

> … the original archive is only thirty years old or so, and it was purpose built as an archive, so it's got an air conditioning plant, but the cladding that was used, which was original from thirty years ago, is not brilliant anymore, and flammable, basically. There were other things which we have addressed, like fire dampers etc, but these things take a long time to get through. (University archive)

The building is 150 years old. So, I mean, you know, they built them to last in those days. So structurally it's sound but, nevertheless, in a building that's 150 years old there are things that you have to be aware of; we're also Grade 2 listed because we're in a conservation area so again, from a building maintenance point of view that gives us challenges. (Public library)

... we're surveying library buildings at the moment, fitness for purpose, ... we acknowledge that a lot of library buildings, well, a lot of museum, archive and library buildings are in atrocious condition. We need some building maintenance here. That's actually probably the biggest single cause of disasters, either poor electrics maintenance or roof leaks or floods and blocked drains so, that's a problem. (National MLA)

Substandard building work, basically, that hadn't been quality checked properly by whoever. We thought it was all fine, and it wasn't. Building works, that's the thing we learnt from that exercise really ... (University archive)

... Major problem is lack of preventative maintenance of our buildings – constant minor problems with blocked drains causing flooding into building – easily preventable but Estates don't do the work. (University library)

Building maintenance is the huge sticking point for the whole museum service. There is no programme of maintenance because, they tell me, there is no money. We are now in the farcical situation of having to do massive roof works – one of biggest issues in the museum is roof leaks ... we are supposed to be half way through replacing the roof and at the moment our roof leaks are probably worse than ever mainly because we have contractors on the roof and therefore it is a building site which means they have all their tools, empty drinks bottles, crisp packets, etc. which get into the gutters and block them. We had requested that we should have mesh put into the top of down pipes so that they couldn't get blocked, because we get bird poop in there as well, some of that has been done and some hasn't been done, so that isn't helping. And it is really only having to be done to the extent that it is because for years no one has done any maintenance on the roof. It is all fire fighting, be it reluctantly. (Local Authority museum)

We have a number of locations now where they are not our buildings and we are tenants, there may well be campus plans attached but we have no specific safety plan or disaster plan for any, working on the premise that there is nothing there that's not replaceable. (Public library service/record office)

Not all paint a gloomy picture:

Well I think we do our buildings very well, I think you can see that. Things like, even like the electricals from outside, not on the ground floor, half way up, so that water won't affect it, access from outside so they don't need it inside the building, because once an incident happens, the fire brigade come in, they take control of the building, and we can't do anything, they're in control. So if we do need access, we can't get access until we get the ok from them anyway, but we can go in very quickly, fairly easily. (National library)

Equipment

It is worth noting that the UK questionnaire survey found that regular checks of fire and electrical equipment were the most frequently reported disaster management related activities undertaken in archives, libraries and museums. Regular checks of electrical equipment were performed in 84 per cent of archives/libraries/museums (over 90 per cent in institutions in the national category and /or in institutions where there had been a disaster in the previous years).

Fire and Police Service

In terms of protecting the building or property, it is important as part of risk assessment, to seek advice from appropriate external agencies, which should include fire and police services. 59 per cent of managers reported their archive/ library museum had obtained advice from police or fire services. Museums in general (71 per cent), particularly local authority museums (84 per cent), archives/ libraries /museums in the National institution category (82 per cent) and where there has been a disaster in the previous five years (70 per cent) most frequently obtained police and fire service advice. Such advice will influence activity relating to protection and security of buildings. Respondents and interviewees reported differences in availability of fire service advice; in some cases they would advise the institution should contact a consultant. In the UK, this may be due to recent changes in legislation and role of the fire service

> Certainly their awareness has shifted clearly over the years and certainly in the last few years there's been a very noticeable strategic awareness at senior levels that the fire brigade act at of the uniqueness of heritage collections and heritage buildings and the need to prioritise those to a greater level than previously. However, the fire officer who was assigned to liaise with us from the early '90's was actually incredibly aware and incredibly sort of keyed in and to an extent certainly was, it was a priority. And through him we were, I felt very successfully able to do a whole series of training exercises over the years with the fire brigade, the fire service they prefer to be called now, looking at each one of our buildings in turn. (National museum)

> And so we had to sort of just reign back a little bit so thereafter we concentrated just on doing the tours [with fire service]. Now, quite often they did actually repeat sessions for various stations … and a lot of city centre buildings for

example are covered by two or three stations so we were finding that, a few of them where finding it a bit repetitive anyway, so it wasn't a bad thing to reign back a little bit. But by continuing with the tours we were covering to the best of our ability both the stores and the public access buildings by just showing them around and raising their awareness and reminding them … liaising with them … We decided to do a more generic exercise based here trying to apply principles and practices that would apply to any of our buildings, so we actually invited curators to come and join in and use it very much as a training exercise both for our own staff as well as the fire brigade. (National museum)

Disasters

Impact on Disaster Planning

Unfortunately, in terms of disaster planning, an actual incident may serve to motivate action as the following examples illustrate:

> … I think an awareness of a lack of preparedness. A lot of library and archive institutions found an awareness that they were not properly prepared if a disaster were to strike them and we all were shocked at the Norwich fire, I know it was several years ago now, but I think that was a wake-up call. And also, we have collections here which are unique and priceless, literally priceless and extremely valuable. (Public library service/record office)

> There were some basic plans in place before for the museums but nobody had looked at the archives at all, and within the first six weeks of me starting this job, … we actually had a disaster in the archives here at X which involved … a toilet which is above the main archive store; basically there was a problem with the overflow and it started raining water … brought to the fore that we didn't have any plans in place and that this was something that we needed to look at very quickly . But I think the fact that we were able to respond and cope with that and that nothing was lost or damaged within the emergency procedure – alright things happened when they got wet and had already been damaged within the store – but no extra damage was caused by our actually salvaging stuff so I was quite pleased with that. And having learnt from that, we're now really in place with getting our plans and looking at it as an organization … (Independent museum)

> In terms of terrorism, I think we are generally, as careful as any other major town would be. Probably more so in [town] because we had the bombing ... and that has made us careful of things like suspicious packages. (Public library)

… and I think the 7th July did focus minds more. So it became much more borne out. And also the avian flu thing, the directors were particularly keen that we deal with that aspect, because of the loss of staff and what would happen then, so we've been through that one as well. (National museum)

Well I suppose in some respects having had a disaster has helped I think. (Independent museum)

You always get a sense there's an attitude of 'it'll never happen'. It just takes something to happen. (National record office/National museum)

Region-wide Disasters and their Impact

Recent catastrophic region wide disasters (see Chapter 2) have had major media coverage and have served to warn cultural heritage organisations that they need to think beyond the institution – what impact will such a disaster have on archives, libraries and museums, and the people who work there? What planning can they undertake to mitigate the impact and facilitate recovery.

… Because there was a major flood disaster in the city, which put the main police and fire stations under water, and cut power to TV, radio stations and transmitters, alarm systems, mobile phone masts, and because falling trees blocked roads and cut phone (land) lines, they were very isolated. We in museums in the county, couldn't have got through to X to help, even if we had known help was needed … Emergency plans need to be as self-sufficient within the organisation as possible, and not reliant on outside organisations and colleagues at other institutions … small organisations need to train up management, committee members, volunteers, etc., who live in close vicinity. Don't expect museums, galleries and archives to be the top civil priority if the disaster is all engulfing. Lives come before objects. (Charity archive)

I saw the heavy down pour, and thought I wouldn't want to rush home, I'd sit and work, then I got a look out of the window, and saw a river outside, then the library caretaker rushing along. He was more aware than [just] the library problems, he knew they'd had many floods in the past, but not on that scale. We walked down the library to discover the worst. He called the fire brigade, but there was such a flood that the fire brigade were very busy …I had never been confronted with such a situation, and my mind was frozen. The fire brigade were so busy with call outs, most of the houses were being flooded, and domestic situations took priority, so we had quite a wait. We had to resign ourselves until the place was pumped out. There was very little that you could do. Which is probably not something that you work out in advance, the realisation gradually dawns, unless you'd seen it before, which I hadn't. (Local Authority archive)

The impact on staff can be huge:

> I was there 5–6 weeks after [Katrina] and people were still in a state of shock, they couldn't concentrate, write a coherent letter for funding, e.g. for attention to roof. Had to sensitise help … They were overwhelmed, demoralised, needed to know that there were people to help them … A widespread disaster remember – they lost their homes too. If a fire, it would be isolated, with Katrina a lot of other factors came into play. [For example, the] mental state of people who've been through a disaster. AIC and NEH 'Train the Trainers' programme about 8 years ago – selected 10 people around the country to train in disaster response – that was the focus, not salvage. I was one of the 10 .. We were trained to train other people. That first mentioned the psychological thing – didn't realise until I saw it how critical it was. In case of Katrina, these people couldn't do it themselves, doing their best but could only see so far – 6 weeks later! (International conservation expert)

> Forget about libraries – you have to be with people and listen to them – keep it going – don't let this fade away – we are with you – you are not isolated. (Professional body)

There is also a need to inform visitors and readers of what is going on:

> [Visitors] don't know what they need – but they need people to help them, make decisions. The most effective thing on 7th July (London bombings) was a whiteboard telling which Underground stations were working. Now we have plasma screens. There was a lack of information for everyone – it was unprecedented that day. That was underlined at the Society of Archivists conference with the presentation on Hurricane Ivan – the people there had no homes (Craig, R., Selzer, T. and Seymour, J. 2006). The priority was home and loved ones. You have to plan but be aware the whole thing can go out of the window. The lesson from the 7th July, and it was put into practice on 21st, was to say we have no more information, but will keep you informed. (National institution)

Storage An issue that was commented upon in relation to the aftermath of a region-wide disaster, is the availability of adequate storage to which objects can be moved before an incident if there is sufficient time before it strikes, or after one, to provide safe, temporary storage. This applies not only to 'national treasures' but is a factor for others too.

> One of the things we looked at very, very, very carefully after, particularly after the 7/7 scares and all the rest of it, was external storage if we were to be hit by a major, major disaster like a bomb explosion or something. And we didn't like any of the scenarios. We looked at sites within a region of about 50 miles

radius of our major museums and in the end we thought no, the collection centre scenario whereby we take stuff and put it in there or put it in another of our own museum sites was much better for us in terms of security, in terms of handling in terms of our control over the system. And to be honest out there there's not a lot of what we wanted, if you wanted emergency storage we looked at underground caves, we looked at army camps we looked at everything. And our decision was to keep it within our own ... (National museum and gallery)

Yes, we want high security, we want high environmental control, you know, we want high degrees of access to it ... [like in] the Second World War when they put all the stuff up in caves in North Wales and slate quarries ... We are not geared up for that. And one of our biggest problems was transport. And we knew that in a case of a major disaster we'd be at the bottom of the pecking order. Hospitals and schools would have advantages over us and therefore, again, it's what we could control ourselves. (National museum and gallery)

Ultimately it will make life a little bit easier for community museums and this site because the ultimate plan is that there will be no stored collections other than at this centre. So that means the only objects we have to worry about are those on display which makes it easier to know where they are and explain to people how to get an object. It also gives us a central store for emergency kit. It also gives us a salvage location. If anything happens at one of the other locations, we now have a secure site that we know objects can go to. And even if there is not enough space within the building we know there is flat space, so we can have temporary buildings. So that is a huge advantage. (Local Authority museum)

Training

Training is essential for effective disaster management; it brings to life the written disaster control plan. Different types of training (for example, desk based, practical) must be considered.

Staff training is so, so important. I can't see enough. (National library)

My observation over many years in heritage collections in [two different regions of England] is that there are too many training sessions and not enough 'doing'. In X ... the most useful part of disaster planning was our frequent exercises with the Fire Brigade. You learned more from half an hour of practical work than in hours of training ... Also talking to other libraries, museums and archives is essential ... (University library)

Our pick up training which was annual, was found not to be enough. So you know, there were just too many, we do have a lot of contract staff here, and so we are going to have to do it on a real time basis if you like as soon as they start they'll have to be trained, rather than waiting to do a bunch every May as we used to. So that was a failure, if you like, of the system. (National museum and gallery)

The disaster happened at about 6pm, and we were still there at midnight, just doing the initial things. We were working about 2 hours before the fire brigade arrived. There wasn't a lot we could do. This is when you're training comes back, you start to do things instinctively, and hope you do the right things – sorting things out, putting polythene out, sorting stuff into categories, beginning to set things up. (Local Authority archive)

Training can play a key role in team building – effective teamwork and communication will be important in dealing with incidents

The issue we have is orientation because it's a big building and multi-site. Dividing into teams .. What has worked is getting everyone together … Although they managed, some were quite creative, and that was interesting, they managed quite well, using the floor under the table for drying lines and various means … the boss, was particularly quite keen on it, as well as the disaster planning side, it was quite a good team building exercise. (University archive)

I am delighted that we've been able to set up training both for the fire brigade, actually designed for the fire brigade, and for our internal staff; and we've now incorporated our internal training programmes into an overall collections management training programme, which encompasses a wide variety of different sort of subject areas which are talked about by different professions within museums. (National museum)

Several respondents commented that experiencing a disaster was the best form of training

… we were able to put it into practice in that we were able to give some assistance to the library next door when they had a serious flood a couple of years ago … I suppose to look at it cynically I suppose it was nice to have something to practise on, without feeling that ultimately it's your responsibility, it was someone else's responsibility, but it was good practice. (Local Authority archive)

… one of the real things to gain experience, is to have an incident, though it's not what you want. (National library)

Exercises/Simulations

Whilst training is generally regarded as a key factor in disaster management, the use of exercises or simulations of incidents and dealing with them is quite low. The UK questionnaire survey found that only 26 per cent of archives, libraries and museums had conducted a disaster simulation /exercise. Those who had undertaken found them useful, if resource intensive:

> I'm a firm believer, I think even the smallest exercise really [like the one at X] threw up so many things in terms of that plan, and they're really very well organised at X, but it also threw up issues for the fire services because in a fire, three fire services would actually be called to an emergency at X, and then it threw up issues for them so they kind of learnt from it. (National heritage organisation)

> So, having the role play and running through is absolutely key to the success of this really, to make sure you keep on improving, that you learn something every time. That's really how the plan fits in with external bodies. It fits in because we keep in contact with them and have those sort of plans … the fire brigade on Monday were saying they'd now like to do a more difficult one for them, which would be in the middle of the building … If we had a big electrical problem, which set off a fire in the middle of the building, it'd be much more complicated for them. So they want to do a more complicated exercise and on that exercise we said we'd perhaps would do it on a Saturday, maybe in the daytime and bring in our own pyramid as well. (National library)

> Well it can be done really quite simply, because we've found that in order to test a plan you don't really need a huge number of objects really, but using things from either, you know, staff flats or room stewards' rooms and things, non-collection items anyway. But you can just set up a few things either in an entrance hall or, you know, another room beyond, whatever, but it tests your actual plan but at the same time you might want to produce sort of fake inventories and things and fake inventory marks on objects and things, you know testing things relatively thoroughly. And the fire brigade are sometimes involved in those exercises, and they too may have an exercise of their own really before the X staff are allowed in, either to try and rescue someone or whatever, negotiate the building in their masks … (National heritage organisation)

> … one of the house staff at X produced a whole load of sort of fake inventory lists so we've got that for any exercises now too if anybody wants to borrow that sort of stuff, and fake plans and marked everything on ……… And then, the other thing we tried to do in the exercises which was an idea really taken from somebody who used to work at X, who's now left, but he had an ex-military background, he devised it so that people were able to experience four different

types of activity in the exercise, which is what we did at the X which people found very useful because a lot of the feedback in the past from training courses had been, you know, 'it was kind of great during the exercise but I was stuck in wherever, and didn't see anything'. (National heritage organisation)

And then we had conservators in who talked through how you would deal with sodden material, whether it was smoke damaged, and we set fire to a few things so you could see what happened. We brought old items – we did a trawl of all the charity stores and brought items that sort of replicated things within the collection, so it was quite good. (Independent museum)

We did an exercise up at X. We learnt quite a bit from that. But also, learning from the fire at the MOMA, what happened there was absolutely fascinating and I actually used that scenario for our own internal business company last week as a desktop exercise to go through, whereby the library has gone up in flames, and take it from there. So the other major issue is salvage, that all museums should have a salvage team. (National museum)

Last year's practical training session was good, but it was very contrived. Everybody had a box with a mixture of archives that had been soaked and they worked out how to dry out different things and how much space you needed. But it would be more useful, I think, to have a realistic simulation where you actually had reference coded boxes, I think that's the most difficult thing – keeping track of your archives … (University archive)

… because we are split over a number of geographic sites it is important, we feel, to sort of bring in the local fire stations to those particular buildings and what we do is we hold four training sessions … We programmed in four training sessions for four different afternoons that allowed each of the four watches of the local stations to come in and participate and literally we would tell them about our emergency planning, we told them how important we feel it is to liaise with them and how important it is that we give them a good idea of the type of collections that we both exhibit and importantly store in the various buildings, and we actually take them on a big tour. Now this is different from their normal building familiarisation tour – it's very much concentrated on objects in the building and literally, we're not trying to teach them the detailed facts, we're trying to show them that these are important and just to give them an awareness of the different types of materials and objects kept in the different buildings. And then we follow that up with a practical exercise where we literally set up a pretend fire in a building. It's very staged I have to say, obviously, and we can't fill buildings full of smoke or anything like that, we have to be very careful making sure security and other types of collection care and maintained during them but we try to make them as, you know other than that, as realistic as we can. And we bring in our own staff too to coordinate with them as they would hopefully in a major incident. So we've tried to do that for all of our buildings, we did quite a few of them, they're quite big and quite sort of cumbersome to organise really but we did that through the '90's. (National museum)

Some institutions record the exercises – this facilitates analysis of how they went – it can add to the comments of observers and let those who participated see examples of good and bad practice they may not have noticed whilst taking part in the exercise. It can lead to a more meaningful debrief.

The X Museum was the main one that we probably recorded first. One of our AV people pretended to be Press, and one of our demonstrators – we tried to make it as real as possible – one of our wonderful demonstrators down at the X Museum was a sort of journalist, so the two of them went around together and tried to nab staff and say "Give us an interview." … Our director … actually came down on site and gave a press interview. And it was really nice to get that level of involvement. We have lots of photographs, because what I tend to do is site observers in key locations, so we actually have participants in the exercises and we have observers and they're usually differentiated visually by armbands so the observers are not part of it, the exercise, at all. They take notes, they take photographs, only interfere if literally there is likely damage to a real object ... (National museum)

Table top exercises, less resource intensive, can also be useful.

Table top exercise is good … most useful is sitting round the table talking about the plan with a cup of tea! When you have an incident that's what you do – sit round being fed information – what are we doing about this …? You get used to talking around a plan. It helps to give people confidence. (National heritage organisation)

The tabletop one was done last week, I wasn't present for that because I was off ill, but I set it up by email, I gave him the edited version as well, I based it around the X fire, but as applied to our library, so the scenario was essentially, fire in the library, probably electrical because we've had two incidents where the electrics have gone. Then the fire brigade come onsite, take it over, the originally mentioned planning group goes over the road, with the basic essentials, and then after discussion with the fire brigade and the business continuity director, they decide to move off site to X. The salvage team have already gone there, they set up the site ready to run and then the group takes over from there. So what do you do, who do you liaise with, how does the recovery information that we've got together so far, that whole package, how does it fit in, how does it work? And a number of questions have come out of that, so that's been quite useful. (National museum)

… we had a big sort of, rush of blood to the head after the 7/7 type disasters and then we all got very excited about doing a lot of this but now that that's sort of faded off a little bit, it's not a priority and now we've got some budget problems it's fading even further into the distance. But what a few of us would have very much liked to have done was literally round the table simulations, which I think would be immensely useful. Just going and saying to one of the warders that somebody has just put a bomb in the corner what are you going to do now? Who do you call? And if he or she didn't know they'll say, 'Well, I'll call my supervisor' – ok, do it. Then you say to the supervisor, he or she's just called you, what are you going to do? And just follow the trail. Well it's actually a brilliant, very quick, dry run scenario, very cost effective, but it also makes everybody think. Ok, there's a guy there he's holding a bomb or he's holding a gun, what are you going to do? Do you close the gallery? Do you not close the gallery? I don't know. So then you can then put that back into their training. But it also then goes right the way up through the chain of command so that you would say, 'Well ok. The bomb went off. It's caused this amount of damage to the pictures and to the electrics – they are all hanging off the wall. What happens next?' And I think it would, that kind of thing, would find out a lot of weaknesses in our system. (National museum and gallery)

I think calling it a simulation exercise is putting it a bit strongly. We had two days with [disaster recovery company]. The first day was a general introduction to disaster management and to our own disaster plan, primarily for team leaders, team officers who might be called upon to actually invoke the plan in the case of disaster. That was a series of presentations by me and by X from [disaster recovery company]. And then the second da6y was a very small scale simulation of what might happen in the event of a flood and how we would react to it. In a sense that was quite useful because we literally had buckets of water and things and wet books. The first thing we immediately realised is how much space you need to deal with the aftermath of a disaster, we ran out of space within about two minutes. But we haven't done any more like that and again I think we need to do more planning in that area and more training. (Public library service/record office)

Whilst training with groups and teams is important, it can be targeted at individuals.

We don't tell them what we're going to do, and they don't know when its going to be, so it is completely sort of ad hoc and random. We don't single people out to test them. And unfortunately one person did have two things happen to her … So it has actually turned into a good way of praising people for how they actually responded. I asked a colleague from another museum, to do it, who is very experienced in security. And he was very impressed – he was 'I don't believe it'. They did a really good job. It's worked out as a really positive exercise and the staff have accepted it. And it does come into people's appraisals. We do remind them that they will be happening in the next year, and that they may be participating. Just to make sure that they've brushed up on all the skills. When they're in the gallery they are responsible for that area. That's worked out well ... we had one person, and we asked one of the casual art handlers who was quite new, and who didn't know the organisation to come in with a carrier bag and to remove a piece of art work off the wall. And X who worked here, she was on the gallery. And he came in, and she was down the other end, and he tried to unscrew the work, and of course she went over to him, and she's like – what are you doing, you can't do that. We were watching on the CCTV ... And, as we saw her go over to him and challenge him, we all ran down to the gallery, and there were some French people, and they were going 'bravo, bravo – she saved the painting'. (National museum)

Needs

(For a list of training needs see Tables 3.10 and 3.11 in Chapter 3.) In spite of increased activity ongoing raising awareness is essential; induction and repeat/ refresher training can play a part in this and emphasise individual's roles in implementing the disaster control plan

Well, if you could call awareness raising training, or awareness training, I think there is a need for that on a cross-site, organization-wide basis, particularly with posts that traditionally wouldn't associate themselves with these kinds of situations, buildings people, for example. (National record office/National museum)

I think probably that the first thing that we will need to do is, once these manuals are completed, is talk to the various groups about how to use the manual, what's in the manual and so forth and what their first response should be. Then I guess the next step would be to go back and try and train staff, and this might be something that the conservator has to set up of course, how to handle materials and things like that. Especially, again, for the small scale emergencies, the water emergencies, which are the most frequent, or mouldy books, occasionally we have something like that. (International museum)

Training needs vary according to staff roles generally and in respect of their involvement in disaster management. Training will need to address a range of factors in that context.

At a very general level and to a certain extent, it depends on who the person is, but sometimes management training, in terms of dealing with people, how to handle people in what could be fraught situations, the whole interpersonal relationship when maybe you're dealing with someone who in a structural, organisational sense – you've got to be aware a lot of these organisations are quite hierarchical – where potentially in a situation you've someone at a relatively low grade telling someone who's maybe three or four grades above them what to do. So it's management in … that kind of personal communication, interpersonal skills training, if there is such a thing, some people can do it naturally, other people will never be able to do it, but I do think some people can be taught to do it. The psychological aspect of a situation which can be fraught and nerve-wracking and make people behave differently than they would on a day-to-day basis, I think there's got to be awareness raising of that as well – basically, the human context. (National record office/National museum)

I think it's such a vast area and you can't actually define or even imagine what it's going to be. I think, priority for me at the moment, we've just had a restructure and we did training for all the new library managers, one of the areas is facilities management, which is ownership of your environment, all the issues around, safety, and prevention, where your potential hazards are going to come from, and how to deal with them. I think we need to do something similar for the Central Library because, either rightly or wrongly, because there is a Buildings Manager, there are caretaker and maintenance staff, there are security, people do not have ownership of the building. You'll go through parts of the building in the morning, lights won't be switched on and you'll say 'is there something wrong with this light', 'Don't know', I'll say 'Have you tried turning it on', 'No', 'Why not', 'I thought somebody else would'. That sort of mentality betrays a sort of attitude that could cause a disaster. 'Is that radiator leaking?', 'Oh I don't know. Yes it looks like it's wet', 'How long has it been doing that for?', 'Oh I don't know, couple of days'. And the bits of the building that people don't go to, and there are some, it only needs to be left a day and now we've got an issue. So I think it needs somebody in management … to resolve. So it's an attitude that there could be a problem, there might not, but if I leave it and don't do anything about it, you know three days down the road, people are going to say, 'did you notice a smell?', 'yes', 'did you hear a noise of dripping?', 'yes', 'Did you do anything?' 'No', and you just look like a fool. The worst case scenario is doing nothing and something horrendous happens. If you have actually intervened and it wasn't required, well that's probably quite a desirable place to be. So that's something we need to do, facilities management for team leaders in central. (Public library service/record office)

Handling and salvaging damaged items was frequently cited to us as a training need – …That's one of the things they all want more training on … It's one of thing they all said they've had training on, but they want more. (National museum)

I think the key thing from my point of view for the Record Office is more training in salvage techniques. We have got so many different formats and material here and we are not necessarily, our conservator certainly isn't anyway, we're not necessarily specialists in all of these formats, for example film archives, we are only just beginning to get support from the local film archive, but it's not immediately accessible for us so we've got to know what you do with film, how it's affected and you have to obviously respond quickly. We have sound archives, every type of photograph you could imagine and everything else, and now electronic records, and I don't think, I'm sure we are not all familiar with the latest recommendations for salvage techniques. I must say our conservator hasn't really had much up to date training ... so we could really do with more up to date conservation expertise. (Public library service/record office)

one thing that we did that we did agree and identify was there was a need for hands-on salvage training ... I'm certainly hoping that come the autumn time that will happen. (National record office/National museum)

... maybe that's an area [salvage techniques] where we need to do some training with people like the cleaners and the security men because if some people come across a pile of wet papers they might think, I'll put them on the radiator to dry them out, that would be then natural reaction for quite a lot of people and maybe some very, very basic salvage training might be useful. (Public library service/record office)

Given that most disasters involve water it's important that cultural institutions understand the [effect of] mould after the event. Ventilation, plastic being used, use absorbent materials, freeze things to buy time. Can freeze almost anything if you have to – often better than alternative. Not all conservators appreciate that. Freeze drying v vacuum drying – can get that in half a day. (International conservation expect)

The whole aspect of disaster management that isn't covered in training for the museum sector is salvage. And it's what people assume they're going to be doing. If you ask people to write an emergency plan, they think you mean a salvage plan, rather than how you man and structure that, which is what the emergency response plan is. Salvage comes second. There's more training on writing the plan than there is on salvage. Quite a lot of training I've come across says you shouldn't salvage unless you've been trained because you can do more harm than good. But there's no one doing that training. If you work for the [national organization], you get that training . But where does the museum profession go? I've got various conservators, that we can call on in an emergency. And lots of people would assume that they would come in and assist with salvage. But a lot of people on that list, as far as I'm aware have never done any salvage training. And it's not something you do as part of a conservation degree. It may be 12 years out of date, but when I did my degree there was nothing about emergency planning on my degree course. (Local Authority museum)

Salvage and Conservation

Along with the need for training in handling and salvaging damaged materials, there was a general concern about salvage – how to go about it, how to deal with different formats so as not to cause more damage, but to facilitate conservation treatment. The concern also included getting documentation relating to salvage right so as to keep track of items during the various stages. There was also a need to understand better the conservation treatment options available for different media.

> Curatorial staff did the training last year – about how to handle objects and so, certainly here when our new emergency plan is in place it'll be training the whole organisation on the plan itself, so how to use it in case of an emergency and then from that bring in some conservators to do how do you deal with wet objects, burnt objects, that sort of thing. Bring in the fire service to do chatting to them and explain what they would do, and I think do some more basic handling training and keep that as an ongoing training policy. (Independent museum)

> One thing I'd nail, is this – the whole issue of treatment and stabilisation, freezing, etc. There's a lot of guidance at events and in the literature. You need to have that conversation with an emergency company at the beginning, i.e. before anything happens – what are the options? We've had a contractor in to give a presentation – one of things they said they could do is come in as Project Manager. For example, they could do the 'dirty' stuff, e.g. contaminated water, and our staff could focus on other things. (National library)

> The bit that I find personally difficult, thinking about it without actually ever having tried it, is how to maintain control over the contents, the archival contents that you're drying or moving or spreading about, if they're badly labelled and packaged for example, lots of loose papers, that's the bit that I can't quite get my head around, and that's the bit I'd like to try out with the next simulation. (University archive)

> Have to decide in a triage system – have to empower people to do their own triage. If you don't know, don't do it, you may do harm – may not have that option in a disaster situation. Some of the things you do to stabilise – short term – can cause problems long term, but … (International museum and library)

> What we do well, I think, is the arrangements for salvage is done well, the understanding of material is good, whether it be the vellums, parchments, paper, books, we have experts at hand who know how to react to situations. We have considered it, we have situations set up, we have areas set up for air-drying, for freeze drying, for freezing. (National library)

Well, we were all sent a template, I wrote the risk assessment, the call out trees, the chain of command kind of things. And all the backups – we've got lists of contractors and procedures, things like that. And then what I decided to do was, I gave a presentation to all the staff at a staff briefing and tried to explain what we were trying to do. And asked people to volunteer to be on the business continuity plan call out list. We got a really good response. Lots of people gave me their contact details, and we also arranged sort of, small workshops – handling art, taught the staff how to take works down, how to wrap works. (National museum)

Space

In order to undertake salvage activities, it is important to have safe and appropriate space to work in. This is not easy to find in most institutions.

… that's what people are finding, they don't realise how much space they need in situations really. (National museum and gallery)

The other issue I suppose was, I don't know whether I'm quite answering your question again, but space within the college to expand into in the event, is a bit of an issue … Even when it didn't affect the contents significantly, just moving all the boxes out, re-boxing lots of things, laying some of it out to make sure it was dry and so on, required quite a lot of space, because we were trying to do it in that storage area. (University archive)

The first thing we immediately realised [in a simulation exercise] is how much space you need to deal with the aftermath of a disaster. We ran out of space within about two minutes. (Public library service/record office)

… security, dealing with things in a safe area, actually salvaging things, and sort of recording things … (National heritage organisation)

Staff

There is a need to keep up staff motivation with regard to all stages of disaster management. Managing staff and being aware of the pressures on them post-incident is vital.

… management training, in terms of dealing with people, how to handle people in what could be fraught situations, the whole interpersonal relationship when maybe you're dealing with someone who in a structural, organisational sense – you've got to be aware a lot of these organisations are quite hierarchical – where potentially in a situation you've someone at a relatively low grade telling someone who's maybe three or four grades above them what to do. So it's management in a very, very ... that kind of personal communication, interpersonal skills training, if there is such a thing, some people can do it naturally, other people will never be able to do it, but I do think some people can be taught to do it. The psychological aspect of a situation which can be fraught and nerve-wracking and make people behave differently than they would on a day-to-day basis, I think there's got to be awareness raising of that as well. Basically, the human context. (National record office/National museum)

There will be a range of people and roles to manage:

I think, really, the way they're chosen is the jobs they do. People in finance, we need to have access to money, and I need to get this company in that will cost money. ICT manager because of course information technology, the estates manager, buildings, that's very complex, health and safety manager because of the risks, preservation and conservation because of the material so all of our roles, we're all key players. (National library)

Not all institutions will have this staffing capacity though:

And we, like everybody else, are so short-staffed, everybody is wearing ten hats, as they call it, and then to add other responsibilities onto that, it's very difficult. We have one conservator and one conservation technician at the moment, and that's it. And it would be her, she would have to direct any kind of effort that went on. (International museum)

Some institutions reward staff for involvement in disaster teams, for example.

One thing that comes up in training days is what's expected of staff. Some are prepared to lay down their life for collections, but will it be safe, will I get paid? There's an HR element. There are cases where it is too much to go in – not insured, for example. material. (Commercial disaster management service)

... I arranged as part of the last pay deal for everyone who's a qualified first aider to get an additional half-day's annual leave a year. It's only half a day, it didn't cost us anything really but it was seen that we were looking after the people who'd volunteered to do something. So doing things like that really, you know, if you're helping us ... (National gallery)

There was a dip last year, in that there were folk on the disaster reaction team who pulled out. Goodwill was lost. I don't know what exactly happened. What happens is, within the administrative grades there can be a high turnover of staff. The younger element coming in and almost refusing point blank – it's not in my job description to do this sort of thing – and we were finding it very difficult to get volunteers. We had made a proposal, which didn't go down particularly well, that perhaps they should be given some sort of bonus payment, a one off payment. It wasn't until the November flood that that proposal then was put back on the table, not that it interfered in anyway, as we were able to get sufficient people out to deal with that particular flood, but I was thinking to myself, what if it were to happen at the end of this year, would we have a core number of people? We then got our new corporate services head to investigate the detailed policies on pay and conditions and he found out it was ok to go ahead. It's the case now that those on the disaster reaction team will get a one off payment of £200. (National record office/National museum)

Due regard must be paid to health and safety of staff during reaction and recovery stages.

One of the key things in our reaction plan is that people's safety is more important than the safety of the building or its contents. Bur given that history seems to indicate that disaster is more likely to happen when the building is shut than open, it's the people who are on site when the building's not formally open to the public who are likely to be the first people to come across it and have to deal with it, so that would be the security staff, the cleaners. So that is an area where we need more training. (Public library service/record office)

Attention should also be paid to staff's physical ability to undertake some tasks.

We had an incident not so long ago, where we closed for a day for a bombing. Head office and HR handled that very well. One interesting point from the last incident, from the volunteers list was about [fitness for] physical work. It was noticed that the volunteers were over 40 or 50. (HE college library)

Conservators

Conservators have key roles to play in disaster control planning and in dealing with incidents. In some areas of the UK a shortage of conservators was reported. In the UK and the US, interviewees reported that there was a need for conservators to have advanced training in dealing with the aftermath of major disasters.

… if you do have an emergency then probably the most valuable person that you can have is a conservator who can assess whether paper needs to be freeze dried or whether it will actually air-dry. I think that's all, you know what to do with wet photographs, and I think you can have all the kind of plans you like but actually need all that expertise on the ground. (National MLA)

Absolutely, with sprinklers and things like that. We got them [conservators] down to do a talk for senior management down here in the early '90s. And the senior management, under our Estates department, because I really wanted us to be seriously considering the installation of sprinkler systems when we renovated or even created new stores. (National museum)

Well, I think, in [country] we have relatively few qualified conservators so I think we have a sort of issue with expertise ... Well I think that's the normal situation in [country] there are very, very few conservators employed in either museums or archives, none that I'm aware of outside the national library in libraries. But we also have very few freelance conservators, I'm not sure exactly how many but I'd be surprised if it was more than half a dozen in the whole country. (National MLA)

The other issue ...and this is an issue which is much broader than just in relation to disaster issues, is the shortage of conservators. There are very few conservators on the ground within [country]. (National record office/National museum)

... and we also deal conservation wise with the Conservation Centre in Liverpool so they would be our first port of call, and also the Lancashire Conservation Service that was formed out of what was the North West Museum Service Conservation Department. So as far as conservators to call we've got quite a strong list. (Independent museum)

Again, just as a conservator, working as an assistant conservator before coming here, part of being a conservator, is having some involvement in disaster planning. In that case, I did a little bit of it as part of my training course, and we did have some training at the record office that I was working at, some hands on training there, and I did have some input into the disaster plan that was being created there at that time. But beyond that, I've not had any kind of formal training, just read around the subjects a little bit, and been on odd, usually practical-based training courses, that's it. (University archive)

Sustainability

Once a plan and related activities are in place it is important to sustain this – this is not always straightforward.

The dilemma is how to keep the momentum up – and time – getting everyone together and away from their day jobs. (National library)

Training was fine when we started – people come along – but the more regularly you do them, the more people cry off (for genuine reasons). We had sessions in the Exhibition Galleries – to see how to open cases and get things out – we've had two but we still have six people to do. So we have to do it 3 times before progress is made. And, you can tell people different things in different sessions leading to inconsistencies – and we <u>are</u> supported by management so [it must be] more difficult for those trying to get it on the agenda. (National library)

In relation to emergency planning, my priority for other staff is trying to keep training relating to the emergency response plan still on the radar. It is to keep them informed, to make sure they remember that it exists. I think it's important that it's not the kind of training we just do once, it needs to happen every 2–3 years. I would hope that I have the opportunity to talk to new staff as they arrive, to make them aware of the emergency planning, but at least doing training – it picks them up. It always reminds the staff who've been here for sometime that it's still here, it's still relevant, it's still something they need to know. It's not something other people do, everyone needs to buy into it. I hope I'm managing to keep it on the seasonal induction plan for the season staff at the community museums. As far as I'm concerned, I'm the person maintaining and coordinating the plan, I'm concerned to make sure I keep up with current thinking. At the moment I feel I'm up to speed, but thinking may change in the next five years, say that we need to focus more on business continuity. You need to think about salvage and how to keep the museum going, so I need to go on more training to understand how to do it. (Local Authority museum)

Various methods are employed to address this issue.

There's continual risk assessments, going on all the time, that's the strategy of the library, we do look at risks on a regular basis. So, disaster planning does come into my remit but it's always part of our business continuity planning group. (National library)

Formalising – training planned for next 18 months, something every or every other month – will involve kick up the backside stuff – this is key/core. And, going back to basics – with everyone. For example, no-one had explained to me how Estates emergency procedures worked and I cascaded it to everyone – there is an assumption you know. There was a distinct gap. I could go to 1-day courses on writing a disaster control plan or how to train other people, but not in salvage training. (National library)

One of the problems with training is actually thinking of doing something different each year, isn't it? Because we don't want to do the sort of wet books every year, we did it for about three years on the trot and then … it's boring for them to come here and do the same thing, we need to think of something different. (University library)

One year we did a simulation exercise, we set a scene, there was fire in the west wing of the library … what do you do, somebody phones Jill, Jill's had three bottles of wine! It did also catch people locally with the disaster plan, who would call who, and what might happen and whether they might have to go and move it, what they might have to take with them, what they might… and as I say, none of this is perfect but I suppose it's different ways of getting people to think about it and pay a bit of attention. (University library)

Collaboration/Networks

Responses to the UK questionnaire survey revealed that managers' perception of formal or informal with regard to networks was not uniform. A third of managers said their archive/library/museum was part of at least one formal or informal network. One interviewee from a national MLA commented:

I think it's disappointing actually the extent to which they [archives, libraries and museums] don't seem to be joining up and working. I think that's an area that we would like to try and foster and encourage and not just within a single authority but across authority boundaries as well.

Interviewees revealed the advantages of collaboration and networks but also acknowledged the difficulties involved in setting up and maintaining them. The latter seems to lead to informal arrangements at local level with individuals and their local contacts central to this.

Advantages include sharing information, offering/receiving advice, learning from others, mutual assistance and the availability close at hand of staff with expertise and experience to help in the immediate aftermath of an incident:

… we have, in [country], a sort of a semi formal/informal linkage with all heritage organisations that have got conservators or people interested in conservation. So that's libraries, archives, National Trust, institutional museums, private museums, private conservators. I organise a sort of newsletter and conferences and programmes like that so that we have an informal arrangement whereby we can call on these people very quickly or they can call on us for help. We tend to act as the centre because we're biggest … So I suppose we act as more of a leader in the field than we do as a coordinator. (National museum and gallery)

In terms of cooperation, the two immediate levels of cooperation that come to my mind – one is learning from each other, information sharing, and the second is helping each other in a worst case scenario. I'm sure there are others, but the learning from each other, there's a limit to what you can actually do through a formal group. It boils down to people … (National record office/National museum)

... most of the advice networking that we've done so far has been based with people. You know, firstly linking up with people who you know and they know that I've done a lot of work and they might come to me for how do you do this, or whatever. But we are a national organisation, which is really pretty well resourced, particularly in comparison to some of our regional neighbours and so certainly we do give advice when asked for. X is a good example because we gave a lot of advice about emergency planning ... We would be more than happy to make that advice more generally available to maximise the use of public funded resources, but also to learn from others. It's a two-way thing isn't it, we don't know all of it ... I might have missed out on really hearing what other people are doing and that might be more efficient than this. (National museum)

To save reinventing the wheel and that sort of thing but it's really that sort of learning opportunity. And of course, actually on a practical basis, do all of the regional museums know that we're here and around, and we need to develop our systems whereby people can, even if it's only on a voluntary basis know that we're here and know our telephone numbers in the middle of the night as in their own museums? But I'm sure most of us here would on a personal basis be quite willing to go out and help in the middle of the night. And also we might well need their help in the middle of the night, you know. An enormous number of benefits that we could be gaining from that sort of partnership (National museum)

... all the details of our grants programme are on our website ... But in terms of eligibility, in addition to individual archives, museums and libraries we do also support professional networks. So there are, for example in [county], a group of museums that work together and we have funded disaster-planning there, boxes of equipment for them to share. (National MLA)

... we do have quite close contact with the university that's next door ... we do actually have quite a close contact with the university and ... under the present emergency plan if our people get called out they actually congregate on the university site next door, next to one of their buildings, and then get called on here. And we are in discussions with them about having a kind of backup control room facility, for them and for us. So that if the library were to be burning down we could have a room in their place with loads of telephones. And then if they were in trouble they could use one of our rooms as a kind of a command place. We aren't a member of anything more regional than that, as far as I am aware. (National library)

Difficulties in establishing formal arrangements include time it can take within bureaucratic organisations, personal drive and relationships between individuals, and staff turnover. Some institutions, by their nature, may feel self-sufficient.

This is an informal group of local authority, universities, national museums, business archives that get together just to discuss problems where we can, such as collection policy agreements. Some years ago we discussed whether there was any possibility of setting up a formal agreement, but I think the general feeling was that it would be difficult to get a formal agreement signed up to. I think part of the problem is that a lot of the members of the group are not at a particular high or senior level in their organisations so it would mean getting their line managers and their line manager's manager to agree. So we have a very informal understanding that if one of us had a disaster we would do our best to chip in by sending a conservator over or any staff we had to spare, share some supplies if we could, but it is an informal understanding. We try and keep in touch and if anyone had been on any recent training or has any new information then they will share it with the group. (Public library service/record office)

… archive or museum, libraries, galleries, we all have common problems, and there are common solutions to those problems, but those common solutions are never actually looked at. I think a lot of it has got to do, quite simply, with people. They're not prepared to look beyond their walls to see what other people are doing and how you can actually collaborate, either because they're so engrossed and the culture of the organisation is so inward looking, and I think that is a characteristic that most cultural bodies do suffer from, or because the people who are involved in these activities tend to be the same people over thirty years, because once you have a specialism you stay there, there's nowhere else to go, if you have a situation where someone can't abide someone else, nothing happens. It doesn't happen here, thankfully, because we know each other, we respect each other, I think we like each other, but I think the effect of those personal contacts is seriously underestimated, be they beneficial effects or negative. (National record office/National museum)

Probably not for us in so far as we are x sites spread all over the whole [country] and therefore, just the shear spread means that we have to really think of ourselves as x museums, each with its own disaster plan and each of whom would be reasonably self sufficient if there was an emergency because it's truly unlikely that anything will happen that will cover, be a disaster on all x sites, basically if it does, it's Armageddon. So we try and make the sites pretty well independent of each other and to organise their own contacts. There has been the MLA, they have tried to make some initiatives whereby we have some kind of centralised services but it's not worked out terribly well and it goes out of date very quickly. Things like transport and our electricity supplies and freezer units and this kind of thing. But it's pretty difficult for them to maintain so they've stopped it. (National museum and gallery)

We try to get formal liaison with the county record office conservator who was very willing, herself, to be there, to be in the plan as an out of hours number as well as a work time number, so if I wasn't available, for example, they could call on a conservator of another institution to help guide them through actual salvage, that was the idea. But it was very difficult at the time to get it through the county archivist, effectively sign this letter and say yes – it just didn't happen and it went on for ages, so in the end I just gave up on that really. We've got an informal agreement, which I have actually put together. Basically, it's the same agreement, it's basically that the conservator here, myself and the one at the county record office both agree to help each other out, and we've both given each other our out of hours numbers as well, although it's not formally agreed. (University archive)

We sort of reached a conclusion that, with the possible exception of X, almost every institution who is a member of [local library collaborative network] has more than one primary site and it would be the second primary site that would, as it where, take the burden in the event of a disaster. We have one big site but we also have a network of 23 smaller community libraries as well, also institutional buildings and offices too. (Local Authority library service/record office)

I think in an ideal world it's fabulous, I think it would just be really hard to make it work in practical terms, because everybody's so busy and … we plan for disasters, you never quite know what it is that you're planning for, you never know quite what you'll be dealing with. We have quite a big staff turnover, perhaps the wrong term, there's quite a lot of internal promotion. There is quite a bit of people moving around the sites and sometimes the disaster teams change, you might get one of the people change and then find that a third of them had moved on the following year. (University library)

Even where initiatives are begun, getting momentum and sustaining this can be an issue as the following example illustrates:

At the moment it's a talking shop and we really need the focus now. We haven't had a meeting in about five or six months and it's the longest period of time since we've had a meeting but there's been, to an extent, a reason for that. We've had a lot on here, and what I certainly want to do over the next couple of months is sit down and actually look at the issues and figure out what could be used as a driver to move things along to stop the status quo. We need something to drive us forward. We've discussed the issues, we've learnt an awful lot, I've certainly learnt a lot from the National Trust, for example in the way that they do business. Much in the same way, to a certain extent, we work our own disaster plan, I think we need to now set the things what is do-able and we need to sit down and say, 'what are the priorities, what can people sign up to?' and make it bite sized … (National record office/National Museum)

The same institution, trying to lead a network, also points to the need for real partnerships that achieve, i.e., they are not just in name only.

> ... read any government museum document, archive document, library document – it will talk about partnerships. I think that this drive towards partnerships, in theory as a means of sharing information, mutual help and cooperation, the hidden agenda I think, is two people, two groups doing the something will be cheaper. It doesn't always work that way and I think the drive towards partnerships is part of this. I happen to think that [country] could, if this was handled in the right way, become a model for cross-domain working. Disaster issues, crisis management issues, crisis care issues. Because there is a relatively small, well defined geographical location and there are relatively few organisations that you've got to deal with. True partnership ... if it's handled properly, demonstrating how it could work and providing a model that the nation or regions within the nation could refer to. I think at the moment, often my concern, when I see partnership I think, this is the cynic in me ... It ticks the boxes. Partnerships have been established, but it doesn't go beyond that to say, what's that partnership doing? And how are the organisations who are part of this partnership demonstrably benefiting from it? It's just that there is a partnership in place. (National record office/National museum)

Business/Service Continuity

In the UK questionnaire survey, only a third of managers (32 per cent) reported that their archive/library/museum plans for service continuity. Archives/libraries/ museums in the National institution category (73 per cent) are most likely to plan for service continuity, with nearly half of archives/libraries/museums where there is a written disaster control plan (47 per cent) also planning for it. Those managers who had received training in providing service continuity and access placed higher importance than others on liaising with civil emergency planners, on the availability of equipment and supplies and on training. A higher proportion of these managers than expected saw arrangements for terrorist threats, vandalism, liaison with civil emergency planners, preparation and review of disaster control plans, availability of equipment and supplies, and training as very satisfactory.

The benefits of training in business/service continuity seem apparent, but many institutions do not practise this and some of those who do are in the early stages and determining what it involves.

> I think one of the outcomes of it was that a lot of them weren't sure what Business Continuity Planning was – they thought that what we'd done with our disaster plan, that was it, there was nothing else to do ... But I think that most senior managers now are aware of what Business Continuity Planning is and what needs to be done. (National gallery)

To be honest at the moment, I don't think people are thinking beyond getting everything in place, you know, in terms of having a recovery plan. Business continuity's probably a step nearer. Colleague: I suspect a lot of authorities may well have business continuity plans because, well we have to produce one, but it was done separately from the disaster plan because the local authority didn't really seem to see much value in the disaster plan looking after the objects; their concern is to keep the services working and keeping the staff employed and that's really what the business continuity plan was about, so they were separate documents. (National MLA)

We've had the disaster plan in place for something like eight years but it was totally revised and rewritten about two years ago ... but we haven't actually got any further with the Business Continuity side of it. We're in the process of it. It's a thing that, really, means that the [institution] have to make somebody responsible for business continuity planning and that was never my goal. My responsibility really, was disaster planning which I was qualified to do but what they're looking at is introducing or giving somebody that's got a part time role as risk manager. It may be me, but if it is going to be me then obviously they have to change my job description and take some of the other work I do away from me if they want me to do it right. (National gallery)

Business continuity planning has to fit in with corporate plans and arrangements.

Importance of integration into corporate disaster planning and business continuity. Risk assessment is they key to contingency planning. (University library)

Our service continuity plans feed into the corporate major incident plan (Public library service)

There's continual risk assessments, going on all the time, that's the strategy of the library, we do look at risks on a regular basis. So, disaster planning does come into my remit but it's always part of our business continuity planning group. (National library)

Its advantages are apparent to those who practice it especially with regard to external factors that might influence business or service continuity. They can be seen in the following comments as can tips on how to go about it.

... we're lucky in so far as the new collections centre, as I say, is fitted out both to handle an IT emergency to relocate essential staff like paying my wages and to handle collections as well. And we would use that for you know, a switch between the major sites. Within this site we would assume that if there's a major hazard in one area, because the building is virtually symmetrical we would transfer to the other side. So, it's all a bit theoretical and it sounds good in theory but at least we thought about it perhaps and thought, 'Well, yes we can re-establish our accounts systems, our finance systems, our IT systems, our conservators within the other areas'. (National museum and gallery)

Looking at avian flu – pre-pandemic planning. I am going to this big course and conference in London, Pre pandemic planning preparation and business continuity meeting … and my IT section head is going to that one there, which is a similar big national thing focusing on IT. So we don't know about avian flu, it's on the horizon, it goes beyond what we've been talking about really to a certain extent because it's talking about the staff themselves – many of them not being available. But what we are doing on that is we are increasing the facilities for people to work from home. We've got staff at the moment who can access their emails from home. What we're hoping to be able to do is to enable them to get into their files, their folders, the documents they created, which will mean we can carry on quite a lot of work. But this is where the web will be important as well. But obviously physical access would be heavily restricted. Because we're so heavily into IT … it's all to do, so much now to do with IT, so we're just contracted by a big new computer system which will take us on a stage as well. So that touches on training and other disasters. Disasters of a different nature really because most of the other things we've talked about have been where something happens in the building rather than a massive loss of staff or where we just say to staff, well it's better if you just stay at home. (National library)

Lots of people did make it in. But we've had a couple of incidents recently. The bomb delayed all the trains, cancelled the transport network. When we had that really bad bout of snow, one Sunday a few months ago, staff couldn't get into work then. And we've had the XX line closed, and there were those type of problems with [local] travel, and there were those tunnel strikes. So I feel fairly battered in terms of transport disaster. (Public library service/record office)

It is more concentrated on physical disasters. Now the staff, myself and the supervisors have the experience of going to decide that we aren't going to open the galleries if we haven't got enough staff because of the insurance and the risk. And also, if office staff can help out on the galleries as well – we've asked for volunteers in the past to help out. There's nothing formally written down there. But we've talked about the bird flu issue. How, if 50 per cent of staff couldn't make it in, office and front of house staff, how we'd make the decision when to close. We decided we could only make those decisions at the time, taking in account the circumstances that were happening. We couldn't particularly plan for things now, but we talked about people work from home using laptops; and training people how to access the website from home. And perhaps – people have moved around, people who used to work on the switch board now do different jobs, so they could perhaps cover something. (National museum)

… we're doing this in consultation and we're being advised and facilitated by our insurers, [to produce] a service continuity plan … At the moment, what we're focusing on is a disaster that could happen in transit. So we're looking at the transportation element of the operation. I was working on that this morning, we're looking at scenarios such as a road traffic accident, single and multiple, a vehicle fire, vehicle breakdown, hijacking (for example, if people knew what was being moved) … So, we're looking at those scenarios, we have a plan to minimise the possibility of them happening, and we've got an operational plan which is broken down into time phases and people, about who does what in the first hour, who does what in the next twelve hours, who does what in twenty four hours. We're looking at that in relation to transport, and when the dust settles and we get into our new storage accommodation which will be at the end of the year, we will be developing that generic approach into the storage. (National record office/National museum)

I did find the DCMS one [guidance on business continuity (DCMS 2005)] a little over-complicated. It's how they actually put one together … It's the idiots' guide to business continuity plans. I wouldn't say it's an idiot's guide … you'd need to be a genius to understand it … It is quite over-complicated, we tried to go more towards flowcharts. When you come down to business continuity, obviously you can get into more detail because you have more time in theory to do a lot of this and a lot of people looking at running the emergency planning side of things. That's the way we try to break up emergency planning is that the emergency plan should consist of just one page of flowchart, this is what you do, and the rest of our emergency plan is really just saying this is your job, in this situation, at this level. (National museum)

… it would depend which building it happened in. Certainly if it had happened in one of our stores it wouldn't really be an issue worrying about keeping access open for visitors but if it happened in one of our public venues then it is a major issue but it is probably one that is wise for me to leave up to others. It is being questioned but I have to admit I'm not too sure where they're up to on that. My feeling I have to say is it's probably something that we could learn a lot about from benchmarking and other organisations who have learnt a great deal. Again, rather than reinventing the wheel I'd really like to see what sort of major commercial organizations do, how they've approached business continuity. (National museum)

There must be a strong relationship between the business continuity plan and the disaster control plan as the following from one institution demonstrates.

Well, we've actually got two things. We've got two documents that help to explain it. One is we've got an emergency plan, which is really as much as we can think of anything to do with what would happen if almost anything happened – if we didn't have electricity, if we didn't have gas, iIf we had a fire. Who gets called in? What detailed services would be used to try and, for instance, freeze the collections if they got water on them? Loads of stuff like that. And we've also got an emerging Business Continuity Plan which is more, slightly more limited really – business continuity strategies which we haven't actually finalised yet. Which is more to do with how we would keep key services going and it prioritises the activity so, I think, it says for instance, that there has to be an element of finance because you would have to keep on paying people to do something. We'd need to try and keep the website going because lots of people access information through the website. We'd have to think about how we would physically maintain some sort of provision. But we wouldn't for instance see opening the exhibition areas as being a top priority. And we wouldn't probably see continuing cataloguing of materials. The business continuity plan focuses on the key bits of the business that we have to continue somehow. The emergency plan tries to go wider than that and almost look at everything you know. It would be freezer vans, where they come around and pick up materials and collections and then what company's might help to drive them out. That sort of thing. (National library)

… the technical side to assist us in location of staff is the bit that came out of the exercise most. Looking wider at disaster management, the other thing that we talked about as part of our business continuity planning is possibly getting a generator – buying a generator. So if you define the disaster as you know, the electricity fails in the whole area for more than an hour or so, then we are able to provide something into the system to run the computers. Because of our big use, we are so dependant on IT now for our catalogues … all of our indices have been computerised … And then the other thing is we've got the web access which is lots of people accessing material through the web and accessing basic information about the library through the web. And we also are storing vast quantities of material digitally now because we've digitised, for instance, our picture collection, we've got about 4000 pictures here. We've got much more than books. We've got manuscripts, photographs, audio visual stuff and films and loads and loads of things. And the pictures have all been digitised and that's what people can access, one of the things people can access, and we want to make sure we don't lose that. So, the storage servers are key. So, that's all just saying why we are, one of our areas of improvement is we are aiming to be getting a generator in the next year to keep us going for a bit longer. .So it's the maintenance, it's the IT maintenance … and finance. Having to keep the IT going, which means keeping the web going … But the business continuity plan is a new thing actually. (National library)

Conclusion

It is evident that effective disaster management must have the support of senior management. It ought to be integrated into overall institutional management. It requires adequate funding – this can be an issue in large and small institutions alike. Activity varies according to the type and size of institution. Buildings and their maintenance are a cause for concern across the board. The occurrence of a disaster, especially if highly publicised, can have a motivational impact on the institution and others to initiate disaster management practices. Region-wide disasters, in particular, can highlight this by underlining the need for in-house resources and plans. Identification of local experts who may be able to help is advisable as is subscription to an external disaster recovery company. The role of training is highly valued and recommended – it provides confidence to those who may be involved in a real disaster. Salvage of damaged items and their conservation was an area where those had been involved in this, wanted further training. The welfare of staff dealing with the aftermath of a disaster is paramount – due account must be paid to health and safety measures and psychological impact. Archives, libraries and museums need to look beyond the sector for lessons. Business continuity is an area that institutions need to develop and where such an approach will help. Where effective disaster management is in place, attention must be paid to its sustainability. New threats need to be identified and incorporated in plans.

A wide range of institutions and individuals from around the world have participated in the various aspects of the research. They have generously provided comment, offered advice, passed on lessons learned and shared their expertise and experience with the authors. They encouraged us, we hope that their words in this chapter, help put what some might regard as theory very much into practice – what actually goes on in archives, libraries and museums. We hope their words, advice and critical comments inspire others as they did us.

References

Anderson, H. and McIntyre, J. E. (1985) *Planning manual for disaster control in Scottish libraries and record offices*, (Edinburgh: National Library of Scotland).

Craig, R., Selzer, T. and Seymour, J. (2006), 'There is disaster planning and there is reality – the Cayman Islands National Archive (CINA) experience of Hurricane Ivan', *Journal of the Society of Archivists* 27:2, 187–99.

DCMS, Business Continuity Planning Guide. Business as usual. A step by step guide to introducing and maintaining a business continuity plan, (London, DCMS), (published online 2005). <http://www.culture.gov.uk/images/working_with_us/10231stegbystepguide.pdf>, accessed 20 Sep. 2008.

Chapter 7
Planning for the Future

Introduction

Throughout the book issues relating to various aspects of disaster management have been identified and discussed. Lesson learned by those in a range of roles involved in disaster management have been incorporated in that. This chapter, based on findings of the research project, and activity since it was completed, summarises key achievements and then moves on to identify aspects of disaster management that need be addressed in planning future activity relating to archives, libraries and museums. Recent and current initiatives are provided as examples of what can be achieved.

Principles Established

The research has underlined that the basics of disaster management for archives, libraries and museums are established. One of our interviewees, inadvertently perhaps, has testified to this:

> ... the book that I think is the best, is the 'Planning Manual for Disaster Control, Scottish Libraries and Record Office', that was written by Anderson and McIntyre, [published in] 1985, I think. That was done 20 years or so ago, and nothing much has changed. It's a great account of disaster preparedness. (National library)

There have been considerable achievements as the three aspects below illustrate, but they equally underline that there is no room for complacency.

Disaster Control Plan

The disaster plan is now generally acknowledged as the blueprint for action, a framework for activity that is at the heart of effective disaster management. Not all institutions, however, have a disaster control plan, and of those that do only a minority regularly undertake exercises to test it. Most institutions that have experienced a disaster reported that there plan was effective. Others qualify this though, noting that in a major disaster it can 'go out of the window' but also acknowledge that the activities involved in putting it together gave them somewhere to start and the confidence to work together to deal with the disaster.

Information and Guidance

There is much published information and guidance available on many aspects of disaster management. Increasingly, this has been disseminated on the Internet. Some have expressed the view that there is too much information and it is difficult to find what is relevant to their situation in the event of a disaster. Others use this to underline that it is necessary to include identification of relevant sources and reading them in the preparedness stage of the disaster control plan. Many sources, in fact, refer, to the same publications and websites. It is often worth talking to others to seek their views on what they have found useful. Many of our respondents referred to sources they found particularly useful. For example, in the UK

> …what I found to be most helpful was the M25 Consortium, and in a sense we took the M25 template and developed that … we looked at some other plans as well that we were able to borrow from people like [local national museum and university library] (Public library service)

> … actual experience, and also I suppose taking to people … over the years. colleagues attending the NPO conferences. One person I remember was X from [institution] and that's how I picked up the idea of the wind tunnels, which have proved to be invaluable. (National library)

> Very often, it's individuals. You know, phoning up the national museum, phoning up the national library … and asking what other people have done. (National library)

This approach can also help prevent people 'reinventing the wheel'. A MLA Adviser acknowledged how they approached this issue:

> I think it's actually sort of mediating the information. We've been working with a local studies library recently who are just starting from nowhere really in terms of their collections management. And, it was actually just sort of picking the half a dozen sites that would give them the kind of basic information they needed to get started but they were in danger of you know, just sort of typing stuff into Google and getting so many hits back, that they just couldn't actually navigate what was there, an authentic and reliable, professionally respected site. So a lot of [my] work is actually pointing people, getting them started, pointing them in the direction of the right place to look. (National MLA)

Training

Training is undertaken, and in a variety of forms, but it can be difficult for many institutions, especially small ones, to resource it and find time for staff to participate. In the UK, at a recent Museums Association (Lansdale and Matthews

2007) seminar on emergency planning, participants from large organisations such as English Heritage and The National Trust, Historic Royal Palaces informed the audience about their training programmes and EmmS REDS advised of their training activities. Participants from a range of institutions reported various providers of training, including consultants, disaster recovery companies, and in-house, and stressed that 'training should be practical and include frontline staff'.

This practical emphasis was a common theme in the comments of interviewees:

> At the end of the workshop, participants get a CD with the tools on, including photographs taken during the exercises, how to handle material, how to read maps of museums, risk perceptions, insurance, local traditions, that could mitigate against disaster, eg construction of building, use of essential oils in museums to avoid pests ... (International organisation)

> ... I [went] on the UCL "Surviving a disaster" course this January, which again gave me some new stuff, but also reinforced what I knew, so that's the main training I've had ... It was fantastic! It's one of the best courses I've been on. It looked at the whole run of emergency planning; it talked about writing an Emergency Plan and what needs to be in it, and then it moved on to salvage with a very practical salvage exercise. (Local Authority museum and gallery)

Recent region-wide disasters have highlighted a need for training for all staff in handling and salvaging damaged items and, for conservators, in selecting and applying appropriate conservation treatments. This need for experienced, trained and committed staff was again underlined in the aftermath of the flooding in England in 2007:

> It must also be noted that this event was part of a wider regional disaster and that we were fundamentally dependent on our own resources and staff team for support rather than any external agency. Without a large staff team able to react to the immediate situation and then commit time to the ongoing support of the salvage team, we ... would have lost a greater part of the collections in our care. (Chumbley 2008)

> Our contacts with and ability to source accredited conservators within the region to work with us from day two undoubtedly saved our collections. (Chumbley 2008)

Lessons Learned?

Whilst basic principles may have been established, how effectively are lessons shared and learned in practice? Accounts of experiences of disasters impacting on archives, libraries and museums appear in the literature and on websites – many reflect on their experience and offer lessons. Whilst institutional experiences will be different, there are lessons that are broadly applicable. There seems to be a growing recognition that it is important and useful to learn from disaster experiences *and* to share these. After Hurricane Katrina, the Library of Congress Preservation Directorate, in collaboration with FLICC [Federal Library and Information Center Committee] and the American Folklife Center interviewed ten of the conservator volunteers who went to help affected institutions, these have been made available on the Library of Congress *Learning from Katrina: Conservators' First-Person Accounts of Response and Recovery* website. The site also offers advice on recovery from various causes of disaster and insurance/risk.

In the UK, following severe flooding, the Heritage Lottery Fund, Yorkshire and Humberside, within weeks of the incident, organised a meeting of representatives from a range of heritage institutions where:

> ... We tried to capture many of the issues while they were still raw – while people were still happy to talk openly, before any blame games started and before people became reluctant to share their experiences while their insurers are watching ... (Spiers 2007, 1)

A report on the meeting suggests that it is not always the case that lessons are learned:

> Communication problems arise in emergency situations as mobiles can be taken off network to allow the emergency service uncluttered airways. This is something which could have been learned from the July 2005 London bombings. (Spiers 2007)

> Disaster planning in many heritage sites failed. What appeared adequate on paper did not work when tested, and had often neither been kept up to date nor practised. Disaster recovery plans appear to have been treated as compliance documents rather than being regularly reviewed as a working tool. (Spiers 2007)

Prevention and Preparedness

Recent large scale disasters have brought about a focus on the reaction and recovery stages of disaster management. This may be temporary but a key lesson is that prevention and preparedness activities should not be overlooked. Straightforward measures such as awareness and vigilance on the part of staff, and reporting procedures are important and need to be sustained:

> There should be an ongoing risk assessment of the building day by day, we don't do formal risk assessment because the building is walked by security staff, it is 24/7 security staffed and they have a thorough walk around every couple of

hours, there is close circuit TV so the building is monitored all the time. Any workers of contractors who come on site have to report to X's office and give a clear indication of what works they are undertaking, what the attached risks might or might not be ... (Public library service)

And vigilance really, in the storage areas, because that leak was something that had happened slowly, it wasn't an obvious thing, and it was a few days before it was noticed because someone happened to be going in there to work, but our cleaner/handyman, he's very good now, we always say, 'just let us know if you see anything', whether it's the insects, or strange patches on the wall or obviously water, and he is quite good at saying [something]. (University archive)

It's mostly environment only so we're talking temperature, humidity, not actual physical building. So had you been here on Tuesday, in fact, this area was completely blocked off because our new toilet sprung a leak and we had sewage spraying all over downstairs. So again, maybe if somebody was doing checks it could have been spotted. (Independent museum)

Institutional Resources

Likewise, it is important that those managing disaster planning in large institutions or where there is a parent organisation (for example, a local authority or university), identify any institution or organisation-wide plans, liaise with those responsible for these and make the most of in-house expertise where it exists. They should strike up relationships with individuals in the organisation who have key responsibilities relating to disaster management, for example, colleagues in charge of estates, finance, and explain the requirements of the archive, library or museum with regard to the different stages of disaster management. This will 'help them understand the real impact on the institution and its mission as a whole of an incident affecting the library [or archive or museum]. Experience indicates that it is not easy to do this in the throes of dealing with an emergency situation' (Matthews 2005, 62). This is often not the case for smaller institutions. The research has shown that small institutions do look to local larger institutions for assistance with disaster management, and indeed, larger institutions offer this in a variety of ways. Smaller institutions should look at possible local contacts and any regional agencies or networks and initiatives that might offer support.

Future Planning and Strategy

The following are aspects of disaster management that need to be addressed in determining strategy for the future. They are broad in coverage. They will apply, to varying degrees, to those leading or involved in disaster management at international, national, regional, local or institutional level. Likewise, whilst archives, libraries and museums have their own requirements, the research has shown that with regard to disaster management, they have much in common. No attempt is thus made to direct what follows at any one domain, or group, policy makers, civil emergency planners, conservators, for example. Those in the cultural heritage sector must develop dialogue with those outside with regard to disaster management, and vice versa. It is hoped that the way the book is arranged and the thematic approach of the section following will help those from different backgrounds identify items of particular interest to them but in the context of the bigger picture.

Working Together

As Taboroff (2003) has pointed out it is important that the cultural heritage sector does not move forward in isolation. It must work with others at all levels from international to local and this should be incorporated in strategy:

> Cultural heritage needs to be factored into overall disaster mitigation and management approaches. Cultural heritage professionals should make themselves known to disaster mitigation professionals and disaster mitigation professionals should invite the participation of heritage professionals in designing response systems. Effective preparedness and mitigation strategies will depend upon government agencies, heritage professionals, and emergency professionals working together … (239–40).

A recent *World Conference on Disaster Reduction* (UNESCO 2005) report echoes this:

> Most speakers indicated the need to integrate concerns for the cultural and natural heritage into the larger management process, not just for the benefit of the heritage, but also to enhance the preparedness for disasters … A number of presentations emphasized, through specific case studies, the close link between a sound management of cultural and natural heritage resources at the international, national, and local levels, and an enhanced preparedness for disasters … It is crucial … that a concern for cultural heritage be integrated into the general framework of development and planning, as well as into existing disaster management policies and mechanisms … The importance of research and training was also strongly highlighted … Along the same lines, networking and sharing of experience was discussed … several [other] important issues emerged including the need for bilateral and multilateral development agencies, to include cultural heritage risk management within their programmes, and the need to demonstrate the economic benefits of the heritage in order to raise financial support for conservation (1–2).

It is thus encouraging to read that objectives of a working conference of the ICBS in September 2006 included:

> ... to strengthen the network between the national Blue Shield Committees on the one hand and between Blue Shield and other cultural emergency assistance organizations on the other ... to improve Blue Shield's international visibility with institutions and authorities that are responsible for cultural heritage' and 'to stimulate joint operations and the efficient coordination of national initiatives. (ICBS *Announcement. Working conference 27–28 September 2006 The Hague, Netherlands.*)

Models and regional networks mentioned in Chapter 4 provide examples of moves towards this collaborative activity and how it can be approached nationally and regionally. The approach to climate change (see below) is also indicative of this. Some of the models in Chapter 4, have a strong central lead and control, others, however, are more regionally driven. In either case, working with others is both desirable and feasible. Some, however, feel there may be advantages of a national approach. This was a theme that came out of discussion at a recent Museums Association event:

> Advantages of national coordination: sharing experiences; networking across similar collections; standardising of equipment and economy of scale; specialist venues for specialist training; driven forward by legislation; more credibility if national e.g. if DCMS-led (Lansdale and Matthews 2007).

However, some concern was expressed: 'Disadvantage: does one size fit all?' (Lansdale and Matthews 2007). This question seemed to reflect a need for flexibility, to take into account local circumstances in any nationally coordinated scheme.

Beyond the Cultural Heritage – Getting on the Civil Emergency Agenda

A key issue in achieving the above is how to establish relationships with others outside the cultural heritage and to convince them of its needs. Factors involved in this are illustrated in extracts from a discussion about the future of disaster management published in a recent issue of the Getty Conservation Institute Newsletter (JIgyasu et al. 2008)

> ... The business community, for example, is thinking about how to build disaster-resistant communities and trying to create coalitions broader than ones they've considered in the past. I went to a U.S. Chamber of Commerce meeting last year and was the only representative from the cultural heritage community. They're thinking about schools and businesses and infrastructure, but they overlook the resources that we have to offer. It's not that they're hostile to us – they're

just not thinking about it. It's only recently that the Department of Homeland Security's National Response Framework, which has annexes for emergency response functions, incorporated cultural heritage into a function for protecting agriculture and natural resources. It's a long process to get our profile raised (Jane Long, Vice-president, Emergency Programs, Heritage Preservation, in Jigyasu et al. 2008)

You are very right to say that heritage is not on the agenda of overall disaster reduction. As you suggested ... disaster reduction is considered a much more humanistic discipline than in the past. There is a growing realization that disasters are not merely natural events to be resisted through technology but are inherently linked to social, developmental, and cultural aspects. Still, cultural heritage as a specific element in a disaster situation is not really addressed. Some initiatives have been taken in the recent past, but the participation of the wider disaster management community is very limited. We, the heritage professionals, are very happy to talk to one another, but the wider world of disaster management – which is huge – either is not interested or not aware that heritage has to be looked at in a specific manner. Coming back to the question that was posed as we started – there is a problem of perception, as heritage is still looked at in a very elitist manner. The question is often raised: "When people's lives are at stake, why are we talking about elitist things – monuments or some remains from the past – that have no relevance today?" The point here is that the whole definition of heritage is really different from the popular perception, no? We in the heritage professions are indeed stressing that the past has relevance in the present – that it is part of community resilience mechanisms and traditional knowledge systems. Therefore, heritage is not passive. Rather, it has an active role to play in reducing disasters. We have to disseminate this broader understanding of heritage to the wider disaster management community. (Rohat Jigyasu, a conservation architect and risk management consultant, in Jigyasu et al. 2008)

One way some have suggested of increasing the cultural heritage sector's profile is to stress to others its potential role, for example, economic and social, and impact in recovery from major incidents. Stanley-Price (2006) has referred to this in noting that the ICCROM Forum in 2005 demonstrated that

... cultural heritage does play an important role in recovery from situations of armed conflict (and, of course, of natural disasters). While humanitarian goals of adequate housing, food and health are supreme in the post-war period, these are most successfully accomplished when their cultural context is fully understood. Moreover, even in the midst of these basic human needs, in many post-war situations there is evidence of a popular concern for immediate restoration of war-damaged heritage and for the revival of obsolescent traditions. This concern seems to answer to a strong psychological need to re-establish the familiar and cherished following a phase of violent disruption of normal life. The crucial role of culture must be recognised and incorporated in the recovery process, for reasons both social and economic. (p.8)

Beyond the individual institution, in major disasters, there can be enormous economic impact. In areas where cultural heritage and tourism are important elements of the local economy, major disasters will cut this income flow. Additionally, in the aftermath and recovery, authorities may divert funding from archives, libraries and museums to help rebuild the wider infrastructure. Amarasiri (2005) in a report on rebuilding libraries in Sri Lanka after the tsunami identifies the kind of the challenges faced in such situations. These illustrate that some are generic and others specific to the circumstances, for example, trauma of librarians, conservation of damaged library material, working with government bureaucracy, working with non-governmental organisations, interaction with politicians, keeping libraries on the agenda, scarcity of land, and internal conflict. Shaheen (2007) writing about libraries after earthquake in Kashmir also touches on this.

It is thus important that archives, libraries and museums look beyond the cultural heritage sector and liaise with those involved in civil emergency planning and disaster management, and that they 'tap into' civil emergency services. In the last six or seven years, information from civil emergency planners for business (for example, business continuity, risk management) and the general public (for example, what to do in case of flooding) has become more widely available. In England, this has been in line with legislation such as the Civil Contingencies Act (2004) (Great Britain 2004). (For further information on the Act and its implications, see UK Resilience *Civil Contingencies Act*.)

Civil Emergency Planners   A good example of a website offering general advice on preparing for and dealing with the consequences of disasters is *Preparing For Emergencies. What you need to know* (HM Government). It is run by the Civil Contingencies Secretariat in the Cabinet Office, and managed by Cabinet Office Communication Group. It comprises the following sections:

- What you [individuals, families, communities] can do
- What Businesses can do
- What voluntary and community groups can do
- What the government is doing
- Advice on specific emergencies
- More information
- It also includes case studies relating to different types of disaster.

In the US, FEMA's website offers information and advice on the major stages of disaster management and mitigation (*Federal Emergency Management Agency*). It also offers links to cultural heritage sites (FEMA *Historic Preservation Useful Links*).

Some are already aware of the usefulness of working with civil emergency planners and others involved:

> There's a lot more scope for working with EPOs [Emergency Planning Officers] for the county. Get people together in a group. E.g. if we have a problem with access to a property, contact the police, they can sort [the roads] – it's all computerised. Fire brigade – [have] integrated risk management planning plan for possible incidents in area. (Heritage organisation)

but this practice needs to be extended.

Fire Service

It is important to seek advice from local fire services about fire prevention Legislation in different countries may determine the level of advice and interaction they can provide. In England participants in the research told of different levels of cooperation. Recent changes in legislation may have contributed to this. This was echoed by participants in a Museums Association seminar (Lansdale and Matthews 2007):

> There are differing responses from individual Fire and Rescue services in terms of the support, advice and willingness to work with museums and heritage organisations. Following recent fire legislation, there is a need to improve relationships with FRSs, working towards a uniformity of approach and standards and interviewees:

> Fire service legislation, Fire and Rescue Service Act brought in new dimension to the work ... A lot of change is going on. Went from intervention to prevention, the way brigades work. Some brigades won't give advice – will refer you to Yellow Pages for a consultant. They now have a responsibility for heritage in the Fire and Rescue [Services] Act (2004). They have to come up with a plan for dealing with heritage properties. The main change is property protection – reducing risk to persons and firefighters by protecting the property. And, a duty to mitigate risk against fire. (National heritage organisation)

The Fire and Rescue Services Act (Great Britain 2004), has given fire services more flexibility to work in partnership with others. The new fire safety rules, affecting all non-domestic and business premises (including charity and voluntary organisations) in England and Wales, were introduced in October 2006 (The Regulatory Reform (Fire Safety) Order 2005 (Great Britain 2005)) and under this responsible individuals must carry out risk assessments and implement a maintain a fire management plan. (For further information, see Communities and Local Government Fire and resilience. Fire safety law and guidance for business.)

In Scotland, a project begun in 2002 has been developing a database of fire risk information on all Category A-listed properties in the country. The project came out of the Scottish Historic Buildings Fire Liaison Group. It is managed by Historic Scotland, accommodated by the Royal Commission on Ancient and Historical Monuments of Scotland (RCAHMS) and is overseen by the Heritage Co-ordinator for the Scottish Fire Services (Haire and Sorensen 2006). A leaflet from Historic Scotland provides information about the project noting that the database will provide fire fighting crews with information about the importance and value of the buildings (Historic Scotland 2005), it also outlines fire risks and gives advice on prevention. The advantages of the scheme are explained by Coull (2006).

Emery (2008) outlines a project at English Heritage:

> Another development is to put the emergency plans on the internet. In this connection, EH is trialling a health and safety fire and security management system. This will allow individual sites to produce specific risk assessments that can be viewed centrally for audit purposes. It will also enable managers to produce emergency plans on a standard template, store them securely and print off copies for the site; again this can be audited centrally. These plans could be accessed by those fire and rescue services with the necessary equipment at the time of an incident. Although password-protected for security, the password could be released to the emergency services if necessary.

As is the case with Scottish scheme above, Emery notes that 'Provision of guidance on heritage buildings to fire and rescue services will assist with their integrated risk management plans (IRMPs)' which they are required to produce setting out the authority's strategy, for, *inter alia*, reducing the number and severity of fires in the area for which it has responsibility.

Region-Wide Incidents

Whilst collaboration with others is important, recent region-wide major disasters, in the UK and elsewhere, have reaffirmed the need for institutions to be prepared to go it alone for some time as emergency services, for example, will be dealing with matters of life and death and the infrastructure. Even if institutions have agreements of mutual assistance from other local counterparts they may not be able to assist if they are in the same situation.

> People are encouraged to have their own absolutely essential supplies at the properties with local emergency contact lists, but certain ones that have made good links with their emergency planning officer for the county feel that they only need an absolute minimum really and that they would be able to contact that person in the event of an emergency and who would be able to ... get most of the supplies, but I don't know really. (National heritage organisation)

That's their plan and that will link into our plan, because we have to be aware that we're in the middle of an industrial area and how it could impact. The main problem on the curatorial side is that the majority of my collections are outside, the [objects] are physically outside so if there was a chemical incident, there's no way you could protect them. (Independent museum)

It seems clear that some individual emergency plans failed when the whole locality was flooded. Plans had assumed the ability to rely on help from neighbours [for materials, staff, storage space, etc.] but the sheer scale of the disaster meant this was impossible when the neighbours had problems of their own. In many cases there was no Plan B. (Spiers 2007)

Different Kinds of Disaster   Cultural heritage institutions are not only at risk from fire and flood – other external incidents or factors can have an effect on them and their business/service provision. An outbreak of foot and mouth or avian flu can restrict people's movements, thus stopping them visiting sites. Last year's floods in England reinforced this.

In August [2007], we [HLF] held a seminar which was a direct response to the concerns expressed by our grantees in the immediate aftermath of the floods – an issue brought into sharp focus not just with the floods but with the recent outbreaks of Foot and Mouth, Blue tongue etc. We wanted to encourage the heritage sector to think the unthinkable – not just Flood and Foot and mouth, but fire, snow, terrorism, Bio-terrorism, contamination etc (Spiers 2007, 1)

Others in the field of disaster management have drawn attention to this and its significance for disaster planning. Quarentelli (2003, 18–19) for example asks:

Can all threats to cultural properties be approached in the same general way? Most self designated disaster researchers draw a distinction between disasters (which are consensus occasions) and conflict situations. The latter refer to such phenomena as wars, ethnic strife, terrorist attacks, riots, and all crisis situations where at least one party involved is deliberately attempting to continue or make a bad situation worse. This distinction does not seem to be made in the cultural properties literature. For example, of the 40 papers presented at the International Congress of Cultural Heritage at Risk in 1999, more than 15 deal with wartime or conflict situations. To be sure all crises have certain aspects or dimensions in common. But there are limits to thinking therefore that all crises can be dealt with in the same way. The very act that some sort of conscious hostile action is always involved in a conflict has major consequences for whatever planning or managing is attempted. Our strong belief is that those interested in protecting cultural properties take the difference into account.

Brinkman's comment (2004, 12–13) may indicate further research into this might be appropriate:

> Looking at emergencies, it may seem there is a great difference between earthquakes, floods or war situations. It is true, of course, that many elements differ, but there are just as many things that may be similar. A fire brings water damage. A war brings fire and sometimes flooding, as in Yugoslavia where the film archive was flooded because of water seeping in after a bomb attack. In all instances, there is the issue of moving objects to safe places. A museum with an emergency plan for evacuating personnel and objects may already be equally prepared for flood, fire or war.

Networks   The key role of networks has been discussed previously. In the UK, there have been recent developments in this area. In 2006, the DCMS set up the London Emergency Planning Group (DCMS *Business continuity planning. Emergency Planning Group)*, comprising most of the heritage organisations based in the area including national institutions and agencies with properties countrywide. The group aims to prepare business continuity and emergency plans. It meets regularly and members have password access to an Intranet through which they can communicate with each other, post notices, store documents and so on.

One of the key objectives of the group is the development of a standardised training course for salvage and treatment of water- or fire-damaged art. It is intended that this would include the creation of realistic exercises, using museum and art gallery collections that have been subjected to heat, smoke and water; writing an emergency plan; priority lists; post-fire and rescue service arrival. Led by experienced trainers, the course will cover pre-incident, incident and post-incident, with emphasis on the pre-incident phase (Emery 2008).

The most well-known collaborative network in England has also taken new steps recently with regard to training. REDS initiated a pilot Emergency Planning training project in 2007. Twelve museums and heritage organisations of various types were selected to participate in the project, funded by Renaissance East Midlands and managed by EmmS (EmmS *REDS (Regional Emergencies and Disaster Support) Service*. The project involved a series of practical training courses and site visits and advice. An experienced external consultant was appointed to lead the training element of the scheme (EmmS 2007). Following an introductory day, participants began work developing their own plans with the support of the REDS coordinator and members of the REDS team who made visits to each of the sites. Another two days focused on putting plans into action and salvage recovery (EmmS 2008a). A review day was also undertaken. It highlighted:

> The need to identify the potential threats to your own building(s) and create a plan that aims to prevent the most likely incidents occurring, and/or minimises the damage where they are beyond your control;

The value of developing an ongoing collaboration with your local fire station ...
The importance of embedding your Plans (and a culture of disaster prevention)
in your organisation – thinking about ways to get your colleagues (staff, trustees,
volunteers) to adopt and use the plan. (Lansdale 2008)

The pilot was successful and a second one will be run 2008–09 for eight non-
Renaissance partner museums or museums services. (EmmS 2008b)

MLA South East with the support of the South East Hub has recently provided
a free training programme for emergency planning and has placed resources
used in this on its website (MLA South East *Renaissance Related Resources*).
It has also established Emergency Response Units (ERUs) (Renaissance South
East *Emergency Response Units*). Trailers with emergency response equipment
are in place across the region backed by teams involving more than 60 museum
staff, volunteers, curators and conservators ready to offer additional help in an
emergency. Museums, libraries and archives can now also submit their emergency
plans for free professional feedback (Renaissance South East 2007). In the planning
stages, the REDS coordinator was consulted for advice.

Action has been prompted elsewhere. As mentioned above, shortly after the
flooding in parts of England in the summer of 2007, HLF Yorkshire and Humber
held a meeting for those affected. As Spiers, Regional Manager of the HLF, noted
in a report (2007) on the impact of the flooding:

There is no funded rapid response team in Yorkshire and the Humber as in some
other regions, and agencies and professional bodies who were willing and able
to offer help were often not contacted.

She also commented that 92 per cent of the attendees said they wished to
investigate a regional response mechanism. Following on from a second meeting
in November, action to facilitate that development was announced. A scheme,
funded by HLF, is to provide 730 training places spread between 31 organisations.
Deputy Council Leader and Cabinet member for Regeneration Culture and Sport,
Denise Jeffery said

We are delighted that the Heritage Lottery Fund is to enable this training to take
place. The terrible floods of last summer showed that few heritage organisations
can deal with a major disaster on their own. With HLF's help, we can now rely
on our own specialist network in the region for practical assistance and training
in Wakefield, Pontefract and Castleford. Thanks to this grant, the 750,000 people
who visit or use our district's museums and galleries every year will benefit from
our improved response to future disasters and emergencies. (Wakefield Council
2008)

Explaining the importance of the award Fiona Spiers, commented

> As the floods of summer 2007 demonstrated, the heritage sector is in urgent need of people who have specific conservation and disaster management skills. This project will provide training for hundreds of people on a wide range of themes, including business continuity, planning for an emergency and salvage and recovery. It's so important that we take care of the nation's heritage because without it we risk losing our sense of self and identity.

> The Federation of Yorkshire Museums and Galleries will provide the network with seminars and practical training on a wide range of themes. This includes emergency planning, business continuity and recovery which will increase each organisation's capacity to reduce damage from a natural disaster and recover more quickly. The Yorkshire Medium Museum Services network (YoMMS) will organise practical disaster training with specialist equipment. (Wakefield Council 2008)

The floods have acted as a driver elsewhere, too. In the West Midlands, another area of England affected by flooding in summer 2007, another network, the Worcestershire Museums Emergency Task Force (WET), supported by Museum and Heritage Group Worcestershire and Renaissance West Midlands,

> ... has been set up as a response to growing concerns over collection care and safety in today's environment . In the wake of 2007's devastating floods, six separate museums from across the county have come together to set up WET. The aim is to create a regional scheme that benefits all museums in Worcestershire and enables us as a sector to respond more effectively to arrange of possible disasters. WET is a scheme open to all museums in the county. Its members have access to a 'communal pot' of equipment purchased with the assistance of the Worcestershire Small Grants Scheme, as well as access to equipment and services belonging to member organisations. In the event of disaster help will be at hand. (Smellie and Spry 2008).

The recent activities of networks outlined above focus very much on training. The purpose of any new networks must be clear, in line with local requirements, and agreed with those participating. Issues that may need to be taken into account when forming such a network may include: 'insurance; public & professional liability; health & safety; ... service level agreements (cost implications of staff helping other organizations, or mutual aid)'. (Lansdale and Matthews 2007)

New Threats

In addition to the wide range of threats mentioned above, archives, libraries and museums must be alert to new threats. One such, that was perhaps surprisingly rarely mentioned specifically during the course of the project (March 2005 – October 2006), was climate change, which since then has been fully in the public eye. In the UK, the publication in 2006 in the UK of a major report (Stern 2006) on climate change is likely to have attracted greater attention to it than there had been previously.

Climate Change   Climate change is, indeed, now receiving considerable attention, generally (see, for example, O'Brien et al. 2006) and in the cultural heritage sector (see, for example, Cassar 2005; Colette 2007; English Heritage 2008; The National Trust *Climate Change*; Noah's Ark *Noah's Ark. Global Climate Change Impact on Build Heritage and Cultural Landscapes*; Staniforth 2006).

In the UK, signs of climate change have been evident in recent years with an apparent increase in region-wide flooding. Lessons from severe natural disasters may well be worth considering by countries which have to date been less affected by them, in terms of both mitigation and recovery. When looking to learn from experience from disasters elsewhere in the world, local circumstances must be taken into account.

The approach taken to investigating climate change and what can be done to address it in the cultural heritage sector will need to be interdisciplinary and multi-agency. In the UK this could involve for example:

- Government departments
- AHRC research clusters
- Noah's Ark project (EU)
- Centre for Sustainable Heritage, UCL
- UNESCO World Heritage Centre case studies
- English Heritage
- The National Trust
- MLA/Regional agencies
- Networks (e.g. M25; EmmS REDS; DCMS London Emergency Planning Group; MLA South East ERUs)
- Civil emergency services
- Commercial services (eg disaster recovery, insurance)
- Professional bodies.

All of those listed are now addressing the issue, albeit to varying degrees but will need to work together and share expertise and knowledge. Scientific and technical research will need to be disseminated not only to the scientific community but also to those working in archives, museums and libraries in a way that can be understood without too much technical expertise.

Buildings   Participants in the research frequently referred to the poor condition of buildings and the need for remedial work and maintenance schedules with regard to disaster management. In addition to comments by interviewees (see Chapter 6), respondents to the UK questionnaire also alluded to this. For example:

> Because of the problem with our building and its services, the Library sustains minor emergencies (effectively water leaks) every few months. (University library)

> Major problem is lack of preventative maintenance of our buildings – constant minor problems with blocked drains causing flooding into building – easily preventable but Estates don't do the work. (University library)

Building condition, maintenance and related issues occurred frequently in 'lessons to pass on to others' suggested by respondents to the UK questionnaire survey. Given that there is considerable mention of water ingress in these, and that one of the predicted impacts of climate change in the UK is more rain and a rise in water levels, they indicate an issue that needs to be addressed:

> On-going maintenance to pick up problems before they arrive. (Local Authority record office)

> Need to ensure that remedial work is adequately completed. (Local Authority local history centre)

> Faulty drains, and faulty building design needs to be sorted out. (Local Authority record office and local history library)

> Roof, drain maintenance is essential. (Local Authority archive)

> Need for building maintenance programme, funded and prioritised. Need for regular inspections of building. (Local Authority record office)

> Maintenance needs improving. (Local Authority archive)

> Need for planned maintenance. (Public library service)

> Effectiveness of central maintenance crew. (University library)

> Make good contact with your Works Department. (Government library)

> Your Estates Department need to be involved at all levels. (University library)

> Check the drains are not blocked. (Research Institute library)

> Don't trust architects to think about collection location. (Special library)

Need for better design of buildings. (University library)

Regular checks of gutters and drains. (Gallery library)

From the outset, insist on a schedule of work and check progress weekly. (Public library service)

Contractors in the building greatly increase the risk of incident. (Independent museum and gallery)

Do not assume that because action has been taken to solve a problem it could not re-occur. (Independent museum)

Keep drains and gutters clear and carry out modifications as required. (Independent museum)

Routine maintenance. (Historic house)

Building maintenance very important. (Local Authority museum and gallery)

Don't rely on your maintenance department to carry out building checks. (Local Authority museum)

Be vigilant – heavy rain is a concern with old buildings. (Local Authority museum and gallery)

Consider building integrity and maintenance. (University museum)

Planned programme of regular maintenance. (Local Authority museum)

Check where leaks have occurred in past. (University museum and gallery)

In catastrophic situations, such as that caused by Hurricane Katrina, extreme cases led to extreme lessons, but with proposed solutions:

Every institution has to have a much enhanced plan of collections whether it's a bunker built into existing structure. When [X] rebuilds – the museum was on first floor – it's gone – it was on stilts washed into a 55 acre debris field. The collection is archaeological relics – they've been able to dig them up – textile shreds, rusting weaponry. [In future], all collection materials will be on the 2nd floor. Administration, public areas, and facilities will be on the 2nd floor. [They] will put in a core area with extra reinforcements. [Y] is planning to do the same thing. A barge is still on top of the site – like taking down a city block. The library here was built, state funded, to withstand hurricanes. Had huge steel 'I' beams sunk into the ground. The building didn't move – everything went through. Some cases couldn't be moved in time – plate glass was screwed in. Another building – a confederate hospital – moved collections into this – brick built, survived previous hurricanes – totally imploded. (International museum and gallery)

Business Continuity

Disasters, large and small, continue to effect archives, libraries and museums. These can cause varying levels of disruption to, even cessation of, business. There is considerable information available on business continuity, but much of this is not directed specifically at cultural heritage institutions. Cultural heritage institutions increasingly operate businesses, and business continuity is also about service continuity: Archives, libraries and museums, particularly those which are part of a larger institution that practices risk assessment and management, are becoming involved in business continuity. Websites such as UK Resilience (see *Business Continuity* web pages), national and regional, offer checklists, instruction sheets, examples of scenario exercises, case studies, guidance on preparing for and dealing with particular kinds of incidents, contacts and so on, and are worth looking at for relevant, helpful material but they could include more obviously material aimed at the cultural heritage sector.

Spiers (2007) gives examples of what can happen if business continuity planning is not undertaken:

> Because salvage and recovery activity was prioritised over other areas of normal operation, the business was interrupted with some financial loss. Some organisations have suffered total and prolonged business interruption, or other unsustainable financial loss. Some disaster plans only referred to the collections and artefacts and had not taken business continuation into account. This means that some venues which rely on admission charges and are now closed or free because of the limited offer have potentially serious cashflow problems.

Whilst digital materials were not within the remit of the research, it is important that those with responsibility for disaster management in archives, libraries and museums liaise with those who have responsibility for digital materials and IT systems in their own institution. They must also include this in business continuity planning as more and more resources are held digitally, records are created and maintained electronically and management systems (for example, finance systems) will have key roles (for example, processing orders, invoices and payments, and staff salaries) to play in the aftermath of an incident.

Risk Assessment Risk assessment must also therefore pay due attention to business continuity. Whilst there is ongoing work on risks and collections (see, for example, Brokerhof 2006; Brokerhof et al. 2007), there does not appear to be the same focus on business continuity and broader aspects of the service.

Insurance

Institutions need to ensure they are appropriately insured. Recent events, such as the floods in England in 2007, have underlined this, for example:

> Insurance issues are moving rapidly up the agenda. Many local authority venues were self-insured ... Not everywhere had the correct sort of insurance – there seems to be a confusion between when contents and when collections insurance would be the most effective ... The lesson is that every venue should have what is appropriate for them, not what is appropriate for their next door neighbour ... Very few venues appear to have business continuation insurance. (Spiers 2007)

> ... most museum collections are insured for conservation costs up to the market value of the object. For many collections (such as social history) there is no tangible or realisable market value in the collections and thus if disaster befalls there is no option other than to dispose. Our insurers understood this issue ... Nevertheless our settlement does not cover the overall cost of conservation and re-storage of the collections ... We feel it is very important that museums with equivalent collections are aware of this issue and are able to take out appropriate insurance for their collections/the nations collections. (Chumbley 2008)

Institutions need to take a more evidence-based approach to this, as one of the respondents to the UK questionnaire put very clearly:

> We need to review our insurance – 'think of a number approach' to annual re-evaluation exercise needs more concrete evidence and support. (University library)

Standards and Benchmarks

An evidence-based approach, applied to disaster management in general, is beginning to take place through the development of standards and developments. In the UK, the need for standards and benchmarks against which to measure progress seems to have been realised. One interviewee commented:

> Yes, very definitely [there should be standards], it won't work unless we have standards because the sort of attitudes tend to be, we'll wait and see what DCMS is doing. (National museum)

There does now seem to be progress.

In England, the National Archives (*Self Assessment*) has recently developed a self-assessment programme. This enables authorities to judge the adequacy of their archive service, measured against the public task of such services, as expressed in the Standard for Record Repositories and the Framework of

Standards. For the first time, it will enable comparisons to be made between authorities. The information from self-assessment will hopefully be useful to employing authorities, archives professionals and the user community. The programme enables The National Archives to reveal regional and other trends, highlight areas of strength and weakness within the archive sector, and to identify individual services that may need other interventions and support. The self-assessment programme is based on a comprehensive questionnaire that examines five areas of the work in local authority archive services: Governance and Staffing; Documentation of Collections; Access Services; Preservation and Conservation; and Buildings, Security and Environment. Included in the survey are questions relating to disaster management. Local authority archive services are asked to indicate which non-statutory policy documentation they have – 'disaster control or recovery plan' is on the list. They are asked for ways in which such policies have been used in the previous year. Other sections of the policy address different aspects of disaster management. Section 5 looks at Buildings, security and environment, and asks, inter alia, respondents to 'assess the likelihood of damage to the building and its contents from each of the hazards, fire and arson, river or sea flooding, vandalism and crime, subsidence, explosion or terrorist attack, wind and storm damage'. The survey asks the condition of aspects of the building and levels of maintenance, fire detection and suppression, water ingress, water sensors and alarms, and security The survey was piloted in 2006 and first undertaken in 2007 – 117 archive repositories out of 125 services responded.

In Northern Ireland, surveys of museum collections have been carried out, one of national museums (Northern Ireland Office 2006) and another more recently of other museums (Northern Ireland Government. Department of Culture, Arts and Leisure 2007). The government minister launching the latter survey report noted:

> This survey provides a valuable insight into the scale of our collections which NIMC are responsible for, ensuring that the millions of artifacts are cared for and preserved for future generations.

> The NIMC objectives in completing the survey of museums collections were to find out the number, type and significance of objects held; establish strengths and weaknesses in caring for collections; and to provide data to assist future work to improve standards and inform planning in museums.

> The Minister continued: 'The report provides a baseline against which those charged with preserving collections can measure improvements. I commend this report to all our museums as it provides a wake up call to those falling behind recognised standards and provides a reminder to others that there is no room for complacency.'

The British Standards Institution (BSI) is currently developing a Code of Practice for Cultural Collections Management, which is cross-domain and which includes emergency planning (BSI 2008).

Sustainability

A key issue is that when disaster management is well practised, it must then be sustained. This must take account of results of testing plans, either in training or for real, and new developments. Nationally, the Society of American Archivists has come up with an interesting way of keeping the profile of good practice high, thus facilitating sustainability:

> MayDay [May 1] is a time when archivists and other cultural heritage professionals take personal and professional responsibility or doing something simple – something that can be accomplished in a day that can have a significant impact on an individual's or repository's ability to respond. (Society of American Archivists 2006)

Ideas for activities are suggested – they include: create or update contact information, review or establish emergency procedures, conduct a disaster drill, invite local fire fighters to visit repository, inventory emergency supplies.

Research

A significant factor in sustainability is research. Research should contribute to the practice of disaster management. Research needs have been identified in several areas and research is underway as evidenced by recent projects:

Conservation Techniques   Hurricane Katrina emphasised the need for research into mass drying and sterilization protocols for library materials damaged by flooding. Work is has been undertaken by a team of international partners, including the British Library, the National Library of the Czech Republic and the University of Utah Marriott Library (see, National Centre for Preservation Technology and Training *Disaster recovery by the book*; Silverman et al. 2007). Similar work has gone on elsewhere, for example in New Zealand (Najar-Simpson 2007).

Salvage and Response   Hurricane Katrina also highlighted the need for research into the handling of different media and formats in the immediate aftermath of severe flooding and the treatment items should then receive:

> It's difficult for people to think about treatment … it needs more research. What treatments can work for different formats. People worry they wouldn't know what to do or who to go to, for say, illuminated manuscripts. External contractors

have more experience. X wondered if stabilisation was more important than treatment. Y said there may be a danger that people send things off to the wrong people for the wrong treatment ... Research should be broader than drying techniques, e.g. guidance on costs, what's user friendly. Do you have flexibility, do you want 'perfect' or 'usable'? It's a difficult subject – on reflection, was that the right thing to do? It's sensitive. (National library)

Mould was a particular feature that needs more investigation:

Mould – still ... If you can stabilise things were mould is dormant and then you can clean, what do you mean by cleaned – what level of toxicity can we give things to public? ... Mould growth was so virulent ... [After different treatments] what warning do we give people handling these and will they be more vulnerable in future – once having had mould, will it happen at lower humidity? (International museum and gallery)

Staff Welfare, Health and Safety The health and safety of staff working to salvage and sort damaged items should be paramount. Interviewees commented on this:

Are there any health and safety hazards to you, such as a marble bust, which looks as if it's quite small sitting on its plinth, if you try to lift it off there, the transfer of weight could literally make it fall to the ground, smash and fill your legs full of glass shards, sorry, marble shards. So that's the sort of thing that we did with them when they came for actual exercises [simulating] a real fire. (National museum service)

... the importance of health and safety as well, because we were lucky it was just water that was pouring in through our ceiling because it was only a pipe that had burst – could well have been sewage as with problem we had earlier on in the week. People have to start thinking, yes, historical objects are important, but your own health and safety is your number one priority, and that you don't just start wandering about in the store knee deep in water/sewage – you have to think those things through. (Independent museum)

You have to be able to protect staff going into contaminated or otherwise unpleasant environments. We have heard a lot about sewage but often with sewage comes discarded works – the protective personal equipment (PPE) for picking up needles and syringes (needlestick gloves, clamps etc.) is something every venue should have, but few do. (Spiers 2007)

Silverman (2004) and Stavroudis (2005) stress this. They identify common risks and how to deal with them.

Staff morale must also be considered. This was one of the lessons from previous incidents elsewhere emphasised by floods in Yorkshire and Humberside in 2007:

> Staff morale can be volatile and difficult to manage – staff may have to go through a grieving process for their loss – they have seen the work of many years damaged or destroyed, and may exhibit a full spectrum of emotions. Different people react on different timescales, there are no guarantees that every member of the team will conveniently synchronise. It can be extremely difficult for managers dealing with their own grief and frustration to recognise this and continue to motivate their staff. (Spiers 2007)

Klasson (2003) has carried out research into the psychological aspects of a library disaster on staff and users but this apart there seems to be little research into this topic with specific regard to the cultural heritage sector. In major, catastrophic disasters staff's personal lives will be affected. If they have suffered personal loss or injury, had their homes destroyed, their children's schooling disrupted, for example, how will this impact on their role in the recovery of archive, library or museum services? Those working in disaster recovery have first hand experience of this. With regard to the population in general, archivists in particular raised the issue of vital records with regard to disaster planning and recovery. Such records include, for example, business, legal, medical, and financial documentation. Loss of birth and death certificates, property deeds, insurance documentation, for example, can complicate attempts to recover from disaster.

Fire   There is perhaps a need for archivists, curators and librarians to become more familiar with the results of research into aspects of fire prevention in order to keep abreast of developments in general terms. For example, the theme of the 2008 National Archives [US] conference was fire suppression, with papers on various aspect of fire suppression technology and risk assessment (National Archives [US] 2008). They will obviously need to take appropriate professional advice and employ specialists if their institutions are undertaking, fire prevention work, for example, but they should have enough knowledge to make an input to plans or proposals from say their knowledge of collections or buildings and storage.

The European COoperation in the field of Scientific and Technical Research (COST) C17 project brought 'together 24 countries with the common goal of setting out consensus guidance on the best approaches to protect cultural heritage from the effects of fire' (*Cost C17*). Findings include a guide to loss statistics, fire detection and suppression technology, insurance and strategies to cope with fire, and the fire threat. The report, *COST Action C17. Built Heritage Fire Loss to Heritage Buildings*, is available from Historic Scotland (Maxwell (ed.) 2007).

Other research in this area has also been undertaken at European level. One such is the Fire Risk Evaluation to the European Cultural Heritage (FiRE-TECH) project, funded by the European Commission, which ran from 2002 to 2005. It aimed to evaluate the risk that fire poses to the cultural heritage and to suggest methods for quantifying and managing the risk using the systems and components available (FRAME *Fire Risk Evaluation to European Cultural Heritage*).

Funding

The research discovered little evidence of funding specifically for disaster management. There were a few examples of major funding supporting capital projects, to install fire detection and suppression systems, for example. To date, institutions have funded activity from general funds or preservation or training funds, or from 'special funds' set aside for in-house funding. More recently, there have been examples of national or regional initiatives, offering limited funding to support development of a disaster control plan, access to consultancy, establishment of equipment and supplies stores, training, for example. Charitable trusts are also potential sources. It would be useful if there was one location, one website, that could be consulted to find details of these and related activities like training events and conferences. In that respect, it was interesting to read an advertisement for a forthcoming event *Poverty is no Excuse: Disaster Preparedness for the Small Library* (Historic Libraries Forum *Historic Libraries Forum Events)*:

> Putting in place structures and guidelines for dealing with disasters of all shapes and sizes is a challenge for the largest and best-resourced of libraries. For those at the other end of the spectrum, small, independent libraries, sole workers, private collectors and those on a very restricted budget, the challenges are often so insurmountable that disaster becomes a dirty word. This year's conference is aimed at looking practically at what can be done with limited time, few staff, meagre resources and no space for a fully-stocked cupboard full of bubble-wrap and mops – helpful, straightforward advice on what to do if you feel at the moment that you can't do anything.

The conference includes case studies which hopefully others can learn from.

Silverman (2006) paints a similar picture with regard to funding in the US as part of his proposal for a national disaster response protocol when he suggests how a National Disaster Center for Cultural Property might be funded. He includes public (National Endowment for the Humanities) and private (foundations) sources. He also mentions federal grants, federal/state/university partnerships, and possible agreements with insurance companies (p.508)

Another aspect of funding, income, is vital and the implications of loss of income should be incorporated in risk assessment and business continuity work

> Many institutions in local government shouldn't just think of preservation but that they provide a service. Museums – a council doesn't have to have unlike a library or archive – could understand service/continuity side better. Having better awareness of things like health and safety. Cultural heritage – complete focus is on the stock – might be better being more dispassionate and look at

other things within the context of whole service they run. Financial aspect of museums is important. One person from a museum at a training event said: 'if the shop burnt down I don't know what we'd do for revenue.' Educational visitors – if the education centre goes up, there's an impact on funding next year. (Commercial recovery service)

People in Archives, Libraries and Museums

At the end of the day, people are essential to effective disaster management. From an individual motivated to draw up a disaster control plan, a group keen to develop simulation exercises, to teams working tirelessly to salvage artefacts following a flood, and the 'leaders' who emerge to direct recovery, they can all inspire others. But if there job is to be made easier, often in difficult circumstances, staff will need to have appropriate skills and communication between them and others involved must be good. One interviewee put this very straightforwardly: 'People need to know what to do.' (International museum and gallery)

The consequences of not having trained staff have also been made clear:

> Not having enough skilled personnel resulted for some in an extended recovery process during which their collections suffered continuing and progressive damage. (Spiers 2007, 2)

But not all institutions have a large staff:

> A major problem for the independent and smaller organisations is lack of people. Where development has been done in projects with project-specific, time limited teams over a long period of time there may not be the core staffing to cope with doing it all again at once, even if the insurance company pays out in full, or to deal with all that needs to be done just to get to a point to start the rebuild. (Spiers 2007)

> … While many in the museum community offered to assist us in our salvage and recovery operation, institutional barriers and bureaucracy often inevitably intervened as did our requirement for people to react immediately to our situation. Our contacts with and ability to source accredited conservators within the region to work with us from day two undoubtedly saved our collections. Many organisations are not (for financial or institutional reasons) able to move this swiftly and experience has shown that the ability to act within the first 72–96 hours was key. (Chumbley 2008)

Conservators

Conservators have a vital role to play in planning for disasters and reacting to and recovering from them. Research findings indicate that they are most effective when collaborating with others, for example in developing a disaster control plan or providing advice on salvage. There seem to be mixed views where conservators are brought in as external consultants to facilitate disaster planning. For example,

> Plans are drawn up by external consultants sometimes, who are just in [country] a few months. Sometimes there are [locals] … on the consultancy group. They are out of the context and it won't work. You have to think of this. (Professional body)

> If do, [bring in consultants, I] bring in as a facilitator rather than doing it. The Conservation Center at [city] has had a programme to help people produce disaster plans and collection management plans. It will review plans and give feedback but doesn't do it. Think this more effective – if you don't own the plan. It serves as a Regional Clearing House, offers resource notebooks. (International museum and gallery)

Some interviewees queried whether there were sufficient conservators in their country or region and were concerned as they appreciated their expertise and the directions they could give to others:

> Salvage and recovery of items post disaster was frequently an issue for those on the scene without conservation expertise. Already, perhaps in shock, they were unsure as to what to do with different types of material and needed expert advice from experienced conservators either from the public or private sector. The sector needs to determine whether it has sufficient expertise of this kind. In the aftermath of Hurricane Katrina, Heritage Preservation recently published a practical guide to emergency response, a short handbook with accompanying DVD with illustrative examples of dealing with different kinds of materials. (Heritage Preservation 2006)

Ongoing training for experienced conservators is required too. The recent initiative led by the AIC (c.2007) to train conservators and produce '60 collections emergency response team members trained to assess damage and initiate salvage of cultural collections after a disaster has occurred' has been outlined in Chapter 4. This reflects attention being paid to developing rapid response teams with expertise, equipment and funds to be dispatched to disaster scenes (see Frost 2006). Consideration of related issues such as local emergency protocols for command and control, health and safety requirements, setting up mutual aid agreements must be addressed.

One of the authors has recently further investigated the role of conservators in salvage in the UK (Knowles 2007). In a survey of museums, she found that 34 per cent of respondents felt they needed training in salvage of collections. For many 'salvage' means the very basics of handling and moving – not decision making on initial treatments and with regard to different materials. She also found that while there is a lot of information on salvage of collections, it is hard to find specific information, and information is not available equally for different material types, for example there is a lot on paper but not so much on textiles, ceramics and organic material.

Conclusion

There is a growing range of incidents that we all face, with the possibility of reputational damage: some large scale and unexpected (eg terrorism); others [we] may be aware of [the] possibility (eg flu pandemic); and new ones (eg climate change). However, the conference has demonstrated that collaboration, networking, and sharing information/knowledge can provide positive support and outcomes (in addition to institutional activity). There is a great deal of experience and expertise about; this needs to be moved forward through information and skill sharing, and perhaps holding more events and conferences?

There is a clear need for benchmarking, common standards, and a glossary of terminology, to ensure that we are all talking about the same things using the same language. Emergency planning and preparedness need to be integrated across the whole organisation – it is *everyone's* responsibility. It should also be integrated with appropriate external agencies.

Prevention is as important as salvage and recovery; both need to be covered practically in training, and plans need to be tested.

Storage provision needs to be addressed.

Heritage organisations need to engage more with others in their communities, including Local Authorities and Regional Resilience Teams. (Lansdale and Matthews 2007)

The above extracts from a summary of discussion at a recent Museums Association event, represent a concise overview of where disaster management in archives, libraries and museum is at the moment, and what it needs to do to move forward. One of the participants (Wisner in Jigyasu et al. 2008) in a recent discussion about the future of disaster management, highlights another key factor – learning from each other:

So we're learning all the time. I refer to this as hybrid knowledge. You have various forms of local knowledge, and you also have external specialists' knowledge. If you have a relationship of trust and a good institutional framework, you can actually marry the two. (Jigyasu et al 2008)

From speaking with people, from listening to them and reading the literature, those who have been involved in disaster management, particularly those who have had to deal with major incidents, have a positive, determined and imaginative attitude, when they might have been expected to have been more pessimistic and uncertain, but they need support appropriate to their circumstances. They have demonstrated tremendous resilience – but no matter what the disaster, preparedness helps:

We did not accept the defeatism which says that when disaster happens on the scale of the June flooding, it is so overwhelming that nothing else could have been done. Not even the heritage sector can control the weather but we can be prepared, we can be significantly more ready in future than we were. (Spiers 2007, 1)

As respondents to the UK questionnaire advised early on in the research:

Be prepared. Be practical. Be trained (University library)

but

Always expect the unexpected (Independent museum).

We hope that this book does justice to those who have provided us with an insight into their experiences of various aspects of disaster management and that it facilitates understanding of the subject within and without the sector.

References

AIC (c.2007), *AIC Collections Emergency Response Training* (Washington: AIC), (published online c.2007) <http://aic.stanford.edu/education/workshops/documents/certdes.pdf>, accessed 7 Aug. 2008.

Amarasiri, U. (2005) 'Tsunami affected libraries in Sri Lanka: rebuilding process and challenges' in IFLA PAC ASIA and National Diet Library (2005*), Open seminar on the documentary heritage damaged by the Indian Ocean Tsunami and the meeting of Directors of the IFLA/PAC Regional Centres in Asia and others*, National Diet Library, Tokyo, 6 Dec. 2005 (Tokyo: National Diet Library) [website], (updated c.2005) <http://www.ndl.go.jp/en/iflapac/news.html>, accessed 14 Aug. 2008.

Anderson, H. and McIntyre, J. E. (1985). *Planning manual for disaster control in Scottish libraries and record offices* (Edinburgh, National Library of Scotland).

Brinkman, M. (2004) 'Introduction', in Menegazzi, C. (ed.) (2004), *International symposium on cultural heritage disaster preparedness and response, 23–27 November 2003, Salar Jung Museum, Hyderabad, India.* (Paris: International Council of Museums), 11–13 (published online), (updated 2004) <http://icom. museum/disaster_preparedness_book/index.html>, accessed 31 Aug. 2008.

Brokerhof, A. W. (2006), 'Collection Risk Management – The Next Frontier', in CMA (2006), (published online 2006) <http://www.musees.ca/protection/en/ presentations/Brokerhof.pdf>, accessed 5 Dec. 2008.

Brokerhof, A., et al. (2007), 'Advancing Research in Risk Management Applications to Cultural Property', *ICCROM Newsletter* 33, 10–11, (published online June 2007) <http://www.iccrom.org/eng/02info_en/02_03newsl_en/ newsl_en/newsl33_en.pdf>, accessed 5 Sep. 2008.

BSI (2008) *PAS 197, Cultural collections management – Code of practice* (London: BSI), (published online), (updated 2008) <http://www.bsi-global.com/en/ Standards-and-Publications/How-we-can-help-you/Professional-Standards-Service/PAS-197/>, accessed 12 Sep. 2008.

Cassar, M. (2005), *Climate change and the historic environment* (London: Centre for Sustainable Heritage, University College London), (published online 2005) <http://eprints.ucl.ac.uk/archive/00002082/>, accessed 5 Sep. 2008.

Chumbley, A. (2007), 'The Floods of 2007 and the impact on museums in Sheffield', in *Don't Panic! Planning an Effective Disaster Response* [presentation based on report to MLA]. The Midlands Federation of Museums and Art Galleries, RAF Museum Cosford, Shifnal, Shropshire, 2 July 2008.

CMA (2006), *Cultural Property Protection Conference*, Ottawa, Canada, 16 January 2006 (Canadian Museums Association), (published online 2006) <http://www.museums.ca/protection/en/presentations.html>, accessed 6 Sep. 2008.

Colette, A. (2007), *Case Studies on Climate Change and World Heritage* (Paris: UNESCO World Heritage Centre), (published online 2007) <http://whc. unesco.org/documents/publi_climatechange.pdf>, accessed 5 Sep. 2008.

Communities and Local Government, *Fire and resilience. Fire safety law and guidance for business* {website], (updated c.2007) <http://www.communities. gov.uk/fire/firesafety/firesafetylaw/>, accessed 22 Aug. 2008.

Coull, M. (2006), *Background to the Scottish Historic Buildings National Database, Historic Scotland Board Meeting 18 December 2006*, (published online 2006) <http://www.historic-scotland.gov.uk/nationalfiredatabasehsb3206-2.pdf>, accessed 22 Aug. 2008.

DCMS, *Business continuity planning. Emergency Planning Group* [password required] [website], (updated 2008) <http://www.culture.gov.uk/working_ with_us/business_continuity_planning/default.aspx#collaboration>, accessed 6 Sep. 2008.

Emery, S. (2008), 'Heritage fire safety', *isurv* May 2008, (published online 19 May 2008) <http://www.isurv.com/site/scripts/news_article.aspx?newsID=25>

EmmS (2008a), *EMMS News* 29, January 2008.

EmmS (2008b), *EMMS News* 32, July 2008.

EmmS (2007), *EMMS News* 27, September 2007.

EmmS, *REDS (Regional Emergencies and Disaster Support Service)* [website], (updated n.d.) <http://www.emms.org.uk/reds.htm>, accessed 6 Sep. 2008.

English Heritage (2008), *Climate Change and the Historic Environment*, (London: English Heritage), (published online 2008) <http://www.helm.org.uk/upload/pdf/Climate-change.pdf>, accessed 5 Sep. 2008. [Supersedes an earlier version published in July 2006.]

FEMA, *Federal Emergency Management Agency* [website], (updated 2008) <http://www.fema.gov/>, accessed 5 Sep. 2008.

FEMA, *Historic Preservation Useful Links* [website], (updated n.d.) <http://www.fema.gov/plan/ehp/hp/hplinks.shtm>, accessed 5 Sep. 2008

Fire and resilience [website], (updated n.d.) <http://www.communities.gov.uk/fire/firesafety/215642/fire/>, accessed 15 Sep. 2008.

FRAME, *Fire risk evaluation to the European Cultural Heritage*. [Programme funded by European Commission, Research Directorate, General Directorate Environment Key-Unit "Urban sustainability and Cultural Heritage" Fifth framework program – Environment and Sustainable Development; Key-Action City of tomorrow and cultural heritage], [hosted by] F.R.A.M.E. Fire Risk Assessment Method (for) Engineering, (published online n.d.) <http://www.framemethod.net/firetech.html>, accessed 5 Sep. 2008.

Frost, G. (2006) 'Lessons from Katrina: recovery of cultural collections', *Archival Products News* 13:2, 1–4.

Great Britain (2004), 'Civil Contingencies Act 2004 Chapter 36', *Office of Public Sector Information* (London: The Stationery Office), (published online 2004) <http://www.opsi.gov.uk/acts/acts2004/ukpga_20040036_en_1>, accessed 12 Sep. 2008.

Great Britain (2004), 'Fire and Rescue Services Act 2004 Chapter 21', *Office of Public Sector Information* (London: The Stationery Office), (published online 2004) <http://www.opsi.gov.uk/acts/acts2004/ukpga_20040021_en_1>, accessed 12 Sep. 2008. (For further information, see Communities and Local Government.

Great Britain, 'The Regulatory Reform (Fire Safety) Order 2005. Statutory Instrument 2005 No. 1541' (London: The Stationery Office), (published online 2005) <http://www.opsi.gov.uk/si/si2005/20051541.htm>, accessed 12 Sep. 2008.

Haire, S. and Sorensen, C. (2006), 'Fire database project', in RCAHMS (2006) *RCAHMS Annual review 2005–06 In partnership,* (Edinburgh: Scottish Executive), 24–7 (published online 2006) <http://www.rcahms.gov.uk/pdfs/AR0506_24_27.pdf>, accessed 22 Aug. 2008.

Heritage Preservation (2006), *Field guide to emergency response* (Washington, D.C.: Heritage Preservation) [With instructional DVD].

Historic Libraries Forum, *Historic Libraries Forum Events* [website], (updated 2008) <http://www.historiclibrariesforum.org.uk/hlf/events.html>, accessed 15 Sep. 2008.

Historic Scotland (2005), *Fire safety: creating an awareness of the fire threat (Inform: Information for historic building owners)* (Edinburgh: Historic Scotland), (published online 2005) <http://www.historic-scotland.gov.uk/ informguides-fire-2.pdf#xml=http://web1:10700/texis/webinator/pubssearch/ pdfhi.txt?pr=publications&prox=page&rorder=500&rprox=500&rdfreq=5 00&rwfreq=500&rlead=500&rdepth=0&sufs=0&order=r&id=48ae01ba7>, accessed 22 Aug. 2008.

HM Government, *Preparing For Emergencies . What you need to know* [website], (updated Aug. 2008) <http://www.pfe.gov.uk/index.shtm>, accessed 5 Sep. 2008.

ICBS. *Announcement. Working conference 27–28 September 2006 The Hague, Netherlands. Towards a solid organization: infrastructure and awareness. The challenge of an effective cooperation* [website], (updated 4 Sep. 2006) <http:// www.ifla.org/VI/4/conf/Conference09-2006.htm>, accessed 5 Sep. 2008.

Jigyasu, R., et al. (2008), 'Putting heritage on the map: a discussion about disaster management', *Getty Conservation Institute Newsletter* 23:1, (published online 2008) <http://www.getty.edu/conservation/publications/ newsletters/23_1/index.html>, accessed 29 Jul. 2008.

Klasson, M. (2003), 'Psychological aspects of disaster management', in Matthews, G and Feather, J. (eds.), 143–68.

Knowles, G. (2007), *Disaster salvage: are UK conservators ready to react?* MA Dissertation [MA Conservation of Historic Objects], Lincoln School of Art and Design, University of Lincoln.

Lansdale, S. (2008) [E-mail to G Matthews, 8 April 2008].

Lansdale, S. and Matthews, G. (2007), 'Notes of group and plenary discussions', *Safe and Sound: new approaches to emergency planning*, Museums Association conference, National Council for Voluntary Organisations, London, 21 May 2007.

Library of Congress, *Learning from Katrina: Conservators' First-Person Accounts of Response and Recovery; Suggestions for Best Practice* [website], (updated 3 Sep. 2008) <http://www.loc.gov/preserv/emergprep/katrinarespond.html>, accessed 4 Sep. 2008.

Matthews, G. (2005) 'Disaster management and libraries; planning into action; the institutional perspective', in Wellheiser, J. G. and Gwinn, N. E. (eds.) (2005), *Preparing for the worst, planning for the best: protecting our cultural heritage from disaster. Proceedings of a conference sponsored by the IFLA Preservation and Conservation Section, the IFLA Core Activity for Preservation and Conservation and the Council on Library and Information Resources, Inc., with the Akademie der Wissenschaften and the Staatsbibliothek zu Berlin.*

Berlin, Germany, Jul 30 – August 1, 2003, IFLA Publications 111 (München: K G Saur), 61–77.

Matthews, G. and Feather, J. P. (eds.) (2003), *Disaster Management for Libraries and Archives* (Aldershot: Ashgate).

Matthews, G. et al. (2004), *An investigation into the work of REDS (Regional Emergencies & Disaster Squad). A report to East Midlands Museums, Libraries and Archives Council (EMMLAC)* (Birmingham and Leicester, Centre for Information Research (CIRT), University of Central England in Birmingham, East Midlands Museums, Libraries and Archives Council (EMMLAC)), (published online 2004) <http://www.mlaeastmidlands.org. uk/templates/temp_cor_rep_index.rm? category=keywords_root.taxonomy. corporate.documenttype.Report&category=keywords_root.taxonomy. corporate.subject.Collections&id=589&sort_type=date&num=5&term=&sub mit.x=11&submit.y=13&from=6>, accessed 14 Aug. 2008.

Maxwell, I. (ed.) (2007), *COST action 17: built heritage fire loss to heritage buildings. Final report.* 3 vols. (Edinburgh: Technical Conservation, Research and Education Group, Historic Scotland, COST, European Science Foundation).

MLA South East (2008), *Renaissance Related Resources* [website], (updated 19 Aug. 2008) <http://www.mlasoutheast.org.uk/museums/renaissance/>, accessed 6 Sep. 2008.

Najar-Simpson, P. (2007), 'Cooperative disaster salvage and recovery in New Zealand: a case study of vacuum freeze-drying services', in *Coping with Disaster in Asia and Oceania, Asia and Oceania Section, World Library and Information Congress, 73rd IFLA Conference and Council,* Durban, South Africa, 19–23 Aug. 2007, IFLA, Coping with Disaster in Asia and Oceania, Asia and Oceania Section, World Library and Information Congress, 73rd IFLA Conference and Council, Durban, South Africa, August 2007, (published online 2007) <http://www.ifla.org/IV/ifla73/papers/140-Najar-Simpson-en.pdf>, accessed 14 Jul. 2007.

National Archives [US] (2008), *The ABCs of modern fire suppression in cultural institutions, 22nd Annual Preservation Conference, March 10, 2008, Washington* [website], (updated 2008) <http://www.archives.gov/preservation/ conferences/2008/details.html#exhibitors>, accessed 15 Jul. 2008.

National Center for Preservation Technology and Training, *Disaster Recovery by the Book* [website], (updated 18 Jul. 2007) <http://www.ncptt.nps.gov/NCPTT-Notes/Issue-45/Disaster-Recovery-by-the-Book.aspx>, accessed 5 Sep. 2008.

Northern Ireland Government. Department of Culture, Arts and Leisure (2007), *Minister Poots Launches Survey of Museum Collections.* (published online 20 December 2007) <http://www.dcalni.gov.uk/news_details. htm?newsRef=702>, accessed 6 Sep. 2008.

The National Trust. *Climate change* [website], (updated 2008) <http://www. nationaltrust.org.uk/main/w-chl/w-countryside_environment/w-climate_ change.htm>, accessed 5 Sep. 2008.

Noah's Ark, *Noah's Ark: Global Climate Change Impact on Built Heritage and Cultural Landscapes* [website], (updated n.d.) <http://noahsark.isac.cnr.it/>, accessed 5 Sep. 2008.

Northern Ireland Office (2006), *Collections management in the National Museums and Galleries of Northern Ireland. Report by the Comptroller and Auditor General HC 1130, Session 2005–06, 8 June 2006* (London: The Stationery Office), (published online 2006) <http://www.niauditoffice.gov.uk/pubs/MAGNI/FullReport.pdf>, accessed 6 Sep. 2008.

O'Brien, G., et al. (2006), 'Climate change and disaster management', *Disasters* 30:1, 64–80.

Quarantellli, E. L. (2003), *The protection of cultural properties: the neglected social science perspective and other questions and issues that ought to be considered. Preliminary paper # 325* (Newark, Delaware: Disaster Research Center, University of Delaware), (published online 2003) <http://dspace.udel.edu:8080/dspace/bitstream/19716/734/1/PP325.pdf>, accessed 5 Sep. 2008.

Renaissance South East, *Emergency Response Units* [website], (updated 21 Aug. 2008) <http://www.museumse.org.uk/sharing_skills/emergency_response_units.html>, accessed 10 Sep. 2008.

Renaissance South East (2007), 'South East Hub Sharing Skills. Crisis back-up', *Renaissance South East News* 7:2, (published online 2007) <http://www.museumse.org.uk/generic_docs/renaissance_newsletter.pdf>, accessed 10 Sep. 2008.

Shaheen, M. (2007) 'Academic Institutions and Libraries of Pakistani Administered Kashmir: A Pre and Post Earthquake Analysis', in *Information Providers Coping with Disaster in Asia and Oceania, Asia and Oceania Section, World Library and Information Congress, 73rd IFLA Conference and Council*, August 2007, Durban, South Africa, IFLA, (published online Aug. 2008) <http://www.ifla.org/IV/ifla73/papers/140-Shaheen-en.pdf>, accessed 14 Jul. 2008.

Silverman, R. (2006), 'Toward a national disaster response protocol', *Libraries and the Cultural Record* 41:4, 497–511.

Silverman, R. (2004), 'A litany of "Terrible, no good, very bad" things that can happen after the disaster', *International Preservation News* 33, 8–15, (published online 2004) <http://www.ifla.org/VI/4/news/ipnn33.pdf>, accessed 5 Sep. 2008.

Silverman, R., et al. (2007), 'Comparing mass drying and sterilization protocols for water-damaged books', *International Preservation News* 42, 22–9, (published online 2007) <http://www.ifla.org/VI/4/news/ipnn42.pdf>, accessed 13 May. 2008.

Smellie, C. and Spry, K. (2008), 'W.E.T. (Worcestershire Museums Emergency Planning Task Force) Museums: a county-wide approach to disaster planning', in *Don't Panic! Planning an Effective Disaster Response* [based on report to MLA]. The Midlands Federation of Museums and Art Galleries, RAF Museum Cosford, Shifnal, Shropshire, 2 Jul. 2008, (unpublished).

The Society of American Archivists (2006), *MayDay Saving our archives May 1 2006*, (published online 2006) <http://www.archivists.org/mayday/MayDayActivityList.pdf>, accessed 5 Sep. 2008.

Spiers, F. (2007) *Notes from Beyond the Deluge: Towards Recovery* [meeting organized by] HLF Yorkshire and the Humber, Aug. 2007.

Staniforth, S. (2006), 'The Impact of climate change on historic libraries', in *Turning the library inside out*, Uppsala University Library, Sweden, 4-8 Jul. 2006.

Stanley-Price, N, (2005) 'Culture and disaster recovery'. *ICCROM Newsletter* 31, 2–4 (published online Jun. 2005) <http://www.iccrom.org/eng/02info_en/02_03newsl_en/newsl_en/newsl31_en.pdf>, accessed 5 Sep. 2008.

Stavroudis, C. (2005) Health and safety. 'Getting prepared', *Western Association for Art Conservation* [waac] *Newsletter* 25:3, 12–15, (published online 2005) <http://palimpsest.stanford.edu/waac/ttl/wn27-3-special.pdf>, accessed 20 Aug. 2008.

Stern, N. (2006) *The economics of climate change. The Stern Review* (HM Treasury, Cabinet Office, Cambridge University Press), (published online 2006) <http://www.hm-treasury.gov.uk/independent_reviews/stern_review_economics_climate_change/sternreview_index.cfm>, accessed 5 Sep. 2008.

Taboroff, J. (2003) 'Natural disasters and urban cultural heritage: a reassessment', in: Kreimer, A., Arnold, M. and Carlin, A. (eds.), *Building safer cities: the future of disaster risk* (Washington D.C.: World Bank), 233–40.

TNA, *Self-assessment* [website], (updated 2008) <http://www.nationalarchives.gov.uk/archives/self-assessment.htm>, accessed 23 Aug. 2008.

UCL Centre for Sustainable Heritage Short courses at CSH [website], (updated 2006) <http://www.ucl.ac.uk/sustainableheritage/short_courses.htm>, accessed 5 Sep. 2008.

UK Resilience. *Business Continuity* (updated 16 May 2006) <http://www.ukresilience.gov.uk/preparedness/businesscontinuity.aspx>, accessed 6 Sep. 2008.

UK Resilience. *Civil Contingencies Act* [website], (updated 16 May 2008) <http://www.ukresilience.gov.uk/preparedness/ccact.aspx>, accessed 12 Sep. 2008.

UNESCO (2005), *KOBE REPORT draft. Report of Session 3.3, Thematic Cluster 3. Cultural Heritage Risk Management. World Conference on Disaster Reduction. 18–22 January 2005, Kobe, Hyogo, Japan*, (published online 2005) <http://www.unisdr.org/wcdr/thematic-sessions/thematic-reports/report-session-3-3.pdf>, accessed 31 Aug. 2008.

Wakefield Council (2008), News. Press releases. Emergency training grant boost for local heritage, (published online 14 May 2008 <http://www.wakefield.gov.uk/News/PressReleases/news/PR1782.htm>, accessed 14 Sep. 2008.

Chapter 8
Sources of Information

Introduction

One of the authors provided a select guide to sources of information, in, Matthews, G. and Feather, J. (eds.) (2003), *Disaster Management for Libraries and Archives* (Aldershot: Ashgate) 213–28. The intention here is to update that list and add sources relevant to museums. Some key sources appear in both guides. Subject coverage relates to that of the project. Disaster management of digital materials, for example, is excluded. References at end of chapters should also be consulted.

Bibliographies

There are several bibliographies that provide details to various types of source, current and older, covering many aspects of the topic.

Brown, K. E., 'Emergency Management Bibliography NEDCC Preservation leaflets', *Emergency management 3.5*, (Andover, MA: NEDCC) (published online), (updated 2007) <http://www.nedcc.org/resources/leaflets/3Emergency_Management/05EmergencyMgmtBibliography.php>, accessed 29 Jul. 2008.

ICCROM, *ICCROM Online library catalogue* [website], (updated n.d.) <http://library.iccrom.org/Libris/index.html>, accessed 5 Aug. 2008.

J. Paul Getty Trust, *Online bibliography* [website], (updated 2007) <http://gcibibs.getty.edu/asp/>, accessed 29 Jul. 2008. [Provides access to ICOM's Museums Emergency Programme, Preparedness and Response in Emergency Situations database.]

Kulzack, D. and Lennertz, L. (1999), 'A decade of disaster: a selected bibliography of disaster literature, 1985–1995', *Library and Archival Security*, 15:1, 7–66.

Special Libraries Association, *Disaster Planning Portal* [website], (updated Jul. 2007), <http://www.sla.org/content/resources/inforesour/sept11help/disip/index.cfm>, accessed 29 Jul. 2008. [Portal is '…dedicated to the librarians who were killed or injured on September 11th, 2001.']

Teygeler, R., with the cooperation of de Bruin, G., Wasink, B. and van Zanen, B. (2001), *Preservation of Archives in Tropical Climates: An annotated bibliography* (Paris, The Hague, Jakarta: ICA, National Archives of the Netherlands, National Archives of the Republic of Indonesia), (published online), (updated 2004) <http://www.knaw.nl/ECPA/ grip/publications.html>, accessed 3 Jun. 2006. [The bibliography contains an overview of preservation and conservation in tropical climate resources. See Chapter 6, Disaster preparedness, Part One Preservation of Archives in Tropical Climates, and Chapter 6, Disaster preparedness Part Two Bibliography. 'The webversion is derived from a revised version of the bibliography, published in Comma, 2001.3–4, Paris: ICA.']

General

Guides (whole books and chapters and short articles) to disaster management and/ or specific aspects of it relevant to archives, libraries and museums include:

Aitchison, K. (2004), *Disaster Management Planning for Archaeological Archives, Institute of Field Archaeologists Paper No 8*, (Reading, IFA) (published online Sep. 2004) <http://www.archaeologists.net/modules/icontent/inPages/docs/ pubs/paper8.pdf>, accessed 20 Jul. 2007.

Alire, C. (ed.) (2000*), Library Disaster Planning and Recovery Handbook* (New York: Neal-Schuman Publishers) [Based on experience at the Morgan Library, Colorado State University campus, devastated by a massive flood.]

American Museum of Natural History, *Museum SOS: A comprehensive resource for museum disaster preparedness and response* [website], (updated 2 Sep. 2005) <http://museum-sos.org/htm/index.html>, accessed 29 Jul. 2008.

An Chomhairle Leabharlanna (The Library Council), *COLICO. Disaster planning* guide [website], (updated n.d.) <http://www.librarycouncil.ie/colico/disaster_ guide.shtml>, accessed 30 Jul. 2008.

Bolger, L., 'Scared or prepared? Disaster planning makes the difference', *Information Outlook*, (published online July 2003) <http://findarticles.com/p/ articles/mi_m0FWE/is_7_7/ai_105515115/pg_1?tag=artBody;col1>, accessed 31 Jul. 2007.

Doig, J. (1997), 'Disaster Recovery for Archives, Libraries and Records Management Systems in Australia and New Zealand', *Topics in Australasian Library and Information Studies, Number 12* (Riverine Wagga Wagga, New South Wales: Centre for Information Studies, Charles Sturt University).

Dorge, V. and Jones, S. (comps.), *Building an Emergency Plan. A Guide for Museums and Other Cultural Institutions*, (Los Angeles, California: GCI), (published online 1999) <http://www.getty.edu/conservation/publications/ pdf_publications/emergency_plan.pdf>, accessed 14 Aug 2006.

Dean J. F. (2004), *Getting started* [website], (updated 2004) <http://www. library.cornell.edu/preservation/librarypreservation/meolda/management/ gettingstarted.html> (Management and Planning, Disasters), accessed 31 Jul. 2008. [Produced by the Department of Preservation and Collection Maintenance, Cornell University, The site also contains a tutorial for Iraq and the Middle

East   <http://www.library.cornell.edu/preservation/librarypreservation/mee/ index.html>, accessed 31 Jul. 2008.]

Easthope, L. and Eyre, A. (2008) Planning for and Managing Emergencies: a good practice guide for higher education institutions (Bristol: The Association of University Chief Security Officers and the Higher Education Funding Council for England), (published online 2008) <http://www.aucso.org.uk/uploads/File/ THE%20GUIDE%20FINAL_1%20JUNE%2008.pdf>, accessed 31 Jan. 2009. [Of possible interest to those involved in disaster management in university libraries.]

EmmS (2001), *The EmmS Emergency Manual for Historic Buildings and Collections* (Nottingham: East Midlands Museums Service) [Available as interactive CD Rom; for further details see: www.emms.org.uk.]

Ertürk, N. (2005) 'Earthquake preparedness at the Istanbul', in Wellheiser, J. G. and Gwinn, N. E. (eds.) (2005), 53–59.

Ertürk, N. (2005), 'Protection of the cultural heritage against earthquake in the museums of Istanbul', in: *ICOM-CC 14ʰ Triennial Meeting*, The Hague,12– 16 Sep. 2005, (published online) <http://www.icom-cc2005.org/programme/ speech/nevra_erturk/>, accessed 5 Aug. 2008.

Fox, L. L. (1998), *Disaster preparedness workbook for U.S. Navy libraries and archives, prepared on behalf of Northeast Document Conservation Center for the U.S. Naval War College Library,* (Newport, R.I.: the Library), (published online 1998) <http://matrix.msu.edu/~disaster/disasterman.html>, accessed 6 Aug. 2008.

Fullerton, J. (2004), 'Disaster preparedness at the National Library of Australia', *Alexandria* 16:3, 175–89.

Haines, J. (comp.) (2002), *A disaster preparedness plan for small public libraries*, [State Library of Ohio, Libraries] [website], (updated Jun. 2005) <http://winslo. state.oh.us/services/LPD/disaster_frnt.html>, accessed 30 Jul. 2008.

Halstead, D. D. (2005), *Disaster planning: a how-to-do-it manual for librarians with planning templates* (New York: Neal-Schuman).

HDRS, *Document recovery after fire, flood and explosion. Disaster consultancy planning and tips.* [website], (updated 2007) <http://www.hdrs.co.uk/ disasterplanning.html>, accessed 2 Aug. 2008 [Provides downloadable disaster plan template for museums or libraries/archives.]

Heritage Preservation (n.d.), *Emergency response and salvage wheel, rev. edition.* (Washington DC: Heritage Preservation).

Heritage Preservation (2006), *Field guide to emergency response* (Washington, D.C.: Heritage Preservation, 2006) [With instructional DVD].

Historical Manuscripts Commission (2002), *Protecting Archives and Manuscripts against Disasters, Advisory Memorandum No.6*, (London: Historical Manuscripts Commission).

Hoffman, C. (2005), 'After the flood', *Museums Journal*, 105:4, 32–3, 35. [Dresden State museums.]

ICA/PDP, *ICA Study 11 – Guidelines on Disaster Prevention and Control in Archives Guidelines on disaster prevention and control in archives*. (Paris: ICA), (published online 2007) <http://www.ica.org/en/node/30653>, accessed 21 Aug. 2008.

ICOM, *Guidelines for Disaster Preparedness in Museums* [Off-print from *Museum Security and Protection: A handbook for cultural heritage institutions* (1993), ICOM and the International Committee on Museum Security ; edited by Listen, D. (London, New-York: ICOM in conjunction with Routledge)] [website], (updated n.d.) <http://icom.museum/disaster_preparedness.html>, accessed 31 Aug. 2008.

Jenner, S.-J. (2006), 'From disaster plan to action plan' [The British Library], in Koch, C. (ed.) (2006), 34–38.

Kahn, M. B. (2003), *Disaster Response and Planning for Libraries*, 2nd edition (Chicago: American Library Association).

Kuuben, I. (2003), 'Early days of Disaster Recovery Planning in the Estonian Historical Archives', *International Preservation News* 31, 19–25, (published online Dec. 2003) <http://www.ifla.org/VI/4/news/ipnn31.pdf>, accessed 5 Aug. 2008.

LISC (NI) and Public Record Office of Northern Ireland (PRONI). *Disaster plan manual*, (published online 2006) <http://www.liscni.co.uk/images/Disaster_Plan_Manual.doc>, accessed 4 Jan. 2008.

Listen, D. (ed.) (1993), *Museum Security and Protection: A handbook for cultural heritage institutions* (London, New-York: ICOM in conjunction with Routledge). [Off-print available at ICOM (n.d.)], *Guidelines for disaster preparedness in museums.* [website], updated n.d.) <http://icom.museum/disaster_preparedness.html>, accessed 6 Aug. 2008.

Mansell, H. (2003). 'The disaster control plan', in Matthews, G and Feather, J (eds.), 13–40.

Martin, D. (2005), 'Damage control', *Museum Practice* 29, 44–6.

Matthews, G. and Eden, P. (1996), 'Disaster Management in British Libraries. Project report with Guidelines for Library Managers', *Library and Information Research Report* 109 (London: The British Library).

Matthews, G. and Feather, J.P. (eds.) (2003), *Disaster Management for Libraries and Archives* (Aldershot: Ashgate).

McIlwaine, J., *IFLA Disaster Preparedness and Planning. A Brief Manual.* (International Preservation Issues Number 6), (Paris: IFLA PAC), (published online 2006) <http://www.ifla.org/VI/4/news/ipi6-en.pdf>, accessed 14 Aug. 2006.

McIlwaine, J. (comp), *FIRST DO NO HARM: A Register of Standards, Codes of Practice, Guidelines, Recommendations and Similar Works relating to Preservation and Conservation in Libraries*, [IFLA Preservation and Conservation Section] (Paris: IFLA PAC), (published online March 2005) <http://www.ifla.org/VII/s19/pubs/first-do-no-harm.pdf>, accessed 14 Jul. 2008. [Emergency planning/disaster preparedness 14–19.]

Menegazzi, C. (ed.) (2004), *Cultural Heritage Disaster Preparedness and Response. International Symposium Proceedings. Salar Jung Museum, 23–27 November 2003, Hyderabad, India.* (Paris: International Council of Museums), (published online 2004) <http://icom.museum/disaster_preparedness_book/index.html>, accessed 31 Aug. 2008.

Millar, L, *Emergency Planning for Records and Archives Services* (*Managing Public Sector Records: a Study Programme*), (London: International Records Management Trust), (published online 1999) <http://www.irmt.org/Images/documents/educ_training/public_sector_rec/IRMT_emergency_plan.pdf>, accessed 31 Jul. 2008.

Museum Practice (2005), 'Knowledge' [Special issue], *Emergency planning,* Spring, 2005. [Articles on different aspects of emergency planning and museums, e.g. risk assessment, writing a plan, prioritizing objects for salvage.]

National Archives of Australia (2000), *Disaster Preparedness Manual for Commonwealth Agencies*, (Canberra: National Archives of Australia), (published online 2000) <http://www.naa.gov.au/images/disaster%20manual_tcm2-4789.pdf>, accessed 14 Aug. 2008.

NEDCC, *dPlan™: The Online Disaster-Planning Tool* [website], (updated 2006) <http://www.dplan.org/>, accessed 23 Aug. 2008.

Oxford University Library Services. *Conservation and Collection Care Service, Information – Emergency Control Planning* [website], (updated 2005) <http://www.bodley.ox.ac.uk/dept/preservation/information/emcp.htm>, accessed 27 Jul. 2008. [Also see Short-Traxler, K. (2005).]

Pennsylvania Historical and Museum Commission. *Disaster Planning & Vital Records* [website], (updated 2008) <http://www.portal.state.pa.us/portal/server.pt?open=512&objID=2631&&PageID=312506&level=3&parentCommID=2631&menuLevel=Level_3&mode=2>, accessed 30 Jul. 2008. [Includes: disaster plan template appendices disaster plan template, and vital records plan template.]

Rice, D. B., 'First Response to Disasters for Small Museums and Libraries', *PNLA Quarterly* 70:3, 13–18. (published online 2006) <http://www.pnla.org/quarterly/Spring2006/PNLA_Spring_06.pdf>, accessed 29 Jul. 2008.

Routledge, D. (1999), *Planning For Emergencies: A Procedures Manual (Managing Public Sector Records: a Study Programme)*, (London: International Records Management Trust) (published online <http://www.irmt.org/Images/documents/educ_training/public_sector_rec/IRMT_emergency_plan_proc.pdf>, accessed 31 Jul. 2008. [Based on materials developed by the National Archives of Canada.]

Short-Traxler, K (2005), 'Developing an emergency control plan for Oxford University libraries', *SCONUL Focus* 35, 45–51.

Söderlund, K., *Be Prepared: Guidelines for Small Museums for Writing a Disaster Preparedness Plan,* (Canberra: Commonwealth of Australia), (published online May. 2000) <http://sector.amol.org.au/__data/page/44/beprep.pdf>, accessed 23 Aug. 2008. [Guidelines for small museums for writing a disaster preparedness plan.]

SWMLAC (2006), *Emergency Planning (Signpost factsheet 5)*, (published online 2006)   <http://www.mlasouthwest.org.uk/docs/Signposts-Factsheet-5.pdf>, accessed 3 Aug. 2008.

Te Papa National Services (2001). *Resource Guides: Emergency Procedures (Wellington:* Museum of New Zealand Te Papa Tongarewa), (published online Jun. 2001) <http://www.tepapa.govt.nz/NR/rdonlyres/ 3ECB70FF-7948-4E26-B976-E6F09CFBDF06/0/Emergency.pdf#Page=3>, accessed 26 Jul. 2008.

Te Papa National Services (2001). *Resource Guides. Preventive Conservation (Wellington:* Museum of New Zealand Te Papa Tongarewa), (published online Jun. 2001) <http://www.tepapa.govt.nz/NR/rdonlyres/ 017BFB88-80F4-4F1F-AE0879C94A25CC5A/0/Conservation.pdf# Page=2 >, accessed 26 Jul. 2008.

Te Papa National Services (2001). *Resource Guides. Minimising Disaster (Wellington:* Museum of New Zealand Te Papa Tongarewa), (published online Jun. 2001) <http://www.tepapa.govt.nz/NR/rdonlyres/961F6489-3130-47DB-B53F-BE5C94475C48/0/MinDisaster.pdf#Page=2>, accessed 26 Jul. 2008.

TNA, Protecting archives and manuscripts against disasters, (published online Jun. 2004), http://www.nationalarchives.gov.uk/documents/memo6.pdf, accessed 31 Jul. 2008.

Tremain, D. (2004), 'Developing an emergency response plan for natural history collections', in *SPNHC 2004*, American Museum of Natural History, New York City, 14 May. 2004 [website], (updated 2005) <http://museum-sos.org/htm/strat_developing_an.html>, accessed 31 Jul. 2008.

Wellheiser, J. and Scott, J. (2002), *An Ounce of Prevention: Integrated Disaster Planning for Archives, Libraries and Archive Centres*, 2nd edition. (Lanham, Maryland: The Scarecrow Press Inc. and Canadian Archives Foundation.)

Websites

There are many websites published around the world that provide helpful information. The following are examples that the authors have found useful:

General/International

CoOL, *Disaster Preparedness and Response* [website], (updated 26 Mar. 2008) <http://palimpsest.stanford.edu/bytopic/disasters/>, accessed 6 Aug. 2008. [Produced by the Preservation Department of Stanford University Libraries, it has an emphasis on North American sources but also includes much of broader worldwide interest either in its content or via links. It provides information/ links to resources on disaster management (by organisation/author), disaster plans, case histories, and bibliographic resources.]

UNESCO, *Memory of the World Programme* [website], (updated 29 Jul. 2008) <http://portal.unesco.org/ci/en/ev.php-URL_ID=1538&URL_DO=DO_ TOPIC&URL_SECTION=201.html>, accessed 23 Aug. 2008.

[UNESCO's *Memory of the World Programme, Preserving Documentary Heritage* offers access through its website directory to wide-ranging information on preservation of worldwide interest. The site (available in English or French) offers information on news and events, links and publications (basic texts, databases, CD-ROMs). See also, its *Safeguarding the documentary heritage* website, a guide to standards, recommended practices and reference literature related to the preservation of documents [website}, (updated 2000) <http:// www.ifla.org/VI/6/dswmedia/en/index.html>, accessed 6 Aug. 2008).]

UNESCO, *Archives Portal. Disaster Preparedness and Recovery* [website], (updated 24 May. 2006) <http://www.unesco-ci.org/cgi-bin/portals/archives/ page.cgi?d=1&g=942>, accessed 23 Aug. 2008. [Provides links to various resources ranging from primers on disaster management, a journal on contingency planning to institutional guides and emergency response action steps from FEMA.]

National

Many websites of national or regional associations, organisations and libraries will contain information of potential interest and use to those in countries elsewhere. The following are examples that contain a variety of information, but it should be noted that many refer to the same resources and to each other.

United Kingdom

Collections Link, *Emergency Planning* [website], (updated 2006) <http://www. collectionslink.org.uk/plan_for_emergencies>, accessed 6 Aug. 2008. [Links to various resources, including from outside the cultural heritage sector.]

M25 Consortium of Academic Libraries, *Disaster Control Plan*, [website], (updated 2004) <http://www.m25lib.ac.uk/m25dcp/>, accessed 6 Aug. 2008. [Coverage includes a template with commentary.]

MLA South East, *Renaissance* [website], (updated 19 Aug. 2008) <http:// www.mlasoutheast.org.uk/museums/renaissance/>, accessed 6 Aug. 2008. [Resources include templates for different size/type of museum.]

NPO, *Disaster/Emergency Planning* [website], (updated n.d.) <http://www. bl.uk/services/npo/disaster.html>, accessed 6 Aug. 2008. [General guidance provided.]

UKIRB, United *Kingdom and Ireland BLUE SHIELD Organisation* [website], (updated n.d.) <http://www.bl.uk/services/npo/blueshield/overview.html>, accessed 6 Aug. 2008.

UK Resilience, *Welcome to UK Resilience* [website], (updated 8 Aug. 2008) <http://www.ukresilience.info/>, accessed 23 Aug. 2008. [For civil protection practitioners dealing with emergency preparedness.]

United States

ALA, *Disaster Preparedness and Recovery* [website], (updated 31 Jul. 2008) <http://www.ala.org/ala/washoff/woissues/disasterpreparedness/distrprep. cfm>, accessed 6 Aug. 2008. [Offers links to the disaster planning resources, collection valuation, collection preservation and recovery, and other resources.]

California Preservation Program, *Emergency Preparedness and Response* [website], (updated Feb. 2008) <http://calpreservation.org/disasters/index. html>, accessed 6 Aug. 2008. [Resources include: generic disaster plan workbook, template, exercise, resources.]

CoSA. *Archives Resource Center – Emergency Planning and Recovery* [website], (updated 17 Jan. 2008) <http://www.statearchivists.org/arc/states/res_disa. htm>, accessed 6 Aug. 2008. [Links to resources in individual states.]

FEMA, *Federal Emergency Management Agency*, [website], (updated 2008) <http://www.fema.gov/>, accessed 6 Aug. 2008. [Provides advice and information on a range of emergency management topics. 'The primary mission of the Federal Emergency Management Agency is to reduce the loss of life and property and protect the Nation from all hazards, including natural disasters, acts of terrorism, and other man-made disasters, by leading and supporting the Nation in a risk-based, comprehensive emergency management system of preparedness, protection, response, recovery, and mitigation.']

Heritage Emergency National Task Force, *Alliance for Response: A National Program on Cultural Heritage and Disaster Management* [website], (updated c.2007) <http://www.heritagepreservation.org/PROGRAMS/AFRmain. HTM>, accessed 6 Aug. 2008.

Heritage Emergency National Task Force, *Heritage Emergency National Task Force* [website], (updated n.d.) <http://www.heritagepreservation.org/ PROGRAMS/ TASKFER.htm>, accessed 6 Aug. 2008. [The Heritage Emergency National Task Forces is co-sponsored by Heritage Preservation and Federal Emergency Management Agency. Offers a range of resources on may aspects of disaster management, including preparedness and response resources, current disaster information, and initiatives.]

Library of Congress, Preservation. Emergency Preparedness [website], (updated 3 Sep. 2008) <http://www.loc.gov/preserv/emergprep/prepare.html>, accessed 8 Feb. 2009. [Sections on: insurance / risk management; earthquake recovery; fire recovery; flood recovery; hurricane recovery; mudslide recovery; tornado recovery; publications; web links; other organizations.]

Minnesota Historical Society. *Emergency response: Conservation* [website], (updated 2008) <http://www.mnhs.org/preserve/conservation/emergency. html>, accessed 25 Jul. 2008. [Links to flood response and recovery resources.]

NEDCC, *Services: Disaster Assistance* [website] (updated n.d.) <http://www. nedcc.org/services/disaster.php>, accessed 6 Aug. 2008. [Offers 24/7 telephone assistance, emergency management preservation leaflets, links to other resources and dPlan™: the online disaster-planning tool.]

Australia

Heritage Collections Council, *recollections. Managing Collections. Counter-Disaster Planning* [website], (updated 2000) <http://archive.amol.org.au/recollections/4/6/index.htm>, 6 Aug. 2008.

National Archives of Australia. *Disaster Preparedness Manual for Commonwealth Agencies* [website], (updated 2007) <http://www.naa.gov.au/records-management/publications/disaster-manual.aspx>, accessed 3 Aug. 2008.

National Library of Australia, *Preservation* [website], (updated 2008) <http://www.nla.gov.au/preserve>, accessed 3 Aug. 2008. [The National Library website offers a range of useful information under its Preservation Activities pages, for example, its collection disaster plan.]

Netherlands

Netherlands Institute for Cultural Heritage. *ICN* [website], (updated n.d.) <http://www.icn.nl/Dir003/ICN/CMT/homepage.nsf/HFS?readform&language=English&menu=600>, accessed 23 Aug. 2008.

Disasters – Experiences

The experiences of others in dealing with disasters can be useful sources of information and advice. A selection is included below; others are indicated in publications and websites elsewhere in this guide to sources.

Aarons, J. (2003), Hurricanes: 'Nature's Weapon of Mass Destruction', *International Preservation News* 31, 11–18 (published online Dec. 2003) <http://www.ifla.org/VI/4/news/ipnn31.pdf>, accessed 14 Jul. 2008.

Aarons, J. (2005), 'Hurricanes and disaster response: lessons learned in Jamaica from "Gilbert"', in and Wellheiser, J. G. and Gwinn, N. E (eds.) (2005), 117–125.

ALA (2002), *Loss and Recovery: Librarians Bear Witness to September 11, 2001*, Video/DVD, (Towson, Maryland: ALA/Library Video Network). [Interviews with librarians working in or near the World Trade Center when terrorist attacks occurred. They recall the effects on information and library services and how they have recovered personally and professionally.]

ALA, *University of Hawaii Student Chapter, Hamilton Library Flood* [website], (updated 8 Nov. 2004) <http://www.hawaii.edu/ala/flood.php>, accessed 30 Jul. 2008. [Image archives, news articles, blog relating to a flash flood that destroyed part of the University of Hawaii Hamilton Library in 2004.]

Battersby, R. (2005), 'Recovering from disaster – the loss of Edinburgh's AI Library', *Library+Information Update*, 4:3, 36–8.

Clareson, T. and Long, J. (2006), 'Libraries in the eye of the storm: lessons learned from Hurricane Katrina', *American Libraries* 37:7, 38–41.

Corrigan, A. (2008), 'Disaster: response and recovery at a major research library in New Orleans', *Library Management* 29:4/5, 293–306.

Craig, R. Selzer, T. and Seymour, J. (2006), 'There is disaster planning and there is reality – the Cayman Islands National Archive (CINA) experience with Hurricane Ivan', *Journal of the Society of Archivists* 27:2, 187–99.

Cullhed, P. 'The Linköping Library fire', *International Preservation News* 31, 4–10, (published online Dec. 2003) <http://www.ifla.org/VI/4/news/ipnn31.pdf>, accessed 14 Jul. 2008.

Cullhed, P. (2006), 'Foreseeing and dealing with the unforeseen – library disasters in perspective', in Koch, C. (ed.) (2006), 29–33, published online 2006 <http://www.ifla.org/VI/4/news/ipi7-en.pdf>.

Diamond, T. (2006), 'The Impact of Hurricanes Katrina and Rita on Three Louisiana Academic Libraries: A Response from Library Administrators and Staff', *Library Administration and Management* 20:4, 192–200.

Ellis, J. (2007), 'Lessons learned: the recovery of a research collection after Hurricane Katrina', *Collection Building* 26:4, 108–111.

Eng, S. (2002), 'How technology and planning saved my library at ground zero', *Computers in Libraries* 22:4, 28–35.

Farooq, M. U. (2006), 'Earthquake and the libraries of Azadjammu and Kashmir', *Pakistan Library and Information Science Journal* 37:1, 28–30.

Frost, G. and Silverman, R. (2005), 'Disaster Recovery in the Artefact Fields – Mississippi after Hurricane Katrina', *International Preservation News* 37 December, 35–47.

H-Museum, *H-Museum's Current Focus: Floods in Europe. Damage to museums, history places, archives and libraries* [website], (updated 12 Oct. 2002) <http://www.h-net.org/~museum/flood.html>, accessed 13 Jul. 2008.

Hanson, E. (2006), '"Six feet of water in the streets …": Reflections on the destruction of cultural resources on a massive scale. New Orleans after Katrina', in *Cultural Property Protection Conference*, Ottawa, 16 Jan. 2006, Canadian Museums Association, (published online 2006) <http://www.museums.ca/protection/en/presentations/hanson.pdf>, accessed 3 Aug. 2008.

Heritage Emergency National Task Force, *Hurricanes 2005* [website], (updated 2005) <http://www.heritagepreservation.org/PROGRAMS/Katrina.HTM>, accessed 23 Aug. 2008.

Heritage Preservation (2002), 'Cataclysm and challenge. Impact of September 11, 2001, on Our Nation's Cultural Heritage'. A report from Heritage Preservation on behalf of the Heritage Emergency National Task Force, [Project Director Ruth Hargraves,] (Washington, DC: Heritage Preservation), (published online 2002) <http://www.heritagepreservation.org/PDFS/Cataclysm.pdf>, accessed 29 Aug. 2008.

Hewison, H. (2005), 'Disaster planning and recovery – the Caribbean experience', *Legal Information Management* 5, 188–93.

Holden, P. (2004,) '"Heaven helps those who help themselves": the realities of disaster planning', *Journal of the Society of Archivists* 25:1, 27–32.

Holderfield, A. (2007), 'A Library disaster', *Illinois Libraries* 86:4, 11–15.

ICOM, *ICOM News Thematic files: Risk management* (2005), [website], (updated 2005) <http://icom.museum/risk_emergency.html>, accessed 31 Jul. 2008. [Various articles on risk assessment and disasters in museums.]

Kidd, S. (ed.) (1995), *Heritage under Fire: a Guide to the Protection of Historic Buildings*, 2nd edition, (London: Fire Protection Association).

Knoche, M. (2005), 'The Herzogin Anna Amalia Library after the fire', *IFLA Journal* 31:1, 90–92.

Knoll, P., Peek, M. and Cremers, T. (2005), 'Case study', *Museum Practice* Spring, 56–9. [The Rijksmuseum Twenthe in Holland was badly damaged by an explosion in a fireworks factory.]

McIntyre, G. and Neale, S. (2006), 'Lessons Learned: The New Normal: Post Disaster Reflections: the Peterborough [Ontario] 2004 flood', in *Cultural Property Protection Conference*, Ottawa, 16 Jan. 2006, Canadian Museums Association, (published online 2006) <http://www.museums.ca/protection/en/presentations/Microsoft%20PowerPoint%20-%20McIntyre%20-%20Neale%20PowerPoint.pdf>, accessed 3 Aug. 2008.

Miller, W. and Pellen, R. M. (eds.) (2006), *Dealing with natural disasters in libraries* (Binghamton, NY: The Haworth Information Press). [Co-published simultaneously as *Public Library Quarterly* 25:3/4 2006.]

Milles, J. G. (2004), 'Managing a disaster: or there and back again', *Library and Archival Security* 19:2, 35–52.

The Museum of Witchcraft, *Museum of Witchcraft* [website], (updated 2004) <http://www.museumofwitchcraft.com/>, accessed 23 Aug. 2008. [Diary of impact of Boscastle floods in 2004.]

The National Archives [US] (2002), *17th Annual Preservation Conference. Lessons Learned in Emergencies: Not Your Ordinary Disaster Conference, 21 Mar. 2002* [website], (updated 2002) <http://www.archives.gov/preservation/emergency-prep/lessons-learned.html>, accessed 15 Jul. 2008. [The 2002 conference brought together archivists, librarians, and conservators to describe hands-on experience with disaster prevention, recovery, and mitigation. Papers on: fire prevention, fire detection and suppression, emergency response training, fire recovery and techniques, and mitigation, are included and available.]

Norman, J. 'It's back! National Motorcycle Museum reopens year after fire', 24 *Hour Museum* [website], (updated 2 Dec. 2004) <http://www.24hourmuseum.org.uk/nwh_gfx_en/ART25094.html>, accessed 23 Aug. 2008.

Pinhong, S. (2006), 'The urgent need to preserve and conserve ancient books: from the event that ancient books collected in Yongquan Monastery were damaged by a flood. Case study', *International Preservation News* 38, 15–21.

Sakamoto, I. (2005), 'Disaster from great earthquake off Sumatra and subsequent tunamis including damage to cultural heritage', *International Preservation News* 36, 16–20.

Sheffield Industrial Museums Trust. Flood recovery news. Kelham Island Museum [website] http://newkelham.blogspot.com/, accessed 27 Aug 2008 [The museum 'suffered severe flood damage on June 25th 2007'. These pages tell the story of the recovery process [with photographs.]]

Silverman, R. (2004), "A litany of 'terrible, no good, very bad' things that can happen after the disaster", *International Preservation News* 33, 8–15 .

Spafford-Ricci, S. and Graham, F. (2000), 'The fire at the Royal Saskatchewan Museum, Part 1: salvage, initial response, and the implications for disaster planning', *Journal of the American Institute for Conservation* 39:1 (published online 2000) <http://aic.stanford.edu/jaic/articles/jaic39-01-002_indx. html>, accessed 5 Aug. 2008.

Spafford-Ricci, S. and Graham, F. (2000), 'The fire at the Royal Saskatchewan Museum, Part 2: removal of soot from artifacts and recovery of the building', Journal of the American Institute for Conservation 39:1, (published online 2000) <http://aic.stanford.edu/jaic/articles/jaic39-01-003_indx.html>, accessed 5 Aug. 2008.

Štulc, J. (2003), *The 2002 Floods in the Czech Republic and their Impact on Built Heritage*. [Public lecture given at the British Library by Conservator General, National Institute for Heritage Preservation, Czech Republic and President, Czech ICOMOS] British Library, London, 15 May. 2003, (published online 2003) <http://www.bl.uk/services/npo/blueshield/pdf/floods.pdf>, accessed 31 Jul. 2008.

Swartz, N. (2005), 'Katrina devastates Gulf records', *Information Management Journal* 39:6, 24–6.

UNESCO, *Floods in Europe: Damages to libraries and archives* [website], (updated 15 Mar. 2007) <http://portal.unesco.org/ci/en/ev.php-URL_ID=3603&URL_DO=DO_TOPIC&URL_SECTION=201.html>, accessed 23 Aug. 2008.

WWW Virtual Library Sri Lanka (2006), *Tsunami – Worst ever tragedy disaster in Sri Lanka History* [website], (updated 2006) <http://www.lankalibrary.com/news.htm>, accessed 23 Aug. 2008.

Zhang, Z. and Zhao, D. (2007), 'Hot water damage: a case study of the Library of the Culture Palace for Nationalities', *International Preservation News* 41, 22–5.

Co-operative Activity

A local or regional network of mutual support with other archives and libraries can relieve a sense of isolation and provide access to advice and expertise not available within the organisation. Central purchase and storage of emergency equipment and supplies and joint training activities may have cost benefits too.

Davis, S. and Kern, K. (2003), 'Co-operative activity in the USA, or misery loves company', in Matthews, G. and Feather, J. (eds.) (2003), 117–41.

Lashley, B. (2003), 'Co-operative Disaster Planning for Libraries: a Model', *International Preservation News* 31, 26–33.

Matthews, G. (2005), 'Disaster management: sharing experience, working together across the sector', *Journal of Librarianship and Information Science* 37:2, 63–74.

Matthews, G. et al. (2004), *An investigation into the work of REDS (Regional Emergencies & Disaster Squad). A report to East Midlands Museums, Libraries and Archives Council (EMMLAC)*, (Birmingham and Leicester: Centre for Information Research (CIRT), University of Central England in Birmingham, EMMLAC), (published online 2004) <http://www.mlaeastmidlands.org. uk/templates/temp_cor_rep_index.rm?category=keywords_root.taxonomy. corporate.documenttype.Report&category=keywords_root.taxonomy. corporate.subject.Collections&id=589&sort_type=date&num=5&term=&sub mit.x=11&submit.y=13&from=6>, accessed 27 Aug. 2008.

Human Aspects

Effective disaster management relies upon people. To achieve this all staff must be properly trained with regard to their particular roles. Health and safety regulations must be observed. Experience of major disasters also shows that appropriate counselling should be available during and after disasters.

Klasson, M. (2002), 'Rhetoric and realism: young user reactions on the Linköping fire and its consequences for education and democracy', *Library Review*, 15:3/4, 171–80.

Klasson, M. (2003), 'Psychological aspects of disaster management', in Matthews, G. and Feather, J. (eds.) (2003), *Disaster Management for Libraries and Archives* (Aldershot: Ashgate) 143–68.

Silverman, R. (2004), 'A litany of "Terrible, no good, very bad" things that can happen after the disaster', *International Preservation News* 33, 8–15, (published online 2004) <http://www.ifla.org/VI/4/news/ipnn33.pdf>, accessed 5 Sep. 2008.

Stavroudis, C (2005) 'Health and safety. "Getting prepared"', *Western Association for Art Conservation* [waac] *Newsletter* 25:3, 12–15, (published online 2005) <http://palimpsest.stanford.edu/waac/ttl/wn27-3-special.pdf>, accessed 20 Aug. 2008.

Security

Security is an integral part of disaster management that permeates all its aspects, for example, from buildings and facilities, vandalism and theft, to computer networks and systems.

Centre for the Protection of National Infrastructure, *Welcome* [website], (updated 3 Jul. 2008) <http://www.cpni.gov.uk/>, accessed 3 Aug. 2008. [UK government authority; offers advice 'to reduce the vulnerability of the national infrastructure to terrorism and other threats'.]

Collections Link, *Take Care of Security* [website], (updated 2006) <http://www.collectionslink.org.uk/take_care_of_security>. [These web pages provide a range of advice for libraries, archives and museums in the UK, including, for example, security specifications, government indemnity scheme and invigilation guidance.]

Jirásek, P. (2004), 'Museum security, including disaster preparedness', in Boylan, P.J. (ed.) *Running a Museum: a Practical Handbook*, 177–197, (Paris: ICOM), (published online 2004) <http://unesdoc.unesco.org/images/0014/001410/141067e.pdf.> accessed 27 Aug. 2008.

Re:source; the Council for Museums Libraries and Archives (2003), *Security in museums, archives and libraries: a practical guide* (London: Resource). (Also available from Collections Link.)

Business/Service Continuity

Business, or service continuity, is a topic that archives, libraries and museums are beginning to address. There is little in the literature on this topic that focuses on archives, libraries and museums. There is much information available on it in general as the following two sources illustrate.

BSI (2006), BS 25999-1:2006 Business continuity management. Code of Practice (London: British Standards Institution).

Business Link, *Crisis management and business continuity planning* [website], (updated 2008) <http://www.businesslink.gov.uk/bdotg/action/layer?r.s=sl&topicId=1074458463>, accessed 3 Aug. 2008.

DCMS, (2005), *Business Continuity Planning Guide. Business as usual: A step by step guide to introducing and maintaining a business continuity plan*, (London: DCMS), (published online Jul. 2005) <http://www.culture.gov.uk/images/working_with_us/10231stegbystepguide.pdf>, accessed 3 Aug. 2008.

Insurance

Talking to insurers is essential but there are some guides that provide general information, and articles that relate the experience of others.

Breighner, M, Payton, W. and Drewes, J. M. (2005), *Risk and insurance management manual for libraries* (Chicago: ALA).

Graham, R. and Prideaux, A., *Insurance for Museums*, (London: MLA), (published online 2004) <http://www.mla.gov.uk/resources/assets//R/risk_insurance_pdf_5879.pdf>, accessed 22 June 2008.

Hitchcock, L. (2004), 'Making a claim: disaster follow-up at the Oboler Library', *Idaho Librarian* 55:3, (published online Feb. 2004). <http://www.idaholibraries. org/newidaholibrarian/200402/contentsA.htm>, accessed 23 Aug. 2004.

Howes, R. (2003), 'After the disaster: drawing up the insurance claim', *Aslib Proceedings* 5:3, 181–7.

Risk Management

There are publications that address risk and collections but fewer that consider broader issues relating to archives, libraries and museums. General sources on the topic may also be of use.

Blanco, L, et al. (2007), *Mitigating disaster: a strategic guide to risk management in heritage collections* (Kingston, Jamaica: UNESCO).

BSI (2008), BS31100:2008 Risk management. Code of practice (London: British Standards Institution)

Cannon, A. (2003), 'Risk management', in: Matthews, G. and Feather, J. (eds.) (2003), 41–72.

ICCROM-CCI, Preventive conservation: reducing risks to collections, international course. Sources of information for cultural heritage risk management, (published online 2007) <http://www.iccrom.org/eng/prog_en/01coll_en/archive-preven_ en/2007_06risks_biblio_en.pdf>, accessed 5 Aug. 2008. [Contains sections on: risk management outside the heritage field, within the field – general, specific to emergency preparedness, by agent of deterioration.]

Prideaux, A. (2007), 'Risk Assessment and Insurance for Museums', (AIM Focus Papers), (Bristol: AIM), (published online 2007) <http://www.aim-museums. co.uk/images/cms/focuspapers/Focus%20.Risk%20Management.pdf>, accessed 27 Aug. 2008.

War, Civil Unrest and Terrorism

Unfortunately, there is an increasing number of publications which consider the impact of war, civil unrest and terrorism on archives, libraries and museums.

They include those that reflect on past examples and current events.

Bogdanos, M. (2006), 'Casualties of War: The Looting of the Iraq Museum', *Museum News* March/April, (published online 2006) <http://www.aam-us.org/ pubs/mn/MN_MA06_casualties.cfm>, accessed 5 Aug. 2008.

Breitkopf, S. (2007), 'Lost: The Looting of Iraq's Antiquities', *Museum News* January/February, (published online 2007) <http://www.aam-us.org/ pubs/mn/ MN_JF07_lost-iraq.cfm>, accessed 5 Aug. 2008.

Hitchcock, A. (2004), 'Lessons in the Fog: War and Heritage Preservation', *Museum News* May/June, (published online 2004) <http://www.aam-us.org/ pubs/mn/MN_MJ04_WarHeritagePres.cfm>, accessed 5 Aug. 2008.

Hoeven, H. van der and Albada, J. van (1996), 'Lost Memory – Libraries and Archives Destroyed in the Twentieth Century', prepared for UNESCO and IFLA, CII-96/WS/1, Paris: UNESCO. (published online 1996) <www.unesco.org/webworld/mdm/administ/pdf/LOSTMEMO.PDF>, accessed 6 Aug. 2008.

ICBS, *Working for the Protection of the World's Cultural Heritage (ICBS)* [website], (updated 7 Aug. 2006) <www.ifla.org/VI/4/admin/protect.htm>, accessed 23 Aug. 2008. ['The Blue Shield is the cultural equivalent of the Red Cross. It is the symbol specified in the 1954 Hague Convention for marking cultural sites to give them protection from attack in the event of armed conflict.' See also: The United Kingdom and Ireland Blue Shield Organisation's website (UKIRB, United Kingdom and Ireland BLUE SHIELD [website], (updated n.d.) <http://www.bl.uk/blueshield/>, accessed 23 Aug. 2008) for basic disaster advice with links to web and other useful sources.]

ICRC, *International Review of the Red Cross – No. 854* [website], (updated 2008) <http://www.icrc.org/web/eng/siteeng0.nsf/html/section_review_2004_854?opendocument>, accessed 23 Aug. 2008. [Special issue: Protection of cultural property in armed conflict. Issue celebrating 'the 50th anniversary of the Convention for the Protection of Cultural Property in the Event of Armed Conflict. The various articles explain the significance of the cultural heritage of mankind and shed light on the legal rules established to protect it.']

Johnson, I. M. (2005) 'The impact on libraries and archives in Iraq of war and looting in 2003: a preliminary assessment of the damage and subsequent reconstruction efforts', *International Information and Library Review* 37:3, 209–71.

Knuth, R. (2003), *Libricide: The Regime-Sponsored Destruction of Books and Libraries in the Twentieth Century* (Westport, Connecticut: Praeger).

Knuth, R. (2006), *Burning Books and Leveling Libraries: Extremist Violence and Cultural Destruction* (Westport, Connecticut: Praeger).

Petr, K. (2003), 'The Croatian experience 1991–1995', in: Matthews, G. and Feather, J. (eds.), (2003), *Disaster Management for Libraries and Archives.* (Aldershot: Ashgate) 169–90.

Polastron, L.X. (translated by Graham, J. E.) (2007), *Books on Fire: The Tumultuous Story of the World's Great Libraries* (London: Thames and Hudson).

Rayward, W. B. and Jenkins, C. (eds.) (2006), 'Libraries in times of war, revolution, and times of social change', *Library Trends* 55:3, 361–755. [Special Issue.]

Riedlmayer, A. J. (2007) 'Crimes of war, crimes of peace', *Library Trends* 56:1, 107–32. [Special issue, 'Preserving Cultural Heritage', edited by Cloonan, M. V. and R. Harvey.]

Rose, J. (ed.) (2001), *The Holocaust and the Book: destruction and preservation*, (Amherst, MA: University of Massachusetts Press).

Stanley-Price, N. (ed.) (2007), *Cultural heritage in postwar recovery: Papers from ICCROM Forum held in October 4–6, 2005, Rome. [ICCROM Conservation Studies; 6]* (Rome: ICCROM).

Sturges, P. and Rosenberg, D. (eds.) (1999), *Disaster and After: the Practicalities of Information Service in Times of War and Other Catastrophes.* (London:

Taylor Graham). [Proceedings of an International Conference Sponsored by IGLA (The International Group of the Library Association), 4–6 September 1998, University of Bristol.]

Teijgeler, R. (2006), 'Preserving cultural heritage in times of conflict', in Gorman, G. E. and Shep, S. J. (eds.) (2003), *Preservation management for libraries, archives and museums* (London: Facet Publishing),133–65.

UNESCO (1998), *Emergency Programme for the Protection of Vital Records in the Event of Armed Conflicts*, (Washington: UNESCO). To combat the threat of risks to the archival heritage from recent conflicts ' … UNESCO commissioned the International Council on Archives to develop guidelines to help archives to protect their vital or essential holdings'. The programme includes case study reports from Costa Rica, Croatia and the Gambia, a guide to producing an emergency programme and expert reports on specific issues such as fire safety and building hardening.

Valencia, M. (2002), 'Libraries, nationalism, and armed conflict in the twentieth century', *Libri* 52:1, 1–15.

Wegener, C. and Otter, M., 'Cultural property at war: protecting heritage during armed conflict', *Getty Conservation Institute Newsletter* 23:1 [website], (updated 2008) <http://www.getty.edu/conservation/publications/newsletters/23_1/feature.html>, accessed 30 Aug. 2008.

Index